Delusions of Grandeur

The Olympia & Tenino Railroad

by James S. Hannum, M. D.

Illustrated by Carol B. Hannum

Copyright © 2009 by James S. Hannum, M. D.

All rights reserved. No portion of this publication may be reproduced or transmitted in any form without the express written permission of James S. Hannum, M. D.

Hannum, M. D., James S.

Delusions of Grandeur
The Olympia & Tenino Railroad

Library of Congress Catalog Card Number 2008900647

ISBN 978-0-9679043-6-8

First Edition

Published by Hannum House Publications

Illustrated by Carol Bateman Hannum

Printed in the United States of America by Minuteman Press

Cover photograph: the Olympia, Engine #3 of the Olympia & Chehalis Valley Railroad, from the Washington State Historical Society Museum

Opposite title page: Public Service Commission Map of Washington - 1914

Front of end page: US Geological Survey Map of Chehalis Quadrangle - 1916

Proceeds from the sale of this book are donated to
Providence St. Peter Foundation

Also by the Author

Michigan Bridget: Discovering the Truth Behind the Legend

The Ann Arbor Railroad in 1967 (video)

The Earl and Arrell Families from Ireland to North America

Gone But Not Forgotten-Abandoned Railroads of Thurston County, Washington

The Ann Arbor Railroad-Abandoned Early Lines

South Puget Sound Railroad Mania

Preface

When the Union Pacific and Central Pacific Railroads joined tracks at Promontory Point, Utah on 10 May 1869, few Americans realized how railroads would completely revolutionize their way of life. The change would be most dramatic in areas far removed from heavily populated states in the East and Midwest. Thurston County, in Washington Territory, was one of those remote areas. No longer would it be a backwater, on the fringe of the United States. The arrival of a railroad was expected to integrate Olympia and Thurston County into the mainstream of American life.

Soon after 1869 the Northern Pacific Railroad gave residents of Thurston County ample reason to believe that Olympia was going to be the railroad's Puget Sound terminal. Although the transcontinental route of the Northern Pacific was not completed until 1883, construction of its line north from Kalama, in 1872, pointed directly toward Olympia. In October of 1872, track laying stopped for the winter after the rails reached Tenino. When work resumed the following spring, Olympians were disappointed and outraged to learn that Tacoma had been selected as the terminal.

Business people in Olympia were convinced that without a railroad, prosperity would pass them by. Soon a popular movement arose, which attempted to finance and build a rail connection between Olympia and the Northern Pacific Railroad. The result was a narrow gauge line between West Olympia and Tenino, which opened for business in 1878.

Delusions of Grandeur was chosen as the title for this book because of an attitude displayed repeatedly during the thirty eight years that this railroad existed. Time and again the little line prepared itself to take on challenges that seem absurd when viewed from a twenty-first century perspective. Of these, the most far-fetched delusion was an 1891 plan to become a transcontinental railroad.

It's hard to escape the irony that characterized the relationship between the Northern Pacific Railroad and the line from Olympia to Tenino. Thurston County's little home-grown railroad was conceived and built because Olympians felt they had been snubbed by the transcontinental line. But in 1902, the Northern Pacific actually bought a controlling interest in this short line, and began operating it as part of the Northern Pacific system in 1914. In an unexpected move, the Northern Pacific abandoned most of the line south of Tumwater in 1916. Thus the life of this railroad was eventually snuffed out by the behemoth whose actions in 1872 were the proximate cause for building the line in the first place.

Although the mainline of the Olympia & Tenino Railroad was just fifteen miles long, Poor's Manual of Railroads (Edition of 1890) noted that the line operated seven miles of logging spurs that year. Clearly the railroad played a vital role in the economy of Thurston County. This book will explore these economic relationships while detailing the location of the line. Along its right of way several passenger stations and businesses came into existence and have now mostly disappeared. Knowledge of these enterprises helps to integrate the story of the railroad with the broader history of Thurston County.

I greatly appreciate the expertise provided to me by numerous individuals during preparation of the book. Thanks to: Kurt and Kit Anderson, Clarence Canfield, James C. Dick, F. Mark and Cheryl Dowdy, Roger Easton, Jane Ely, Brian Ferris, Leonard Fitzsimmons, Jim Fredrickson, Stephen Frost, Steven R. Gatke, Ken Graham, Allen Haase, Benjamin Helle, R. Dale Jost, M.D., John Labbe, Ronald Larson, D. D. S., Ronda Larson, Esq., Don Marenzi, Scott McArthur, Sandi McAuliffe, Vicki McKinnon, Lon Michaelis, Norman Montgomery, Ron Nelson, John A. Phillips, Wayne Pitcher, Joe S. Reder, Peter J. Replinger, Greg Richmond, Peter G. Schmidt, Jr., Lorenz P. Schrenk, Lillian Springer, Allen Stanley, Shanna Stevenson, Lanny Weaver and Carla Wulfsberg.

Contents

Preface

Contents

Chronology

Introduction

Portfolio of Illustrations
   1. Port Townsend Southern Railroad Engine #1 Approaches the First Plumb Station i
   2. Olympia & Tenino Railroad Engine #1, the E. N. Ouimette, at the First Tenino Station ii
   3. Port Townsend Southern Railroad Engine #858 at the Olympia Brewery Spur in Tumwater iii
   4. Port Townsend Southern Railroad Engine #6 along the Deschutes River in Tumwater iv
   5. Olympia & Chehalis Valley Railroad Engine #2, the Wallula, at McCorkle Road v
   6. Port Townsend Southern Railroad Engine #858 at the Hercules Sandstone Spur in Tenino vi

Chapters
   1. Planning and Construction of the Railroad - 1870 to 1878 1
   2. Railroad Operation - 1878 to 1909 4
   3. Stations - 1878 to 1916 27
   4. Customers of the Railroad - 1878 to 1916 61
   5. Locomotive Roster - 1878 to 1916 119
   6. Railroad Operation and Decline - 1910 to 1915 129
   7. Abandonment of the Railroad - 1916 to the Present 131

Appendix - Newspaper Articles 136

Bibliography 158

Indices
   People 160
   Places 162
   Locomotives 166
   Railroads, Other Companies, and Organizations 166

Chronology

Between 1878 and 1916, the railroad between Olympia and Tenino was known by several names and had multiple owners. For that reason a "genealogy" of the line is included here as a thumbnail reference that may be useful while reading the main part of the book.

31 December 1870
The Olympia Branch Railroad Company is incorporated. Its principal office is at Olympia, Washington. Marshall Blinn and Elisha P. Ferry are among the trustees. Its purpose is to negotiate with the Northern Pacific Railroad in an effort to make Olympia the Puget Sound terminal of that railroad. It is reported that the Olympia Branch Railroad Company plans to donate 240 acres of land (in the place where Watershed Park is located now) to the Northern Pacific for a railroad yard.

26 April 1871
Olympia & Chehalis Valley Railroad Company is incorporated. Its principal office is at Olympia, Washington. Trustees are John N. Goodwin (an agent of the Northern Pacific Railroad), General John W. Sprague (Superintendent of the Pacific Division of the Northern Pacific Railroad) and John J. Hackney. The company proposes to build a separate railroad from Olympia to a junction with the Northern Pacific near the south boundary of Township 16 in Thurston County. It would then continue through the Chehalis Valley to the Pacific Ocean at or near Grays Harbor.

15 March 1872
The Lake Superior and Puget Sound Company is incorporated in the State of Washington. Its principal place of business is stated to be in Maine. The company's agent is John W. Sprague of Kalama, Washington. The Northern Pacific Railroad used this subsidiary organization to handle real estate transactions that were indirectly related to the operation of its railroad.

1872
Numerous residents of Thurston County deed property to the Northern Pacific Railroad for railroad construction. The real estate is to be held in trust by Marshall Blinn, pending completion of the railroad to "the headwaters of Puget Sound on Budd Inlet" on or before 1 May 1872. These transactions are recorded in Thurston County Deed Book 9, pages 1-466.

13 August 1873
The Northern Pacific Railroad renounces any and all claims to the Thurston County property being held in trust by Marshall Blinn. That document was recorded in Deed Book 10, pages 277-278.

23 August 1873
The Olympia Railway & Mining Company is incorporated in the State of Washington. Its principal office is at San Francisco, California. Former Territorial Governor Edward Selig Salomon is appointed agent in Olympia. On the same day, Thornton F. McElroy (Mayor of Olympia in 1875) sells the new company 765 acres of land southeast of Tenino (in Sections 29, 30, 31 and 32 of Township 19 N, Range 1 W). Colonel F. A. Bee holds a prominent position in the company.

31 December 1873
The Olympia Railroad Union is organized.

5 January 1874
The Olympia Railroad Union is incorporated. Its principal office is at Olympia, Washington. Capital stock is $200,000. Among the organizers are Marshall Blinn, Thornton F. McElroy and Albert A. Phillips. Hazard Stevens is President.

1874
Most of the properties pledged previously to the Northern Pacific Railroad, with Marshall Blinn as trustee, are deeded to the Olympia Railroad Union. The transactions are recorded in Thurston County Deed Book 9, pages 621-757.

7 April 1874
Grading of roadbed begins.

8 August 1874
To finance further construction, county residents vote to issue bonds backed by Thurston County.

December 1874
Money raised by the bond sale runs out. Construction stops.

4 June 1877
The Thurston County Railroad Construction Company is incorporated. Its principal office is at Olympia, Washington. Capital stock is $250,000. Among the organizers are Marshall Blinn, Thornton F. McElroy, and Albert A. Phillips.

5 August 1877
The Olympia Railroad Union conveys all of its Thurston County real estate to the Thurston County Railroad Construction Company. The transaction is recorded in Thurston County Deed Book 11, page 723.

May 1878
Locomotive #1 arrives in Olympia by sea. The engine is named the "E. H. Ouimette". Rail and spikes for track construction arrive on the same vessel.

1 August 1878
The first passenger train runs from Olympia to Tenino. The official name of the railroad is the Olympia & Tenino Railroad Company.

25 February 1881
The Oregon Improvement Company is incorporated in the State of Washington. Its principal office is at Portland, Oregon.

1 August 1881
At the annual meeting of the Thurston County Railroad Construction Company, stockholders vote to change the name of the corporation to The Olympia & Chehalis Valley Railroad Company. John W. Sprague is elected President of the renamed business. Albert A. Phillips is Secretary.

6 August 1881
The Olympia & Chehalis Valley Railroad Company is incorporated. The principal office is at Olympia, Washington. This is the same name used by Sprague, ten years before, to incorporate a proposed railroad between Olympia and Tenino. However, the newly incorporated entity is not a direct corporate descendent of the entity incorporated 26 April 1871.

3 October 1881
The stockholders of The Olympia & Chehalis Valley Railroad Company vote to increase the capital stock of the company from $250,000 to $500,000. Principal stockholders are John W. Sprague, Otis Sprague, Robert Wingate, F. R. Brown and George H. Foster.

30 July 1886
John W. Sprague sells land east and south of Bucoda, Washington to the Olympia & Chehalis Valley Railroad Company. The land is in Sections 7 and 17 of Township 15 North, Range 1 West. On 31 July 1886 Robert Wingate also sells land in Sections 9, 21 and 22 to the railroad. All these properties are located between Tenino and Centralia in an area with underground coal deposits.

8 February 1887
Thurston County issues bonds for the Olympia & Chehalis Valley Railroad Company. The transaction is recorded in Thurston County Mortgage Book D, pages 368-371.

28 September 1887
The Port Townsend Southern Railroad Company is incorporated. Its principal office is at Port Townsend, Washington.

1889
The Oregon Improvement Company obtains control of the Port Townsend Southern Railroad. The transaction is reported in Valuation Docket #803, Volume 116, page 377 of <u>Interstate Commerce Commission Reports</u> (see Bibliography).

1 July 1889
Elijah Smith, President of the Oregon Improvement Company, contracts with the Port Townsend Southern Railroad Company to build twenty seven miles of railway between Port Townsend and Quilcene, Washington. The contract also authorizes a three mile northern extension of the Olympia & Chehalis Valley Railroad from West Olympia to Butler Cove.

10 September 1890
Operational control of the Olympia & Chehalis Valley Railroad is transferred to the Port Townsend Southern Railroad. The transition is reported in the 19 September 1890 edition of the *Mason County Journal*.

2 June 1891
The official purchase of the Olympia & Chehalis Valley Railroad by the Port Townsend Southern Railroad is recorded in Thurston County Deed Book 25, page 588. The line between Olympia and Tenino becomes the Southern Division of the Port Townsend Southern Railroad.

1 October 1895
The Oregon Improvement Company enters receivership.

6 November 1897
In a foreclosure sale for the benefit of bondholders, the Oregon Improvement Company is sold to, and is reorganized as, the Pacific Coast Company. Properties transferred to the Pacific Coast Company include the Port Townsend Southern Railroad Company, the Pacific Coast Railway, the Columbia & Puget Sound Railroad, the Seattle & Northern Railway and the Pacific Coast Steamship Company.

13 January 1898
The Pacific Coast Company is incorporated in the State of Washington. Its principal office is located at Jersey City, New Jersey.

17 January 1898
The Northwestern Improvement Company is incorporated in the State of Washington. Its principle office is located at Jersey City, New Jersey. It is a wholly owned subsidiary of the Northern Pacific Railroad.

30 November 1902
The Northwestern Improvement Company leases the Port Townsend Southern Railroad.

1906
The Port Townsend Southern Railroad Company surveys and purchases land for a right of way between Plumb Station and Tacoma. A few years later this right of way will be sold to the Northern Pacific Railroad, which will use it to construct its Point Defiance Line. Also in 1906 the Port Townsend Southern Railroad Company makes a new survey for a line to connect its Northern and Southern Divisions (linking Quilcene and Olympia, Washington). Still another branch line is surveyed to "Summit" [Junction] Washington. This is the place in southern Mason County where the Northern Pacific Railroad met the Port Blakely Mill Company's railroad. Neither of the latter two surveyed lines would be built.

1 January 1910
After negotiating a trackage right agreement in the fall of 1909, the Union Pacific Railroad begins freight and passenger service over the Northern Pacific Railroad between Portland and Seattle. The route followed the Prairie Line between Tenino and Tacoma.

25 June 1914
The Southern Division of the Port Townsend Southern Railroad is sold to the Northern Pacific Railroad.

1914
The original Plumb Station (located along what is currently Old Highway 99) is abandoned. It is replaced by a new station, also called Plumb Station, constructed (per Northern Pacific Railroad AFE 869-14) on the nearly finished Point Defiance Line of the Northern Pacific Railroad. The second Plumb Station would be removed in 1927 per AFE 1610-27.

15 December 1914
The first scheduled train runs on the Point Defiance Line of the Northern Pacific Railroad.

1 January 1916
The Union Pacific Railroad operates its first train into Olympia using a new track connecting downtown Olympia with the Point Defiance Line at East Olympia (Chamber's Prairie Station).

12 January 1916
Rail service ends south of Tumwater on the remaining portion of the Olympia & Tenino Railroad. Track is removed later in 1916 per Northern Pacific Railroad AFE 2338-16.

Introduction

Familiarity with some general information about the Olympia & Tenino Railroad may be worthwhile for the reader before exploring the body of the book. Between 1878 and 1916, this fifteen mile line was owned by several different organizations. First, it operated as the Olympia & Tenino Railroad Company. In 1881 it became the Olympia & Chehalis Valley Railroad Company. From 1891 to 1914 it was owned by the Port Townsend Southern Railroad Company and operated as that company's Southern Division. From 1914 until the beginning of 1916 it was the 14th Subdivision of the Pacific Division of the Northern Pacific Railroad.

Taking into account the succession of companies which owned this right of way, I chose to use the name, "The Olympia & Tenino Railroad" as a general or generic designation for the line joining those two towns.

The reader may find it fruitful to refer to the Chronology from time to time while perusing the book. In addition, an Appendix of newspaper articles (following Chapter 7) provides a glimpse of the tenor of a time long gone, when railroads were a primary mode of transportation and commerce.

Two chapters are styled as a journey from Olympia to Tenino. Chapter 3 examines the stations that were located along the way, while Chapter 4 is devoted to businesses served by the railroad.

Certain types of records are mentioned in the text but may be unfamiliar to many readers. An AFE (Authorization For Expense) is a type of document used by many railroads and can be thought of as a work order. Although the Northern Pacific Railroad generated an AFE covering any and every change in physical plant, some of them have been lost. Those that survive usually provide valuable information such as detailed maps. For example, Northern Pacific Railroad AFE 1580-20 (see Figure 7-2 on page 133) authorized removal of a spur that led to the old Olympia Brewery. This was the 1580th AFE issued in the year 1920.

Valuation Maps are another useful but obscure resource. Between 1915 and 1920 the Bureau of Valuation of the Interstate Commerce Commission sought to determine the cost basis for all common carrier railroads in the United States. The Bureau generated Right of Way Plat Maps which were called Valuation Maps. Using this data, the Interstate Commerce Commission produced a series of Valuation Books covering all existing common carrier railroads. Although the Olympia & Tenino Railroad was technically part of the Northern Pacific in those years, it was described separately on pages 361-377 of Volume 116 of the Valuation Books (see Bibliography).

The Northern Pacific Railroad found it practical to possess multiple copies of Valuation Maps which were relative to its own operation. These maps were updated over the years. In their present state, they contain data related to original purchase of right of way, surveys, and documents associated with abandonment. Three separate collections of Valuation Maps covering Thurston County were reviewed in preparation of this book. The collections are located at the Thurston County Assessor's office, the Washington State Archive in Olympia, and the private archive of Jim Fredrickson in Tacoma.

In the 1920s the Northern Pacific Railroad prepared a series of approximately fifteen Joint Facilities Books. This was an attempt to sort out ownership of real estate and track which was being used jointly by the Northern Pacific and either its customers or other railroads. The books contain interesting photographs as well as a history of each described facility.

In the years after 1916 there was inconsistency in the name applied to the right of way between the diamond (a place where two railroads cross at grade) on the west side of what is now Capitol Lake, and Tumwater. Previously, when the 22 November 1914 Northern Pacific Timetable was issued, trains using that track still operated on the "Tumwater Branch Crossing-Track Connection". It stretched from West Olympia, through Tumwater, and joined the new Point Defiance Line at the recently built (second) Plumb Station. The "Track Connection" ended at Tenino and was also known as the 14th Subdivision of the Pacific Division of the Northern Pacific Railroad.

By 1917 the rails ended at Tumwater. The Northern Pacific Timetable from that year labeled the track as "Tumwater Spur-Track Connection". Nonetheless, for years thereafter, some railroad employees referred to this segment of track as the "Tumwater Branch", as can be noted in Figure 7-2.

Most of the images in this book which show railroad grades use a red line for that purpose. However, shorter sections of right of way may be depicted by black or white lines, with arrows at each end.

Armed with this background, understanding the complex development and later deconstruction of the railroad will be made easier.

Illustrations

Port Townsend Southern Railroad Engine #1 Approaches the First Plumb Station

Olympia & Tenino Railroad Engine #1, the E. N. Ouimette, at the First Tenino Station

Port Townsend Southern Railroad Engine #858 at the Olympia Brewery Spur in Tumwater

Port Townsend Southern Railroad Engine #6 along the Deschutes River in Tumwater

Olympia & Chehalis Valley Railroad Engine #2, the Wallula, at McCorkle Road

Port Townsend Southern Railroad Engine #858 at the Hercules Sandstone Company Spur in Tenino

1
Planning and Construction of the Railroad - 1870 to 1878

In 1870 residents of Olympia were hopeful that the Northern Pacific Railroad would select Budd Inlet as its Puget Sound terminal. To further that goal, the Olympia Branch Railroad Company was formed for the purpose of negotiating with the transcontinental line. Thurston County residents pledged several thousand acres of land, held in trust by Marshall Blinn, to the Northern Pacific Railroad. Multiple sites were proposed for a terminal. One, located in West Olympia near Butler Cove, is reproduced in Figure 1-1. The image is courtesy of the Southwest Washington Regional Archives. The map shows Clark's Addition to Olympia as it was platted in 1871. The plat proposed a route for the "North Pacific Railroad" and imagined several wharfs at the northern end of the right of way. In 1876, Brown's Wharf, also known as the West Side Wharf, was actually built slightly south of the wharves proposed in Figure 1-1. Additional information about Brown's Wharf, Olympia's first deep water port, can be found on pages 36 and 37 of <u>Gone But Not Forgotten, Abandoned Railroads of Thurston County, Washington</u>.

In the early 1870s several other Puget Sound communities were competing with Olympia for the prized Northern Pacific Railroad terminal. Although Tacoma came out the winner late in 1872, a furor of land speculation prevailed in Thurston County in 1871. Major players in that real estate frenzy included Ira Bradley Thomas and General John Wilson Sprague. Thomas, representing the Northern Pacific Railroad, bought eighteen properties in Thurston County between October and December, 1871. His unexpected death shortly thereafter has been cited as one of the reasons the Northern Pacific Railroad chose to bypass Olympia. Probation of the Thomas estate was expected to tie up title to properties needed if Olympia were to have been the terminal.

General Sprague was a colorful man whose title was earned during the Civil War. He entered that conflict as Captain of the 7th Ohio Infantry, and finished as a brevetted Major General of Volunteers. After his death in Tacoma in 1893, he was awarded the Congressional Medal of Honor for his actions at Decatur, Alabama on 22 July 1864. Sprague came to Washington Territory in 1870 as a Superintendent of the Northern Pacific Railroad. In the spring of 1871, he and others connected with the Northern Pacific incorporated the Olympia & Chehalis Valley Railroad Company. In general, Sprague's proposed line was similar to the railroad already outlined by the Olympia Branch Railroad Company, with the exception that his corporation planned an extension to Grays Harbor. It's doubtful that Sprague's railroad was

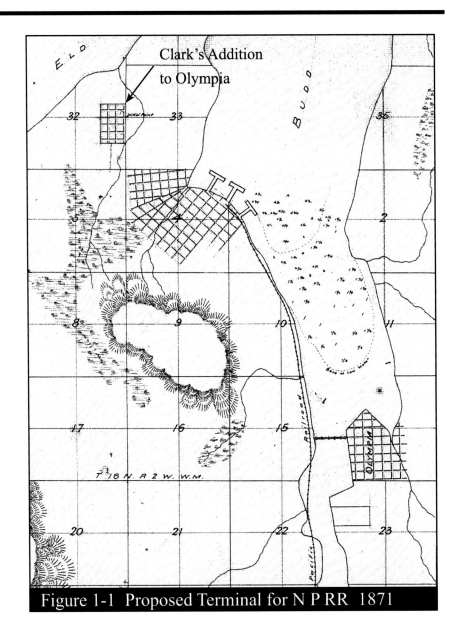

Figure 1-1 Proposed Terminal for N P RR 1871

a private undertaking. Likely this scheme was hatched by the Northern Pacific Railroad as an attempt to manipulate the Olympia Branch Railroad Company.

The name "Olympia & Chehalis Valley Railroad Company" languished in obscurity until 1881. By that time Sprague had become a major stockholder of the Olympia Railroad Construction Company, the organization operating the line between Olympia and Tenino since 1878. At their annual meeting in 1881, the owners of the Olympia Railroad Construction Company voted to change the name of the organization to "The Olympia & Chehalis Valley Railroad Company". Accordingly, the enterprise was reincorporated under that title, this time with a "The" preceding the remainder of the railroad's name.

Crucial events occurred in 1872. With the demise of Ira Bradley Thomas, Sprague began to participate actively in the real estate market. As agent for the Lake Superior and Puget Sound Company, the real estate development arm of the Northern Pacific Railroad, he bought and sold properties in the communities where the railroad considered locating its terminal. At the same time, he appears to be the person who was going to have the final say in selecting the location of the facility. With that advantage in 1872, he no longer needed to promote his Olympia & Chehalis Valley Railroad Company.

In the fall of 1872, when Tacoma was officially declared the terminal of the Northern Pacific Railroad, Olympians were left with animosity toward that railroad. That sentiment continued until the early part of the twentieth century. However, public opinion continued to favor building a rail connection between Budd Inlet and the Northern Pacific Railroad. Tenino seemed to be the logical place for a link to occur. As the organizational structure of the Olympia Branch Railroad Company decayed, a new entity came forward in August, 1873. The Olympia Railway & Mining Company planned to build its line from Olympia to coal fields near Tenino, operate coal mines there, and connect with the Northern Pacific Railroad in that region. Problems developed when many of the people who had formerly pledged land to the Olympia Branch Railroad Company refused to do the same for the new company. In addition, the organization was unable to raise money by selling bonds. In December, 1873 it was clear that the Olympia Railway & Mining Company was incapable of constructing its railroad.

Figure 1-2 Choral Society Benefit Program 1874

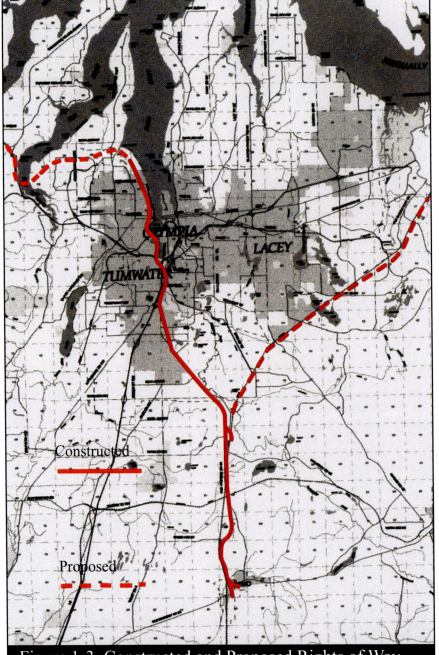

Figure 1-3 Constructed and Proposed Rights of Way

From the ashes of preceding schemes, the Olympia Railroad Union was organized 31 December 1873 and incorporated 5 January 1874. Most of the properties originally pledged to the Olympia Branch Railroad Company were deeded to the new organization. After much debate, the Union decided to build a narrow gauge railroad, believing it would be less costly than one of standard gauge. A route for the line had already been surveyed, and grading of the roadbed began in April, 1874. Most of the early work was done by volunteer business people from Olympia and Tumwater, along with farmers from the countryside. Weekend work parties were festive occasions (see 30 January 1875 in the Appendix). Figure 1-2, courtesy of the Washington State Historical Society Museum, indicates that the Olympia Choral Society raised money for the railroad through a benefit performance. In August, 1874 the voters of Thurston County agreed to back bonds for further construction. By December 1874, funds raised by the bond issue were exhausted and construction was halted.

Though most of the right of way had been graded, it remained without rails for almost three years. In June 1877, E. N. Ouimette spearheaded interest in completion of the line. A member of the Olympia Railroad Union, Ouimette induced the members of the Union to attend a gathering on 1 June 1877. At that meeting, the Thurston County Railroad Construction Company was formed. In little more than a year, the Construction Company was able to finish the work begun in 1874. Winlock Miller, Junior, reported that the rails bought by the company were formerly used by the Central Pacific Railroad, and had been "rerolled" in San Francisco.

The course and mileage of the railroad changed very little over its thirty-eight year lifespan. The solid red line appearing in Figure 1-3 displays all track constructed by the railroad during those years. The first train made a round trip between Olympia and Tenino 1 August 1878. As a memorial to his organizational effort, the first locomotive purchased for the line (Engine #1) was named the E. N. Ouimette.

The completion of the Olympia & Tenino Railroad meant that Olympia and Tumwater would not miss out on the economic boom associated with having a rail connection to the rest of the country. The future looked good. Nothing seemed impossible, both for the people of Thurston County, and their little railroad. This "can do" attitude resurfaced again and again during the next thirty eight years. But when the line was finally abandoned in 1916, these thoughts proved to have been just the first of many delusions of grandeur.

2

Railroad Operation - 1878 to 1909

While studying the operating history of the Olympia & Tenino Railroad, two resources may be helpful. First, Figures 2-1 through 2-13B were prepared from a series of 1930s era aerial photographs of Thurston County. They can be used to locate historical features along the railroad such as stations, spurs, rerouted sections of mainline, and businesses. Second, the Chronology can be used to clarify the Olympia & Tenino Railroad's frequently confusing series of operating names and owners.

When the first scheduled train left Olympia for Tenino on 1 August 1878, the official name of the line was the Olympia & Tenino Railroad Company. It was owned by the Thurston County Railroad Construction Company. The right of way, surveyed in 1874, had a total length of 14.83 miles. It originated in Olympia at a wharf on the bridge carrying 4th Avenue across the West Bay of Budd Inlet, and terminated at the Northern Pacific Railroad's first Tenino Station.

After much discussion, a gauge of three feet had been selected for the track because it was cheaper to build and could negotiate tighter curves. This meant that cars could not be interchanged at Tenino with the standard gauge (4 feet 8½ inches) Northern Pacific Railroad. The Olympia & Tenino Railroad anticipated traffic to consist of passengers, farm products, logs, and coal. Of these, only transportation of logs seemed to have been very profitable. Passenger service consisted of one or two round trips daily between Olympia and Tenino. Figure 2-14 is reprinted from the 16 December 1882 edition of the *Olympia Transcript*. Although the corporate name of the railroad changed in 1881 (see below), it was still referred to popularly as The Olympia & Tenino Railroad.

Before the railroad was built, many county residents believed (erroneously) that the line would soon be carrying coal to Olympia's harbor from mines southeast of Tenino. This notion was revived in 1884 when The Olympia & Chehalis Valley Railroad (as the railroad was then known) planned an extension into those coal fields. Talk of such an extension resurfaced in 1886. In 1887 the idea was combined with a scheme to convert the line to standard gauge and construct an extension to Grays Harbor. Another proposal would have lengthened the line to Butler Cove, north of Olympia, where bunkers would be built for coal exportation. That notion persisted in an 1891 map of Olympia harbor, a portion of which is reproduced in Figure 2-15. Except for the eventual conversion to standard gauge, none of these projects were completed. The implication is that delusions of grandeur formed a large part of the company's vision of the future in the 1880s.

In the 1880s logging was what sustained the railroad. During this decade, previously well established loggers like George Foster and Benjamin Turner probed into timber located far from Puget Sound. They were able to do so partly because the Olympia & Tenino Railroad provided an economical way to transport logs to tideland. Several smaller loggers also used the railroad, and the Tacoma Mill Company had extensive spurs originating from it. The 1890 edition of Poor's Manual of Railroads noted that the railroad (then The Olympia & Chehalis Valley Railroad) had seven miles of logging spurs. Many of these businesses will be described further in Chapter 4.

The official name of the railroad was changed to The Olympia & Chehalis Valley Railroad on 1 August 1881. On that same day John W. Sprague, who had maintained an interest in a railroad between Olympia and Tenino since 1871, was elected President. In 1881, Sprague and Robert Wingate were among the principal stockholders of the company. In 1886 both men owned land southeast of Tenino which contained extensive coal deposits. They sold these lands to their railroad, but obtained no personal benefit when it proved impossible to build a rail extension to the properties.

The Washington State Historical Society has preserved an interesting bit of memorabilia from the Olympia & Chehalis Valley Railroad. Figure 2-16 displays a pass issued in 1889, signed by President Sprague.

In 1886, after eight years of use, the wooden trestle between Warren's Point and the first Olympia Station had become unsafe. Therefore most of the right of way north of Warren's Point was relocated to dry land. This required building a new, much shorter trestle from Warren's Point to Percival's Point. The location of Olympia's Station was moved to the newly aligned grade, southwest of the 4th Avenue Bridge. A trace of the original 1878 trestle can still be seen in the 1936 aerial photograph presented in Figure 2-3B.

In the late 1880s and early 1890s the Olympia & Tenino Railroad underwent a metamorphosis. At the same time, the entire economy of the United States was booming, and Washington and Thurston County were no different. No longer did

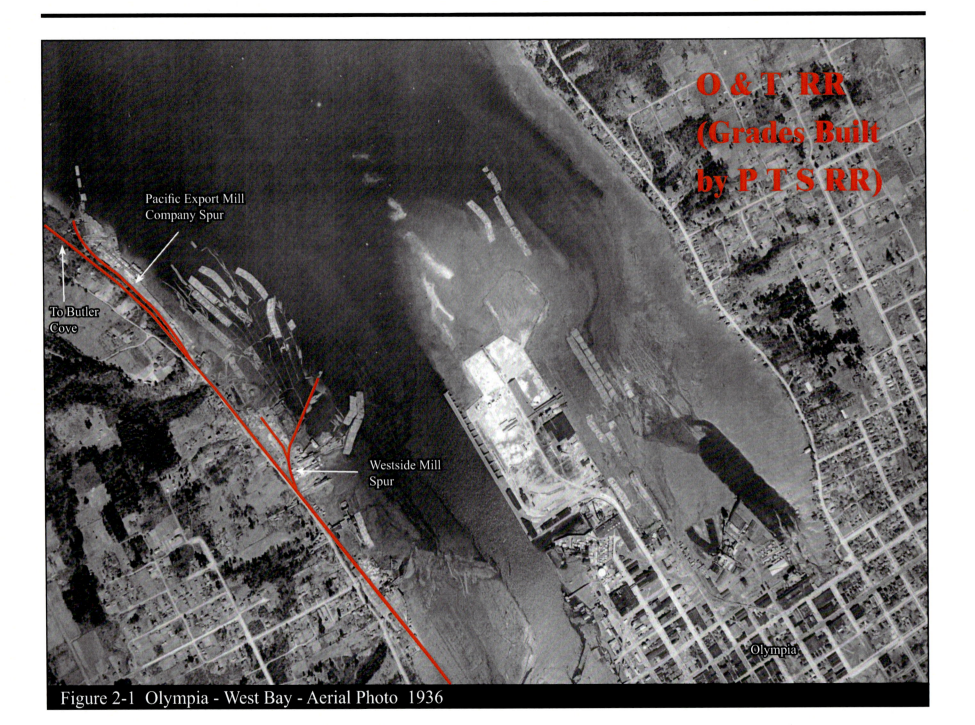

Figure 2-1 Olympia - West Bay - Aerial Photo 1936

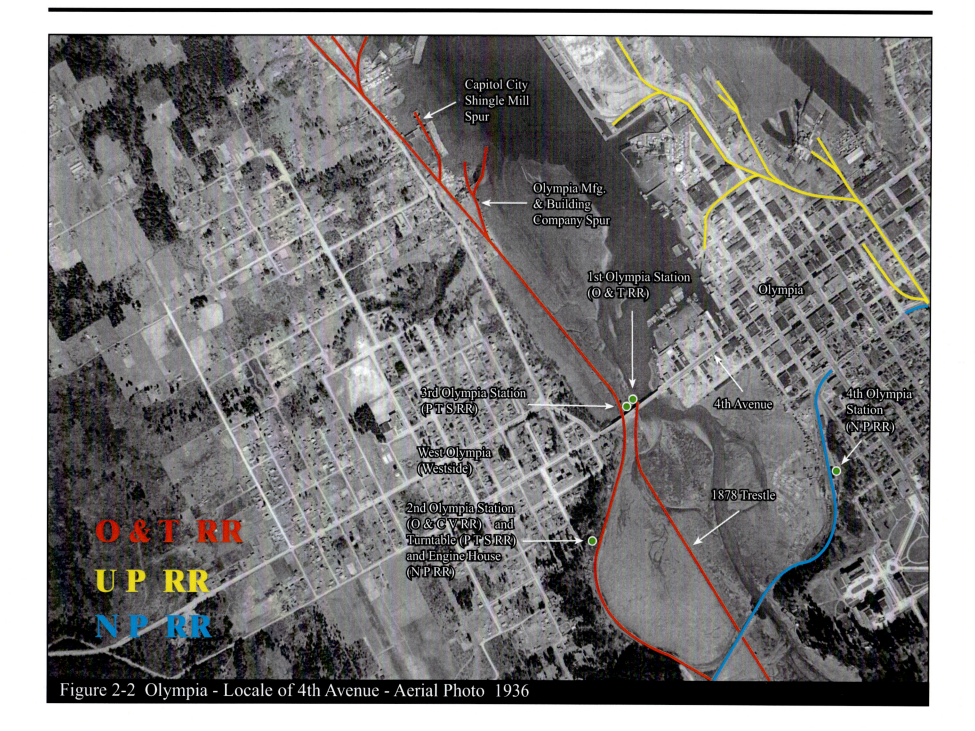

Figure 2-2 Olympia - Locale of 4th Avenue - Aerial Photo 1936

Figure 2-3A Tumwater

Figure 2-3B Aerial Photo 1936

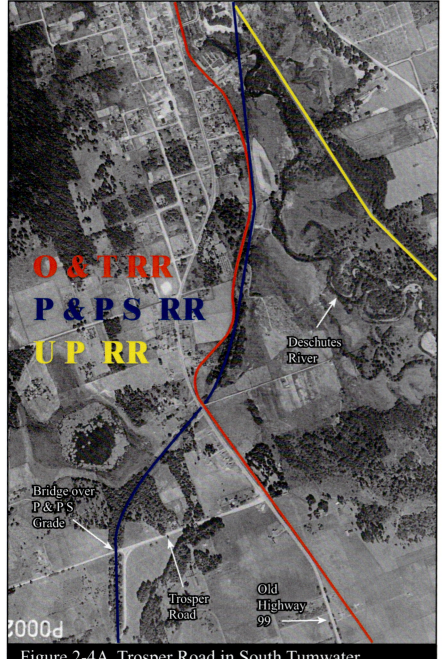

Figure 2-4A Trosper Road in South Tumwater

Figure 2-4B Aerial Photo 1936

Figure 2-5A Old Highway 99 Northeast of Olympia Airport

Figure 2-5B Aerial Photo 1933

Figure 2-6A Old Highway 99 at Rich Road

Figure 2-6B Aerial Photo 1936

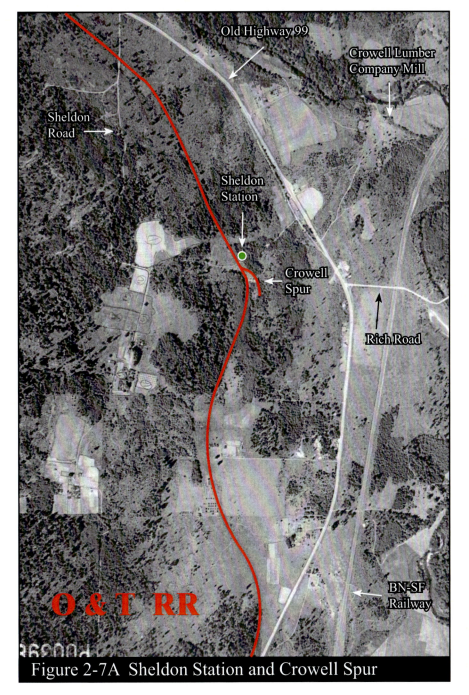

Figure 2-7A Sheldon Station and Crowell Spur

Figure 2-7B Aerial Photo 1936

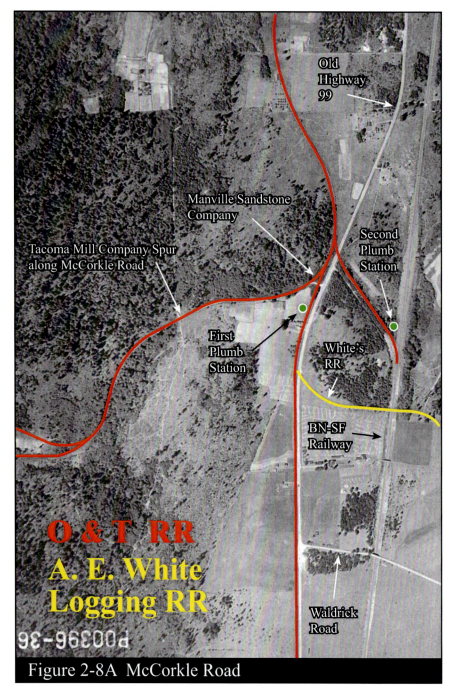

Figure 2-8A McCorkle Road

Figure 2-8B Aerial Photo 1936

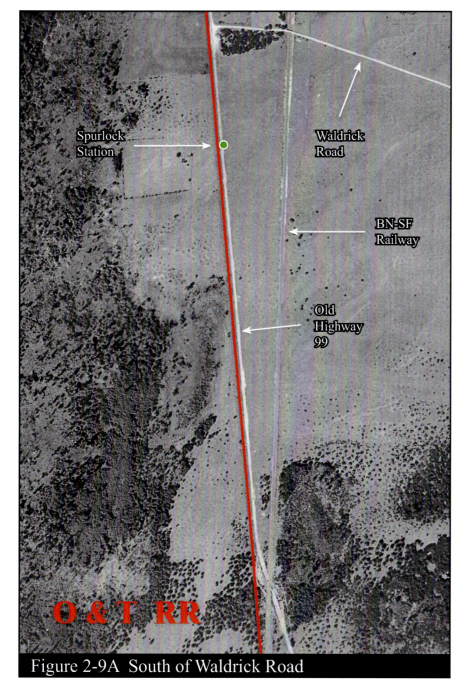

Figure 2-9A South of Waldrick Road

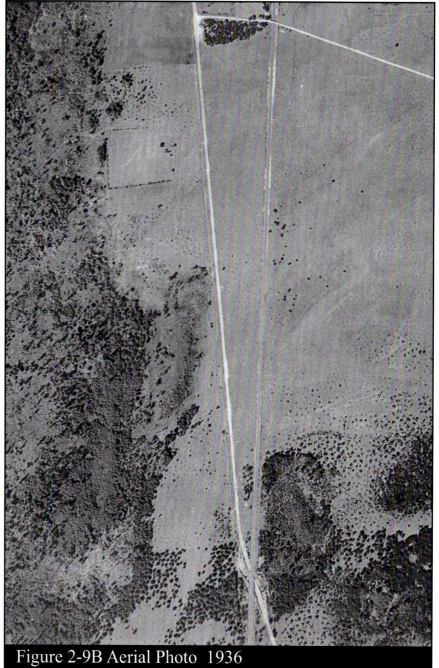

Figure 2-9B Aerial Photo 1936

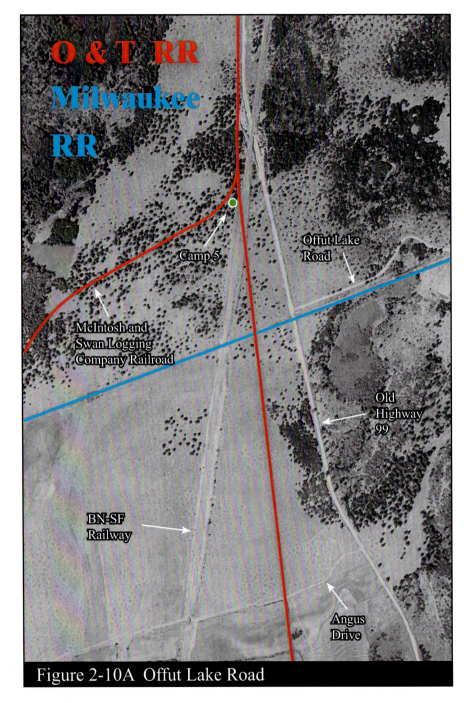

Figure 2-10A Offut Lake Road

Figure 2-10B Aerial Photo 1936

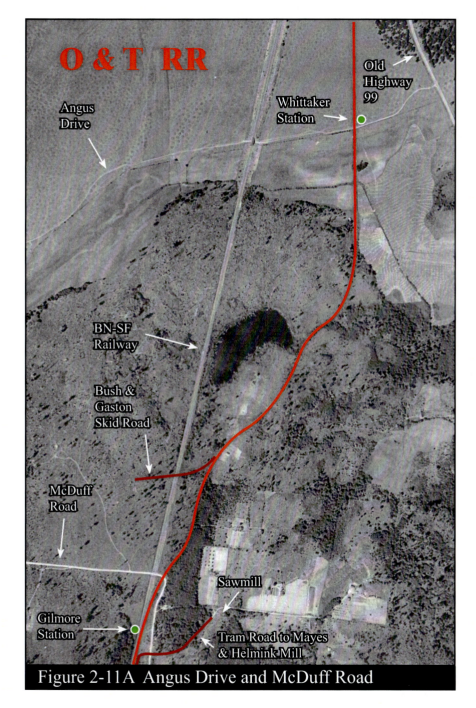

Figure 2-11A Angus Drive and McDuff Road

Figure 2-11B Aerial Photo 1936

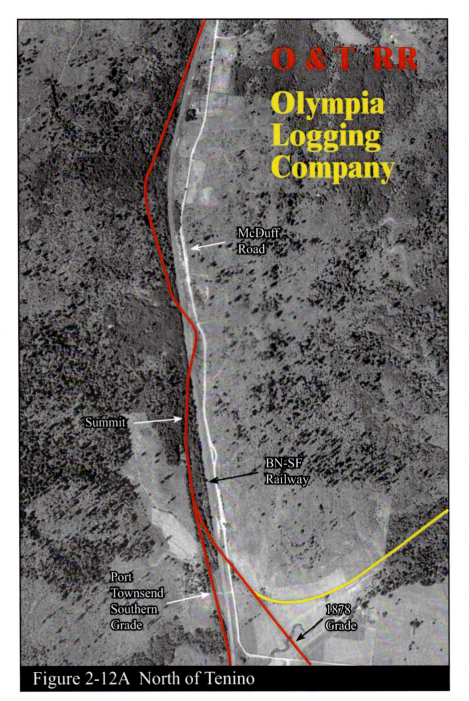

Figure 2-12A North of Tenino

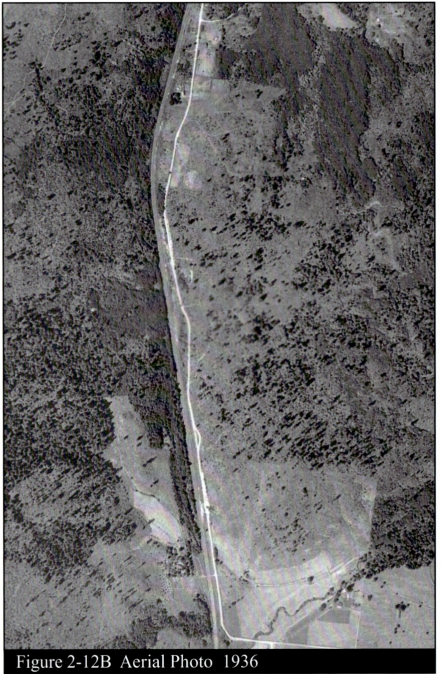

Figure 2-12B Aerial Photo 1936

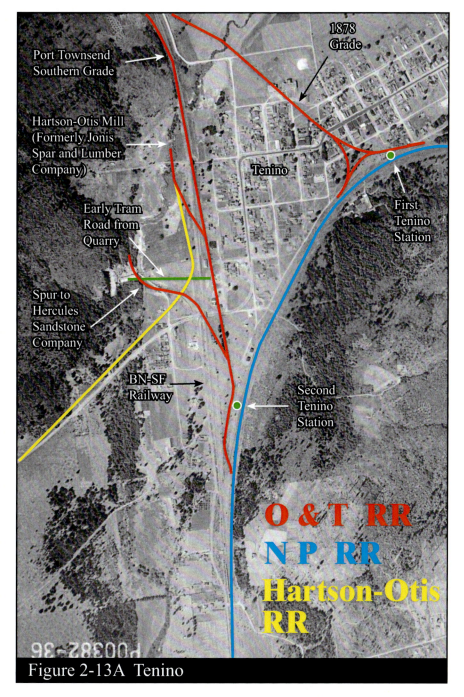

Figure 2-13A Tenino

Figure 2-13B Aerial Photo 1936

Olympia & Tenino RAILROAD.

ON AND AFTER MONDAY, MARCH 20TH, 1882, will run two trains daily, Sundays excepted, until further notice, connecting with the N. P. R. R. at Tenino.

Time Table.

TRAIN LEAVES OLYMPIA AT....	7 A.M.
" " Tumwater at......	7:30 "
" Arrives at Tenino............	9 "
" Leaves Tenino at............	9:15 "
" Arrives at Olympia.........	11:10 "
" Leaves Olympia at.........	12 P.M.
" Arrives at Tenino............	1:45 "
" Leaves Tenino at............	1:55 "
" Arrives at Olympia.........	3:35 "

Figure 2-14 Passenger Train Timetable 1882

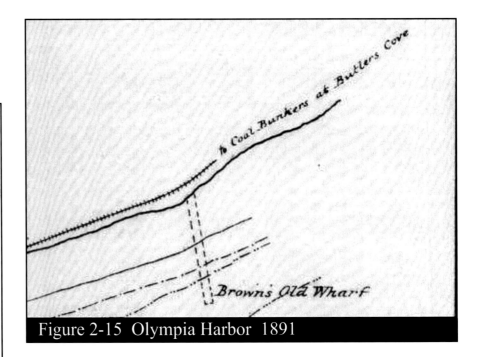

Figure 2-15 Olympia Harbor 1891

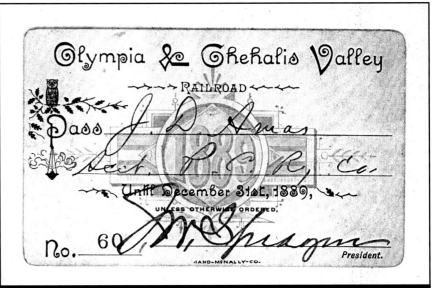

Figure 2-16 Passenger Pass 1889

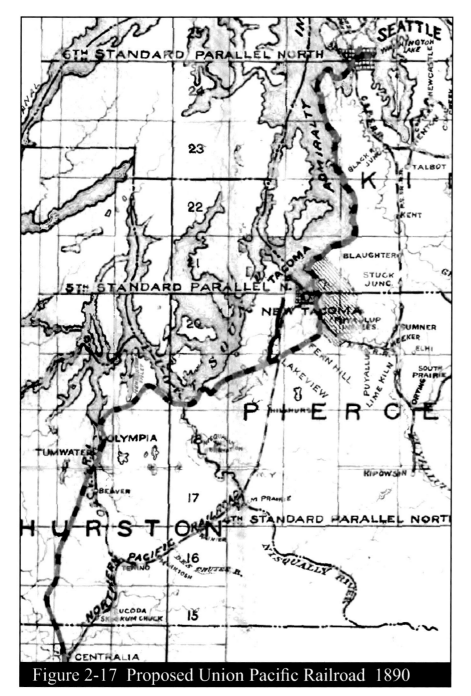

Figure 2-17 Proposed Union Pacific Railroad 1890

Olympia have to beg for a new railroad. Indeed, three new lines wished to serve the Capital city, as Washington passed from territory to statehood in 1889. The Union Pacific, Northern Pacific and Port Townsend Southern all proposed new service for Olympia. Of these, the Northern Pacific and Port Townsend Southern made good on their propositions.

The Union Pacific fell short of its goal. It surveyed the Portland & Puget Sound Railroad and managed to buy and grade a sizable amount of right of way between Portland and Seattle. Figure 2-17 is part of an 1890 Union Pacific map of its Pacific Division. The railroad encountered financial problems in 1891 and had to halt construction before any rail was laid. A tunnel under what would later become Capitol Boulevard was only partially excavated. The tunnel was eventually completed in 1914 when the Union Pacific finally gained entry into Olympia.

The Northern Pacific accomplished its proposal by constructing the Tacoma, Olympia & Grays Harbor Railroad through downtown Olympia in 1891. Figure 2-18 is a Northern Pacific Railroad map from the collection of the Minnesota Historical Society. It indicates the place where the Tacoma, Olympia & Grays Harbor Railroad crossed the Port Townsend Southern Railroad (owner of the Olympia & Tenino Railroad in 1891) on the west side of what is now Capitol Lake.

The Port Townsend Southern Railroad was incorporated in 1887 by Port Townsend businessmen who wanted to make Port Townsend the deep water terminal for a transcontinental railroad. Financing this gargantuan undertaking was clearly beyond the means of the Port Townsend business community. No track had been laid by 1889 when the Oregon Improvement Company bought the enterprise. Late in the same year The Olympia & Chehalis Valley Railroad also came under control of the Oregon Improvement Company. The latter organization planned to integrate that line, from Olympia to Tenino, into the Port Townsend Southern Railroad. The result was to have been a continuous line from Port Townsend south, through Shelton and Olympia, to Tenino. An 1889 map by Charles Baker, called the New Map of Puget Sound, shows the entire length of the projected Port Townsend Southern Railroad between Port Townsend and Olympia. Figure 2-19 reproduces the segment of that map between Shelton and Olympia.

In 1889 the Oregon Improvement Company announced plans for construction of 27 miles of railroad south from Port Townsend to Quilcene. It also called for building approximately 3 miles of line up the west side of Budd Inlet, from the 4th Avenue Bridge to a point immediately south of Butler Cove. Subsequent construction was to have linked these two segments, but financing for that connection could never quite be secured. During its lifetime the Port Townsend Southern Railroad consisted of a

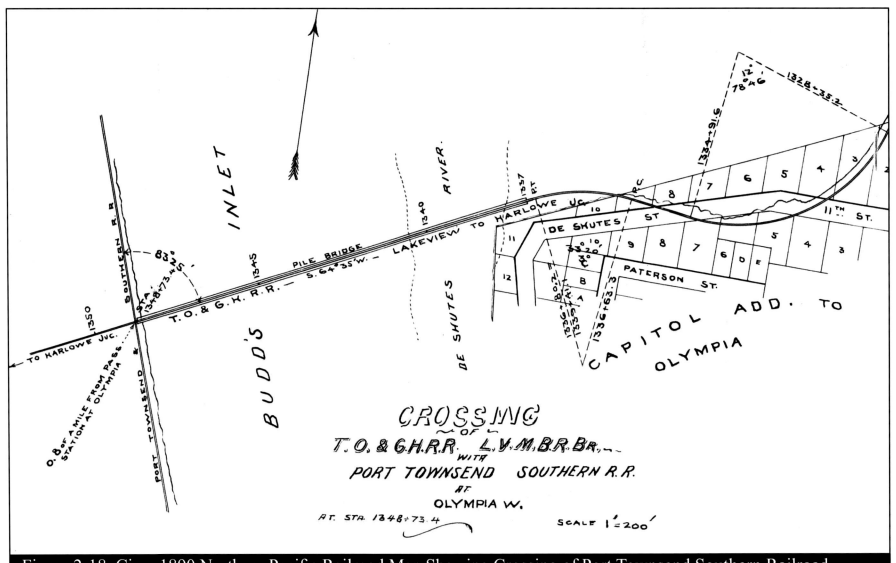
Figure 2-18 Circa 1890 Northern Pacific Railroad Map Showing Crossing of Port Townsend Southern Railroad

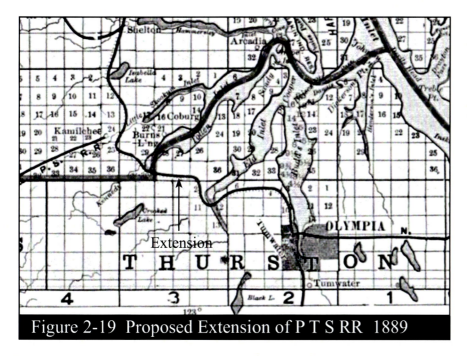

Figure 2-19 Proposed Extension of P T S RR 1889

Northern Division between Port Townsend and Quilcene, and a Southern Division which was the former Olympia & Tenino Railroad.

The extension north from Olympia toward Butler Cove is described in Volume 116 of <u>Interstate Commerce Commission Reports</u>. Page 376 notes that this three mile segment of track was completed in 1891 and abandoned in 1894. The preliminary plan for this right of way placed it on pilings almost all the way to Butler Cove. This is how the grade appeared in the 1890 "Map of Port Townsend and Southern Railroad Company" recorded on pages 52-55 of Thurston County Plat Book #5. When the extension was actually built, it did run on pilings north from the 4th Avenue Bridge. However it came to ground immediately south of the Westside Mill and remained on land all the way to its end, immediately south of Butler Cove.

Figure 2-20 superimposes the right of way on a modern aerial photograph of the region between the 4th Avenue Bridge and Butler Cove. Figure 2-21 looks north at the place where Harbor View Drive diverges from West Bay Drive. Here the grade to Butler Cove began to climb. In the photograph, visible rails do not lie where the Butler Cove extension was located. In 1891 the hill seen on the left had not yet been excavated. It extended far to the right, projecting out into Budd Inlet. Today, the rails north of this point curve right and remain level. The original right of way,

Figure 2-20 Dotted Line Is Extension Built in 1891

Figure 2-21 Harbor View Drive and West Bay Drive

however, cut through the hill, as it existed then, and subsequently hugged the east side of the bluff. In addition, the grade gained elevation as it progressed north.

The old extension may still be seen in a few places along the bluff. Figure 2-22 is a recent photograph taken looking west approximately 500 feet north of the position where Figure 2-21 was obtained. Figure 4-5 represents the topography of this location in 1906, when the Hartson Lumber Company requested construction of a spur.

Farther north along West Bay Drive, at the site of Dunlap Towing, the hillside has been partially removed. Nothing remains of the old grade except at the north end of the excavation. Figure 2-23 demonstrates the cut used by the Butler Cove extension. The photograph was taken looking north.

Another of the best preserved parts of the extension can be accessed by driving north on Crestline Drive and turning right (east) on 25th Avenue NW. The latter road descends to a corner before making a 90 degree turn to the right (south). Figure 2-24 shows the view toward the northeast from a point on 25th Avenue NW, immediately west of that corner. Here the grade can be seen running in a small cut at the lower right side of the picture, before heading out over a large trestle. The origin of the trestle is at the far left side of the picture.

After turning at the corner, 25th Avenue NW runs parallel to Budd Inlet and occupies the old railroad grade. Figure 2-25 was taken looking south along 25th Avenue NW. Page 39 of Gone But Not Forgotten, Abandoned Railroads of Thurston County, Washington contains additional information about the grade north of 25th Avenue NW. To reach the northernmost part of the right of way, drive north to the Oldport community. Follow Anchor Lane to the place where it ends on the south side of Oldport. This spot is also the northern end of the railroad's Butler Cove extension. Immediately to the south, the line crossed a ravine via a high fill. Figure 2-26 is a photograph of the fill, taken looking northeast.

In 1899 the Mason County Logging Company began cutting timber in the Black Hills. A log dump for the company was built on Budd Inlet, north of the Port Townsend Southern station (3rd Olympia Station). Figure 3-15 shows loaded logging cars at the dump. The cars began their journey at Bordeaux, Washington and were then hauled by the Northern Pacific to the west side of Budd Inlet. There they transferred to the Port Townsend Southern for the short trip north to the log dump. The transfer point can be seen in Figure 3-19.

A big change came in 1902 when the Port Townsend Southern Railroad was leased by the Northwestern Improvement Company. The latter organization was a wholly owned subsidiary of the Northern Pacific Railroad. Improvements were made in the

Figure 2-22 View West Along West Bay Drive 2007

Figure 2-24 Extension Seen From 25th Avenue NW

Figure 2-23 View North From Dunlap Towing 2001

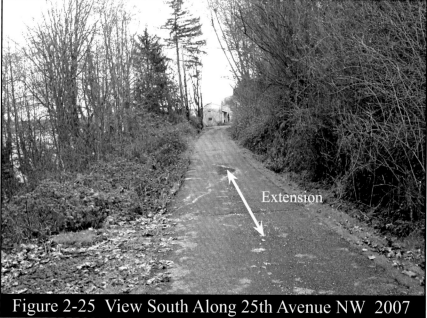
Figure 2-25 View South Along 25th Avenue NW 2007

Figure 2-26 Fill South of Oldport Community 2007

roadbed and a powerful Northern Pacific locomotive, #858, began service on the line. The locomotive appears in Figure 2-27, which is courtesy of the Tenino Depot Museum. The engine was photographed at Tenino after the cab had been repainted to indicate "P. T. S. R. R." Although under control of the Northern Pacific, the Port Townsend Southern was operated with its own distinct name until 1914.

After 1902 a resurgence in logging activity took place in several areas near the railroad. In addition the Hercules Sandstone Company quarry at Tenino began to originate stone shipments on the line. The most ambitious plan of the decade came in 1906 when the railroad caused surveys to be made for three separate lines of new track. The scheme is detailed on page 377 of the same volume of Interstate Commerce Commission Reports mentioned on page 22. The first was to have been a renewed attempt to join the Northern and Southern Divisions of the railroad by completing the segment between Quilcene and Olympia. The second survey was for a route connecting the Port Townsend Southern Railroad to Summit [Junction] Washington. Summit was the place near McCleary where the Northern Pacific Railroad interchanged traffic with the Port Blakely Mill Company railroad. Unfortunately, this survey is known only by the above reference to it. It is not clear whether the junction was to have been with the Northern or Southern Division of the line, or to the projected connection between the two divisions.

The third survey was the most significant from a historical standpoint. It proposed a line between the 1st Plumb Station and Tacoma. Part of that survey is preserved at the Washington State Archives. The Port Townsend Southern actually acquired most of this right of way and eventually sold it to the Northern Pacific for construction of its Point Defiance Line. Even one hundred years later it is impossible to know with certainty whether the Port Townsend Southern really planned, in 1906, to build on this route. At the time, there was speculation that the Northern Pacific, which indirectly controlled the Port Townsend Southern, was using the latter line as a stooge to further its own purposes. In the first decade of the twentieth century, the Northern Pacific tried to block other transcontinental railroads which attempted to enter its exclusive territory.

In 1906 this concern was real because, for the second time, the Union Pacific Railroad was making plans to build its own line from Portland to Seattle. In the same year, the Milwaukee Road began constructing its Pacific Division, and was running trains in Thurston County by 1908. In the fall of 1909 the Northern Pacific Railroad, Union Pacific Railroad and Great Northern Railway decided that a joint operating agreement between the three lines would be in the best interest of each company. On 1 January 1910 the Union Pacific and Great Northern began operating trains on Northern Pacific track between Portland and Seattle. Most of this route was a single track which included the Prairie Line between Tenino and Tacoma. Soon it became clear that the existing railroad would be unable to carry the vastly increased traffic resulting from the new operating agreement. As a result, the Northern Pacific constructed a new double track mainline (the Point Defiance Line) from Tenino to Tacoma and added a second track to its line south of Tenino.

In general, when the Northern Pacific built the Point Defiance Line, it used property acquired by the Port Townsend Southern as a result of its 1906 survey of the route between Plumb Station and Tacoma. Between Gilmore Station and Tenino, construction of the new mainline obliterated most of the earlier railroad's grade.

With the aid of hindsight it seems clear that on 1 January 1910, the process began which led to the demise of the Olympia & Tenino Railroad. Chapter 6 will describe the interval between that first day of 1910 and the date in January, 1916 when train service on the line ceased.

Figure 2-27 Undated Photograph of Port Townsend Southern Railroad Engine #858 at Tenino

3

Stations - 1878 to 1916

An effective way to look at the physical plant of the Olympia & Tenino Railroad is to examine the stations located along the line. These ranged in quality all the way from the traditional depot buildings at Olympia and Tenino, down to mere sheds resembling modern school bus shelters. The railroad maintained its own station building at Olympia, Bush Prairie, Plumb and Gilmore. In Tenino, agreements with the Northern Pacific Railroad allowed the Olympia & Tenino Railroad to use the stations of the Northern Pacific. Three successive stations were constructed in Tenino by the Northern Pacific. In the years when the first two were Tenino's designated passenger depots, they were also used by the Olympia & Tenino Railroad.

All other stations were built and maintained by local residents for their personal convenience. They tended to be named after the owner of nearby land, or for the business located there. Figures 3-1 through 3-10 display a series of maps from 1883 to 1916. Between those years new station names appeared, while others vanished. At least one, known as Sheldon Station, was not shown on any of the maps. In 1905, the First Annual Report of the Railroad Commission of Washington listed the stations maintained by the Port Townsend Southern Railroad (as the Olympia & Tenino Railroad was known at the time). They were located at Bush, Plumb and Gilmore. Station locations are also shown in Figures 2-1 through 2-13B. Those aerial photographs are courtesy of Thurston County Roads & Transportation Services and were made in the 1930s.

In 1878, the railroad erected its first Olympia Station at the northern terminus of the line. Figure 3-11, part of an 1891 map of the Olympia Harbor, locates the depot upon the contemporaneous 4th Avenue Bridge, at the end of a long trestle coming from Warren's Point. Wood from this old trestle could still be seen in 1936 (see Figure 2-3B), before Capitol Lake was formed.

A second Olympia Station was needed in 1886 when a long segment of trestlework north of Warren's Point was relocated. The new right of way crossed Percival Cove on a short trestle and came back to dry land at Percival's Point. Figure 3-12 is part of Whitham & Page's 1890 map of Olympia. It demonstrates the location of the second station, as well as a boardwalk connecting it with the 4th Avenue Bridge. In 1895 the Port Townsend Southern Railroad finished constructing a turntable near the site of the second station. Figure 3-13 is courtesy of the Washington State Historical Society. It is an undated aerial photograph looking west over the Washington State Capitol campus. The second station and turntable are gone, but would have been located on the west side of what is now Capitol Lake (on the right side of the picture).

The Port Townsend Southern Railroad built the third Olympia Station on pilings at a site immediately north of the old wooden bridge carrying 4th Avenue across Budd Inlet. The railroad crossed the bridge at grade. Figure 3-14 is presented courtesy of Peter Replinger. The photograph was taken looking north from the 4th Avenue Bridge. Port Townsend Southern Engine #6 is ready to depart for Tenino with one passenger car and a trailing flat car. The Castle Coal Company, which began doing business here in 1891, can be seen on the right side of the picture. Figure 3-15 is a photograph of the station after 1899, when the Mason County Logging Company, headquartered at Bordeaux, Washington, began using a log dump immediately north of the station.

In 1902 the Northern Pacific Railroad gained control of the Port Townsend Southern, and the latter line's passenger trains began using the Northern Pacific Water Street Station in downtown Olympia. Thereafter the Port Townsend Southern Station operated as a scale house for the log dump. Figure 3-16 is courtesy of Brian Ferris. The photograph was taken in the 1940s and reportedly shows a couple revisiting the place from which they departed on their honeymoon in the 1890s. Figure 3-17 is a 2007 photograph looking north from a position under the current 4th Avenue Bridge. The station was located to the right of the place where the tracks begin to curve left.

Built in 1891, the Northern Pacific Railroad's Water Street Station was Olympia's downtown passenger depot and was used by the Port Townsend Southern after 1902. Figure 3-18 is a 1956 photograph courtesy of Jim Fredrickson. A Northern Pacific passenger train pauses at the Water Street Station, long after the Port Townsend Southern ceased to exist. The original Water Street Station was torn down in 1966. Its replacement was completed in 1968 and occupies the site in 2008.

In order to use the Water Street Station, Port Townsend Southern trains had to transfer to Northern Pacific track on the west side of Budd Inlet. This was done in the vicinity of a diamond constructed in 1891, when the Northern Pacific built its

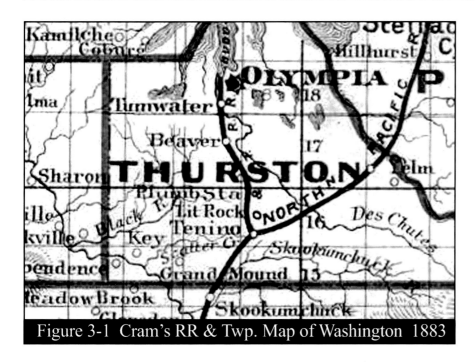
Figure 3-1 Cram's RR & Twp. Map of Washington 1883

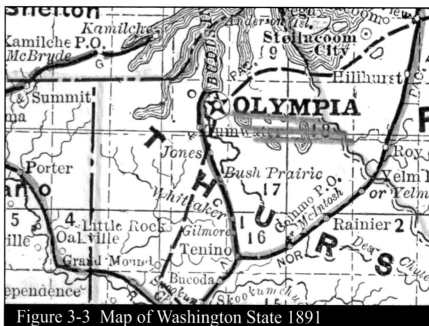
Figure 3-3 Map of Washington State 1891

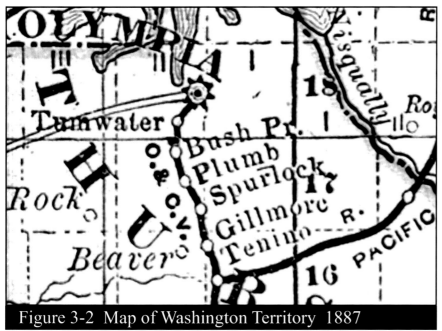
Figure 3-2 Map of Washington Territory 1887

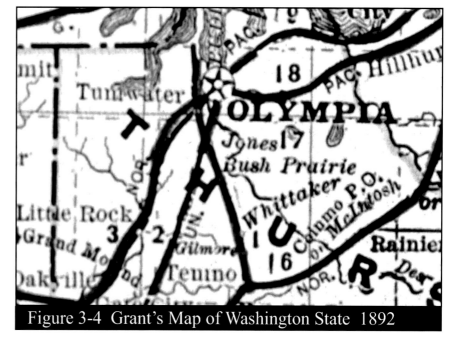
Figure 3-4 Grant's Map of Washington State 1892

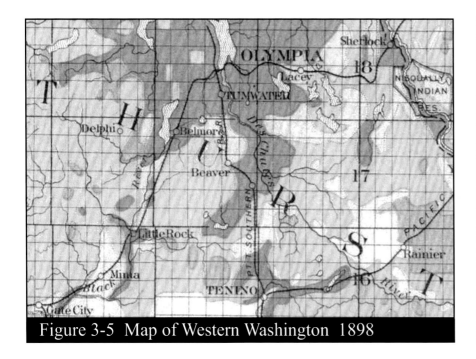
Figure 3-5 Map of Western Washington 1898

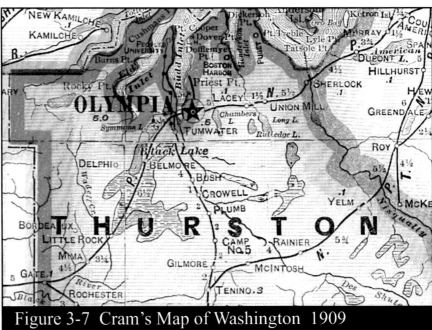
Figure 3-7 Cram's Map of Washington 1909

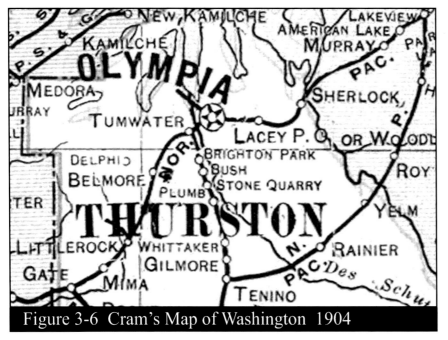
Figure 3-6 Cram's Map of Washington 1904

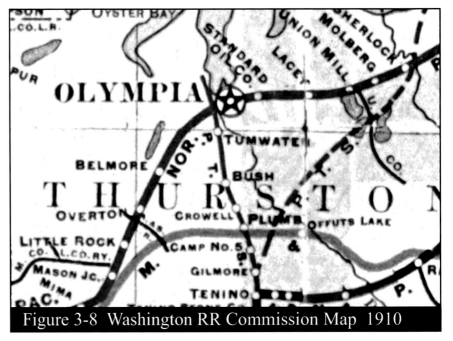
Figure 3-8 Washington RR Commission Map 1910

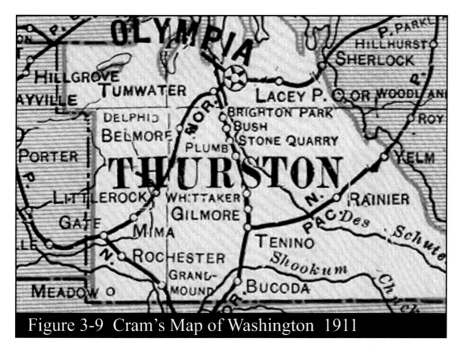
Figure 3-9 Cram's Map of Washington 1911

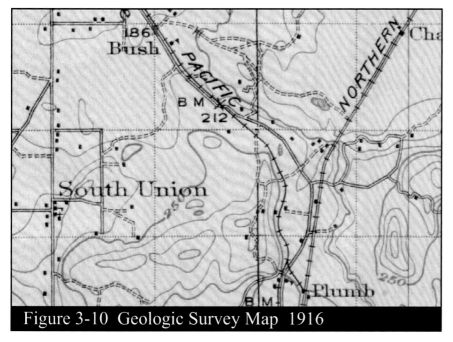
Figure 3-10 Geologic Survey Map 1916

Tacoma, Olympia & Grays Harbor Railroad across the pre-existing Port Townsend Southern grade (see the article dated 28 May 1891 in the Appendix). Figure 2-18 details the original track plan for the diamond. The complete map can be found in Port Townsend Southern Railroad records located in the Northern Pacific Railroad collection of the Minnesota Historical Society.

After 1893, transfer of trains between the two railroads required use of a segment of curved track on the northeast side of the diamond. The segment is visible in Figure 3-19. This figure is part of a 1917 Northern Pacific Railroad Valuation Map. At some later time a similar curved track was placed on the northwest side of the diamond, creating the wye that exists there in 2008. Passenger trains from Tenino executed a specific movement in order to reach the Water Street Station. Initially the train stopped on the Port Townsend Southern mainline, north of both the diamond and the curved track. Then it backed around the curve, crossed Budd Inlet, and entered the station. For the return trip to Tenino, the locomotive was turned using a turntable located near the Water Street Station, then coupled to the opposite end of the train. Finally, it backed out of the station and executed the same movement, in reverse, on the west side of Budd Inlet.

At the southern end of Budd Inlet, Tumwater Station was nothing more than a loading platform. With several homes, businesses, and the Tumwater trolley station nearby, there apparently was no need for a formal depot structure. Figure 3-20 is a photograph taken after 1902 in Tumwater and is provided by the Tenino Depot Museum. The view is northward, at the Tumwater Station, on the west side of the Deschutes River. The conductor, Mr. Ed Kevin, stands on the loading platform next to a baggage car. The locomotive is Port Townsend Southern #858. Contrast this picture with the much earlier photograph, courtesy of the Henderson House Museum, reproduced in Figure 3-21. That view is toward the south and was taken before 1890, when the line (then the Olympia & Chehalis Valley Railroad) was narrow gauge. The largest structure in the center of the picture is the Gelbach Flour Mill, located at the Middle Falls of the Deschutes River. The loading platform at Tumwater Station cannot be seen, but was situated immediately beyond the large white house on the right side of the track.

Figure 3-22 helps clarify these relationships. The figure is part of a Northern Pacific Railroad Valuation Map issued about 1917 and revised subsequently. This version appeared in the 1950s. The Middle Falls of the Deschutes River, the Boston Street Bridge, and a "Depot Cor [ner]" can be identified. Although removed years before, the Tumwater end of the trolley line joining Olympia with Tumwater is still displayed at the east end of the Boston Street Bridge. Passengers from Tumwater who were traveling south could take the trolley to its terminal, cross the Boston Street Bridge,

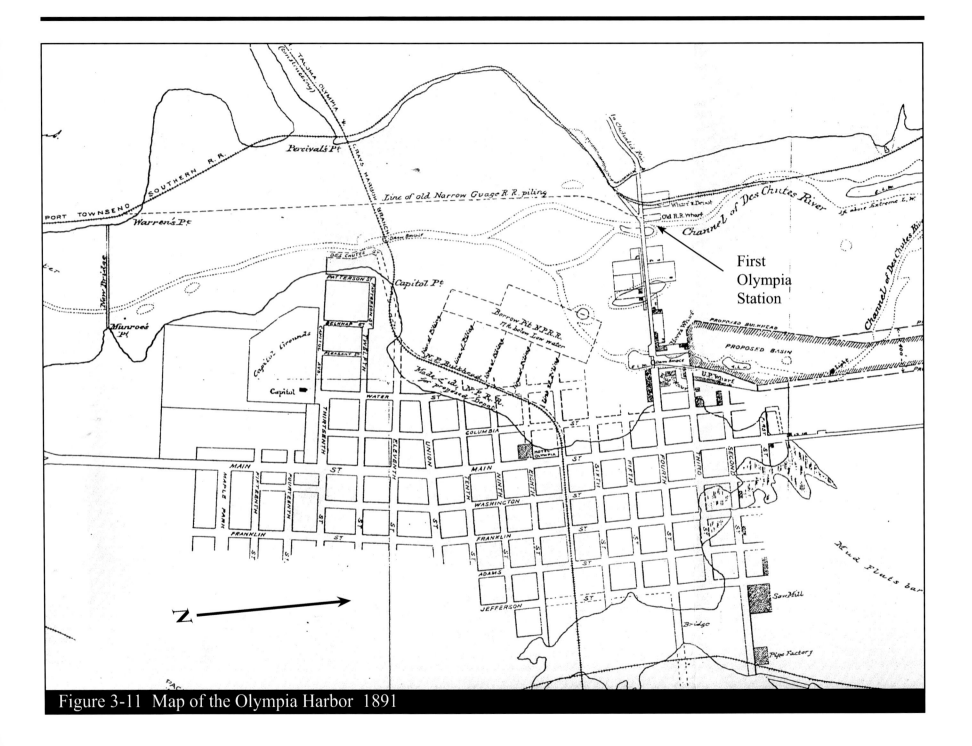

Figure 3-11 Map of the Olympia Harbor 1891

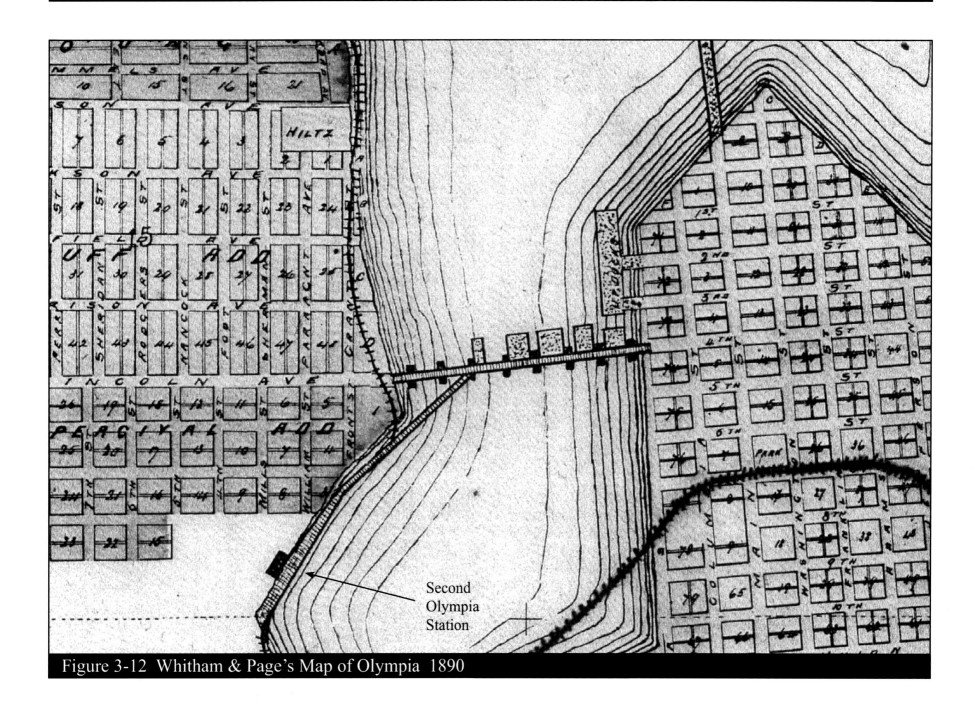

Figure 3-12 Whitham & Page's Map of Olympia 1890

Figure 3-13 Pre-1950s View West Over Budd Inlet (Now Capitol Lake)

Figure 3-14 Port Townsend Southern Engine #6 Prepares to Depart Olympia's Third Passenger Station

Figure 3-15 View North at 4th Avenue Bridge - Third Olympia Station and Mason County Logging Co. Log Dump

Figure 3-16 Third Olympia Station in the 1940s

Figure 3-17 Site of Third Olympia Station 2007

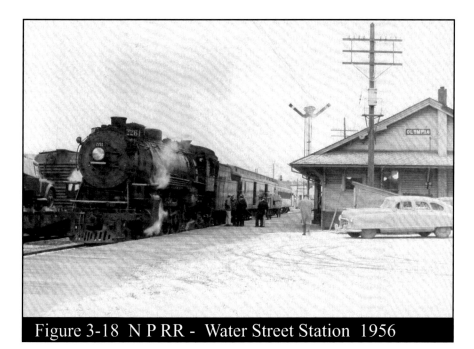

Figure 3-18 N P RR - Water Street Station 1956

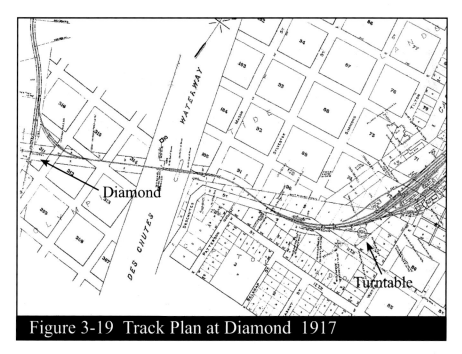

Figure 3-19 Track Plan at Diamond 1917

and walk a short distance north on Reserve Street (now called Deschutes Way) to the Tumwater Station.

Tumwater Station was located approximately 100 yards north of what is now known as the Boston Street Bridge. The earlier wooden bridge at that location is shown in the illustration on page iv. That scene looks northwest over the Deschutes River from a position immediately north of the Upper Falls. Port Townsend Southern Engine #6 heads south to a switching job at the Lea Lumber Company. In 1915 the bridge was replaced by the concrete structure still present in 2008. In 1933 the east end of the bridge was rebuilt when the Olympia Brewery erected a new building on that side of the river, as shown in Figure 3-23, courtesy of the Washington State Historical Society. By that time the track under the bridge terminated at the Tumwater Lumber Company Mill, a short distance south of the place where this picture was taken. The right of way is easier to see in the somewhat earlier photograph reproduced in Figure 3-24, courtesy of the Henderson House Museum.

Construction of Interstate 5 obliterated much of old Tumwater. Nothing remains to identify the location of the loading platform seen in Figure 3-20. The area has been leveled and recontoured. Figure 3-25 is a modern view taken from approximately the place where the platform stood. The view is toward the northeast and shows a remnant of the old grade, immediately west of the current Custer Way Bridge. Immediately north of that point, Figure 3-26 is a modern photograph looking north along the grade as it curves northwest. Around the curve (out of sight) the right of way crossed Simmons Road.

In September 1878, the Olympia & Tenino Railroad began using a turntable at Tumwater. The exact site is unknown, but an examination of local topography suggests a location immediately north of what is now C Street (then called First Street) on the west side of the track. The parking lot and picnic area of Tumwater Falls Park are the current features found in that space.

In 1895 the Port Townsend Southern Railroad built a new standard gauge turntable on the west side of Budd Inlet and the Tumwater turntable was no longer needed. Figure 3-27 indicates the site of the new turntable on page 17 of a Northern Pacific Railroad Valuation Map provided by Jim Fredrickson. The symbol for a turntable (a circle) is located in the lower left corner, with a two stall engine house immediately to the north. The notation "AFE 241-1929" suggests that both turntable and engine house were removed in 1929.

The first station south of Tumwater was known in the early 1890s as Jones Station. It appears in Figures 3-3 and 3-4. Both maps indicate that the structure was located in Township 17 North, immediately south of the place where the Olympia & Tenino

Figure 3-20 Post-1902 Photograph of Northbound Port Townsend Southern Engine #858 at Tumwater Station

Figure 3-21 Pre-1891 View South in Tumwater - Middle Falls of the Deschutes River and Gelbach Flour Mill

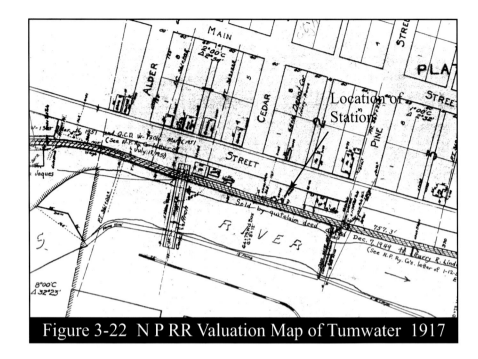
Figure 3-22 N P RR Valuation Map of Tumwater 1917

Figure 3-24 1920s Photo of the Boston Street Bridge

Figure 3-23 1930s Photo of the Boston Street Bridge

Figure 3-25 Location of Tumwater Station 2007

Figure 3-26 South of Simmons Rd. - View North 2007

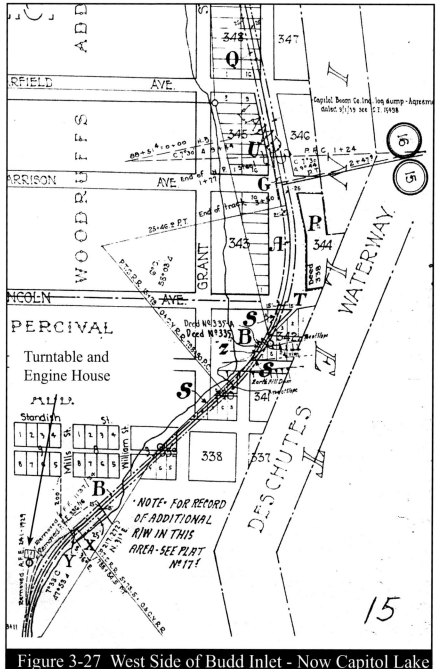

Figure 3-27 West Side of Budd Inlet - Now Capitol Lake

Railroad crossed the right of way of the (never completed) Portland & Puget Sound Railroad. In February, 1891, Erasmus Bennett of Topeka, Kansas recorded a Thurston County land subdivision called Brighton Park, which included the site of Jones Station. Figure 3-28 reproduces part of the Plat Map of Brighton Park. Jones and Bennett Streets run north and south. The "Motor Line" appearing on Bennett Street represents a proposed but never built electric streetcar line called the Olympia, Tumwater & Brighton Park Motor Railway Company. A side branch of the streetcar line was to have ended at the "Depot Grounds" along the "Port Townsend & Southern Railroad." Cram's 1904 Map of Washington (Figure 3-6) indicates that sometime after 1891 the depot became known as Brighton Park Station. Sadly, in the series of aerial photographs (archived at Thurston County Roads & Transportation Services) presented in Figures 2-1 through 2-13B, the photo that should have included the Brighton Park Station could not be located.

Gabriel Jones came west in 1844 in the same party with the George Bush family. In 1851 received a donation land claim which was located near the place where Jones [Brighton Park] Station later existed. However, the namesake of Jones Station was David W. Jones, who owned the farm upon which the station was built. In June, 1890, shortly after David's death, the land surrounding the depot in Section 2 of Township 17 North, Range 2 West was sold to Erasmus Bennett, who subsequently

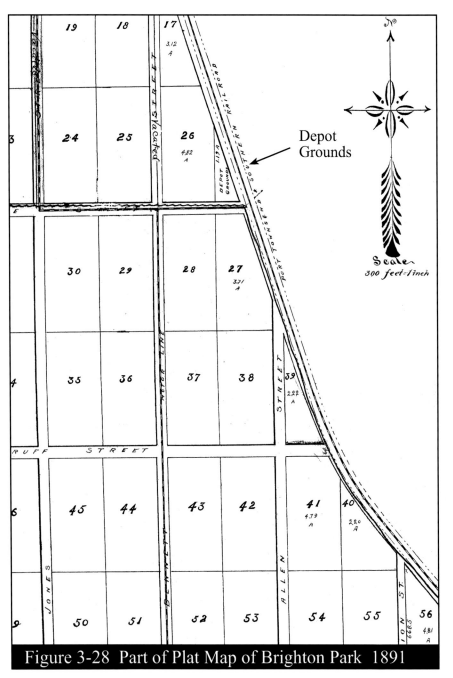

Figure 3-28 Part of Plat Map of Brighton Park 1891

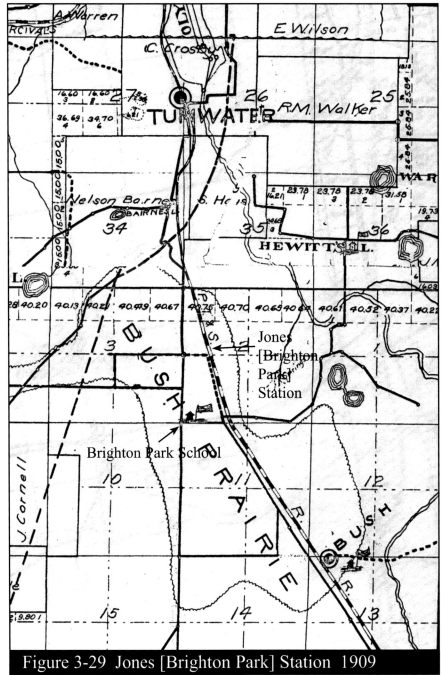

Figure 3-29 Jones [Brighton Park] Station 1909

platted Brighton Park. The region near the station developed into a farming community with enough population to support its own Brighton Park School. The school and location of the Jones [Brighton Park] Station are shown in Figure 3-29, which is part of the 1909 Thurston County Engineer's Map.

Figure 3-30 comes from a Northern Pacific Railroad Valuation Map. It displays the south end of Section 2 in Township 17 North, Range 2 West. The "14 by 20 foot building" was the station, and the "Public Xing" is now 73rd Avenue. Figure 3-31 is a modern photograph of the region where the station was located. The view looks northwest across the junction of Bonniewood Drive and 73rd Avenue SE. The building was located north of 73rd Avenue, in the small sliver of land seen on the extreme right side of the photograph.

Beaver was the original title applied to a station located approximately 1.2 miles south of Brighton Park Station. That name appears on the maps shown in Figure 3-1 (1883) and Figure 3-5 (1898). However Figure 3-2 (1887) labels this depot Bush Prairie, and that designation was then used in Figures 3-3 (1891) and 3-4 (1892). In Figure 3-6 (1904) and all succeeding maps in the series, the station was simply called Bush. Although Figure 2-17 (1890) and Figure 3-5 (1898) again referred to the station as Beaver, it is significant that Bush and Beaver never appeared together on the same map. Clearly, both names indicate the same station.

Between 1859 and 1883, Charles P. Judson maintained a post office at his residence, which was located on his donation claim. The post office designation was Beaver, and it was sited in the Southwest quarter of Section 14 in Township 17 North, Range 2 West. <u>Postmarked Washington: Thurston County</u> reports that in 1873, Beaver was a regular stop on a route that followed the territorial road between Olympia and Astoria, Oregon. After leaving Olympia, the route came south through Beaver and eventually turned west to pass through Satsop on its way to Willapa Harbor and Astoria. After the Olympia & Tenino Railroad was built in 1878, mail to and from Beaver came by train to a place less than one mile from the post office. The railroad called this transfer point Beaver Station. The Beaver Post Office closed in 1883. Figure 3-2 suggests that sometime prior to 1887, the depot previously called Beaver assumed the name of the surrounding geographic area, Bush Prairie.

Bush Station took its name from the Bush pioneer family living nearby. The surrounding prairie was named for George Washington Bush. He settled there in 1845, received a donation claim, and died in 1863. Figure 3-32 is part of the original 1854 survey of Township 17 North, Range 2 West. The Bush farm straddled the "Road from Olympia to the Cowlitz Landing." Less than one half mile north was the residence of Gabriel Jones.

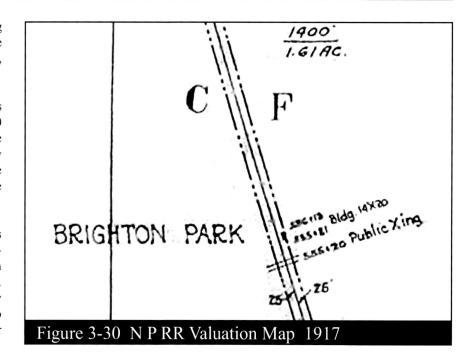

Figure 3-30 N P RR Valuation Map 1917

Figure 3-31 Site of Brighton Park Station 2007

One of George's sons, William Owen Bush, owned most of the George Bush donation claim in 1878, when the Olympia & Tenino Railroad was constructed. Bush Station was located on the east side of the wagon road noted in Figure 3-32. A map of the Tumwater Branch of the Northern Pacific Railroad, dated 28 September 1915 (shortly before track was removed) reveals that the only structure which remained at the station site was a 5 by 10 foot platform located 16 feet southeast of the centerline of what is now 84th Avenue. Currently that spot is occupied by the Pacific Pride gas station at 8406 Old Highway 99. Figure 3-33 looks northeast across the highway toward the place where Bush Station stood. William Owen Bush was engaged in numerous businesses. His activity as a logger will be discussed in Chapter 4.

South of Bush Prairie were stations called Stone Quarry and Crowell. Both were the origin of industrial spurs and will receive detailed descriptions in Chapter 4.

Figures 2-7A and 2-7B include the site of Sheldon Station. It was located immediately north of the place where the Crowell Lumber Company built a spur in the first decade of the twentieth century. As that century began, Albert Elihu Sheldon owned a sizable tract of land in this area. Upon arriving in Washington in 1888, Sheldon settled in Tumwater. In 1890 he bought a majority of the property previously owned by Elihu Plumb, including land surrounding Plumb Station. Approximately one mile north of Plumb Station, and immediately east of his residence, Sheldon put up a shed on the east side of the Port Townsend Southern Railroad. The structure was known locally as Sheldon Station. He also arranged to have Sheldon Road built to his residence from the Olympia-Tenino Road.

One of Sheldon's daughters, Clare, married George Cummins. George eventually rose to the position of Logging Superintendent at the Mason County Logging Company's Bordeaux operation. Another daughter, Lela May, was first married to Charles R. Freitag. He was a fireman on the Port Townsend Southern Railroad and later became an engineer at Bordeaux with the Mason County Logging Company railroad. Freitag died in 1915 and Lela was married for the second time to Marcellus Ross Cummins. Thereafter she resided near the Sheldon home. After Old Highway 99 was first paved (approximately 1921) Lela and her mother, Alice Whitemarsh Sheldon, opened a refreshment stand called Sheldon's Cabin on the west side of the highway. It was a popular stopping place for motorists, and also provided meals for campers visiting the nearby Deschutes River. Lela's second husband ran a service station nearby. Roger Easton provided Figures 3-34A, 3-34B and 3-35, which are 1921 snapshots taken at Sheldon's Cabin. By 1923 (see Figure 3-36) the enterprise had been upgraded and was known as Sheldon's Café. Clarence Canfield recalls

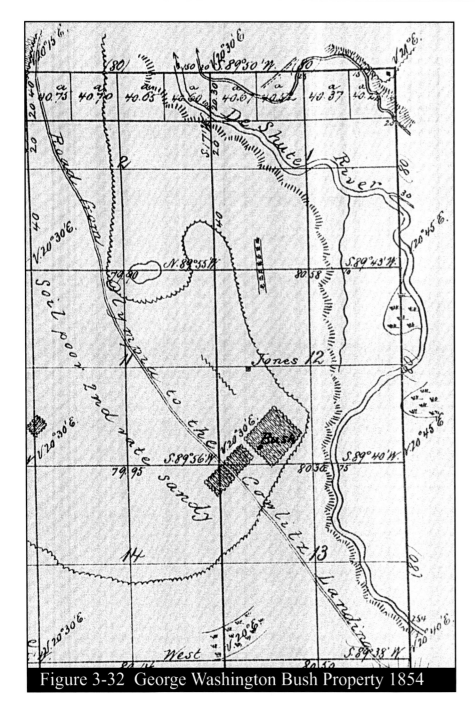

Figure 3-32 George Washington Bush Property 1854

Figure 3-33 Site of Bush Station 2007

Figure 3-34A View South at Sheldon's Cabin 1921

Figure 3-34B Sign at Sheldon's Cabin 1921

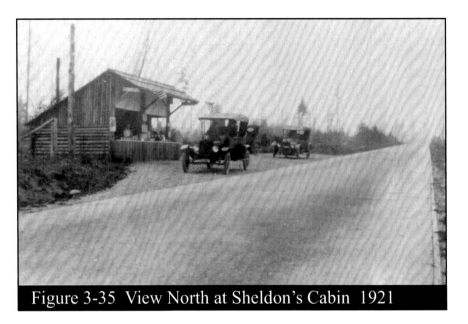
Figure 3-35 View North at Sheldon's Cabin 1921

Figure 3-37 Site of Sheldon's Cafe 2007

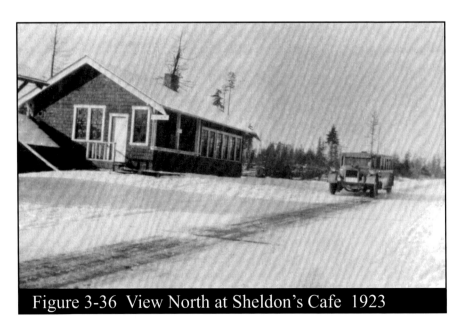
Figure 3-36 View North at Sheldon's Cafe 1923

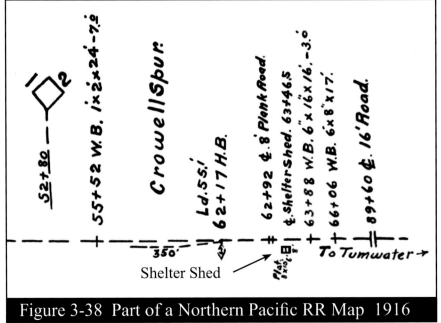
Figure 3-38 Part of a Northern Pacific RR Map 1916

Figure 3-39 Undated Photograph of Passengers Waiting for a Passenger Train at Sheldon Station

that the house at 9609 Old Highway 99 is the former Sheldon's Cafe. Figure 3-37 is a modern glimpse of the structure.

Figure 3-38 is an enlarged view of Figure 7-1. This schematic map was drawn in 1916 and shows Sheldon Station as a "Shelter Shed" precisely 129.5 feet north of the origin of Crowell Spur. The dimensions of the structure were 6 feet by 8 feet. It sat upon a platform 8 feet by 10 feet. Figure 3-39 was provided by the Tenino Depot Museum. Sheldon Station stood on the east side of the tracks in this photograph taken looking northwest. Ron Nelson, an Olympia businessman and lifelong resident of the area near the station, identified the people waiting for the train as members of the Lela May Sheldon Freitag family.

Close examination of the distant part of the right of way in Figure 3-39 reveals that the track curved right while passing through a cut. Figure 3-40 is a contemporary view taken from the top of the bank, on the west side of that same cut. On a snowy day, the photograph looks back toward the site of the station, some 300 feet southeast. Ronda and Ron Larson can be seen standing within the cut.

Figure 3-41 is another modern photograph taken looking west from the place where the shed was located. The visible sign was placed long ago by Earl Shelton, another

Figure 3-41 View West at Site of Sheldon Station   2007

Figure 3-40 View Southeast Along Cut   2007

Figure 3-42 View East at Site of Sheldon Station   2007

Figure 3-43A Aerial Photograph 1933

Figure 3-44 View South at Origin of Crowell Spur 2007

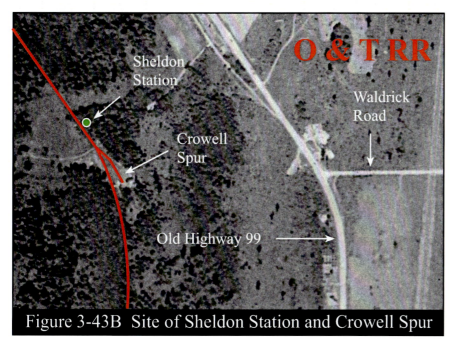
Figure 3-43B Site of Sheldon Station and Crowell Spur

Figure 3-45 Site of First Plumb Station 2007

child of Albert Elihu Shelton. Earl also had a connection to the Mason County Logging Company. At one time he worked as a fireman on that company's railroad at Bordeaux. Looking east from the site of the shed, the residence at 9603 Old Highway 99 is visible in Figure 3-42. The snowy roof of the same home can be discerned in Figure 3-40.

Immediately south of Sheldon Station, recent construction of a pipeline makes it impossible to find the origin of Crowell Spur. Figures 3-43A and 3-43B (which has features added by the author) come from a 1933 aerial photograph of that locale. Figure 3-44 is a recent view looking southeast over the place where the pipeline (which itself was recently rerouted 100 yards farther south) crossed the old railroad grade. Currently there is no public access to the region where Sheldon Station and Crowell Spur were located.

The first of two Plumb Stations was constructed a few hundred feet south of the junction of Old Highway 99 and McCorkle Road. Figure 3-45 is a modern view, looking west, of the place where the station stood. It was situated immediately west of the railroad, on the west side of the county road joining Olympia and Tenino. Although the depot building is long gone, the former grammar school directly across the highway still exists. Known in the past as Plumb Station School, it is now the private residence at 10710 Old Highway 99. The schoolhouse, as it appeared in 2007, is presented in figure 3-46. Contrast this to Figure 3-47, a 1912 photograph provided by the Tenino Depot Museum. The teacher, Clara Mullaney, stands to the left of the students. Frank McCorkle is the lad on the far right, next to Roy Sheldon. The illustration on page i recalls a southbound Port Townsend Southern passenger train preparing to stop at Plumb Station, across the road from the school.

Both station and school were named for Elihu Beman Plumb, who arrived at Rocky Prairie in November, 1861. His family included a foster child, Cordelia E. Ricker, who later became the wife of James Spirlock (subsequently spelled Spurlock). Elihu's brother, William W. Plumb, had previously taken up a donation claim on the west side of Budd Inlet in 1852. By 1870, William had moved to Rocky Prairie and resided immediately south of his brother Elihu.

In 1878, the Olympia & Tenino Railroad was constructed over some of Elihu's land. He operated a post office at Plumb Station between 1879 and 1885. Albert E. Shelton bought the land surrounding Plumb Station in 1890.

In the second decade of the twentieth century, a new location for Plumb Station was required when the Northern Pacific Railroad constructed the Point Defiance Line from Tenino, through East Olympia, to Tacoma. As this work progressed, the Northern Pacific bought the Southern Division of the Port Townsend Southern (the Olympia & Tenino Railroad) in 1914. Track next to the original Plumb Station was taken up. That same year the Northern Pacific (per AFE 860-14) built a new Plumb Station (east of the original one) on the Point Defiance Line. The 1916 Geological Survey Map reproduced in Figure 3-10 indicates the location of the second Plumb Station.

A new track, which connected the second Plumb Station to the remaining part of the former Port Townsend Southern, was placed in service in 1915 (AFE 817-15). It joined the old mainline at the north end of the property at 10525 Old Highway 99. The rails to the second Plumb Station bridged over what is currently Old Highway 99, immediately north of McCorkle Road. An abutment for the bridge can still be seen in Figure 3-48, which looks east over the highway. The right of way between the second Plumb Station and Tumwater was known briefly as the Tumwater Branch of the Northern Pacific Railroad. In early 1916 the entire old mainline track was removed between a siding at the second Plumb Station and the south end of Tumwater (AFE 2338-16).

Figure 3-49 is courtesy of Jim Fredrickson and Brian Ferris. It comes from Northern Pacific Railroad Joint Facilities Book #4. This 1927 photograph was taken along the Point Defiance Line, looking south toward the second Plumb Station. The building uphill from the station was the Eagle Lumber Company's sawmill. Two bridges can be seen in the distance. The closer one was removed sometime after 1927. The distant bridge has been replaced by a concrete span carrying Waldrick Road. The second Plumb Station was removed in 1927 (AFE 1610-27). Figure 3-50 is a recent photograph taken from approximately the same position as was Figure 3-49.

South of Plumb Station was a structure called Spurlock Station. It appears in Figure 2-9A. James Dillard Spirlock owned the property where the station was located. At a later time his descendants changed the spelling of their surname to Spurlock. Ron Nelson, who resides in the original Spirlock residence on Waldrick Road, pointed out the place where the station existed. Figure 3-51 is a photograph taken looking north 0.27 mile south of the intersection of Old Highway 99 and Waldrick Road. Tire tracks occupy the railroad right of way. The depot was sited on the far side of the Mima Mound visible between the tire tracks and the highway.

Spirlock bought farmland on Rocky Prairie in November, 1860. In 1867 he married Cordelia Ricker, the foster child of his neighbor, Elihu Plumb. Thurston County records relating to the formation of McCorkle Road suggest that before the end of the 19th century, a road existed between the Spirlock home and South Union. Although no sign of such a road can be found today, it seems likely that it crossed the railroad at the place known then as Spurlock Station.

Figure 3-46 Plumb Station School 2007

Figure 3-48 Bridge Abutment Over Old Hwy. 99 2007

Figure 3-47 Plumb Station School 1912

Camp 5 appears as a station in Cram's 1909 Map of Washington (Figure 3-7) and in the 1910 Washington Railroad Commission Map (Figure 3-8). It was again present in the 1914 Railroad Commission Map. Unfortunately, the site of this station could not be documented with absolute certainty. Consideration of available information, however, suggests a location at the spot (indicated in Figure 2-10A) where the McIntosh & Swan Logging Company railroad joined the Port Townsend Southern Railroad. This spot is approximately halfway between Plumb and Gilmore Stations, as noted in Figure 3-7. Figure 3-8 seemingly refutes this location, but it's important to note that other gross inaccuracies are found on that particular map. Figure 3-52, part of a 1909 road map of Thurston County, demonstrates a specific error in Figure 3-8. Figure 3-52 provides an accurate location for the future Point Defiance Line of the Northern Pacific Railroad. This route was actually surveyed by the Port Townsend Southern in 1906. The new right of way was supposed to diverge (toward the northeast) from the existing Port Townsend Southern grade, with the separation beginning in the northwest quarter of Section 6 of Township 16 North, Range 1 West. This spot is well north of the intersection of both rights of way with the Milwaukee Railroad. However Figure 3-8 shows the separation commencing south of the Milwaukee, which clearly was not the case. Further information about the McIntosh & Swan Logging Company can be found in Chapter 4.

Figure 3-49 View South at Second Plumb Station 1927

Figure 3-50 Site of Second Plumb Station 2007

Figure 3-51 Site of Spurlock Station 2007

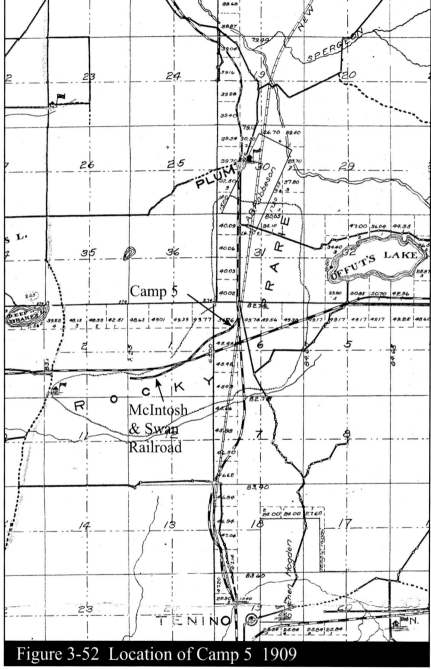
Figure 3-52 Location of Camp 5 1909

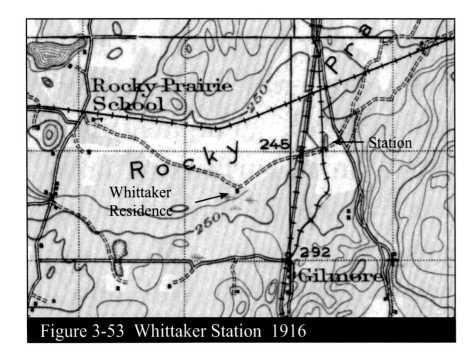

Figure 3-53 Whittaker Station 1916

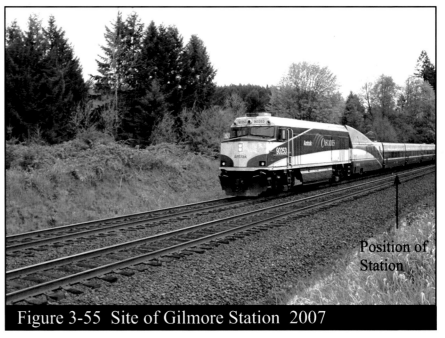

Figure 3-55 Site of Gilmore Station 2007

Figure 3-54 Site of Whittaker Station 2001

Whittaker Station appears in most of the maps (1891-1911) reproduced in Figures 3-3 through 3-9. Two years before the Olympia & Tenino Railroad was constructed, Lemuel Clarence Whittaker bought land at Rocky Prairie. It included the spot where Whittaker Station would later be located. Figure 3-53 comes from the 1916 Geological Survey Map of the Chehalis Quadrangle. A wagon road, in use today as Angus Drive, joined the Whittaker residence with the station. In Figure 3-53, the elongated rectangle on the east side of the railroad locates the station. Rocky Prairie School is identified. It was also built on land previously owned by Whittaker.

Lemuel was a farmer and stock buyer. He operated a sheep loading platform at Whittaker Station, immediately north of Angus Drive. Similar to the situation at Tumwater, it's possible that the platform was the only structure at the station. Figure 3-54 is a modern photograph looking north across Angus Drive. An automobile is parked on the old railroad grade at the approximate north end of the platform.

Gilmore Station was 1½ miles north of Tenino, approximately 700 feet south of the place where McDuff Road crosses the current Burlington Northern-Santa Fe Railway. In a view that looks southeast, the depot building is shown in Figure 3-56. This photograph, courtesy of the Washington State Capitol Museum, suggests that the station was located in a marshy area. Construction of the Point Defiance Line of

Figure 3-56 Undated View Southeast at Gilmore Station

Figure 3-57 First Tenino Station (Right) - Billy Huston's Railroad Hotel (Left) - N P RR Side of Station 1883

the Northern Pacific Railroad destroyed all traces of Gilmore Station. Figure 3-55 is a modern photograph which also looks southeast. The station was located at the position of the first passenger car on this northbound Amtrak train.

Gilmore Station took its name from Henry Harrison Gilmore, who homesteaded the land around the station. When the Olympia & Tenino Railroad was built in 1878, Gilmore had not yet obtained clear title to this property. His ownership was confirmed in 1888 with Homestead Certificate #1466. In 1891 he deeded a right of way over his land to the Port Townsend Southern Railroad.

Tenino was the southern terminal of the Olympia & Tenino Railroad. When the line was first constructed, the Northern Pacific Railroad allowed its (first) Tenino Station to be used by the new railroad. Figure 3-57 is courtesy of the Tenino Depot Museum. This circa 1883 photograph looks northeast across the Northern Pacific's Prairie Line in Tenino. The station is on the right and the Billy Huston Hotel is next to it, on the left. Unseen, behind the station, is the terminal track of the Olympia & Tenino Railroad. Figures 3-58, 3-59 and 3-60 were made available by the Minnesota Historical Society. They clarify the relationships between the station, hotel, water tower and the two railroads mentioned in regard to Figure 3-57. The illustration on page ii imagines the scene in 1878 as Engine #1 (the E. N. Ouimette) of the Olympia & Tenino Railroad arrives at the first Northern Pacific Station in Tenino. Figure 3-61 comes from the Special Collections of the Digital Archive at the University of Washington Libraries. This circa 1885 photograph was taken from a position northwest of the first Tenino Station. The view is toward the southeast with the E. N. Ouimette and two passenger cars ready to depart for Olympia. The Northern Pacific Railroad freight house can be seen on the far left. In the background, track of the Northern Pacific's Prairie Line is visible at the right side of the station.

The first Tenino Station was gone in May, 1928 when the photograph in Figure 3-62 was taken. The picture was provided by Brian Ferris and Jim Fredrickson and comes from Northern Pacific Railroad Joint Facilities Book #3. The view is northeast along the Prairie Line in Tenino. A grade crossing in the foreground, identified by the letter "A", is now the driveway leading to the Quarry House at 318 Park Avenue West. The letter "D" denotes the west end of a road that ended there, in 1928. Later it would become part of Park Avenue. The two story frame house on the left side of the photograph was on the east side of Olympia Street. The site of the first Tenino Station would have been halfway between the letter "D" and the number "1". Figure 3-63 is a current photograph made at approximately the same place as the 1928 picture.

Examination of the lower right corner of Figure 3-59 reveals a feature that is unidentified. That this represents railroad track is confirmed by the notation "H.

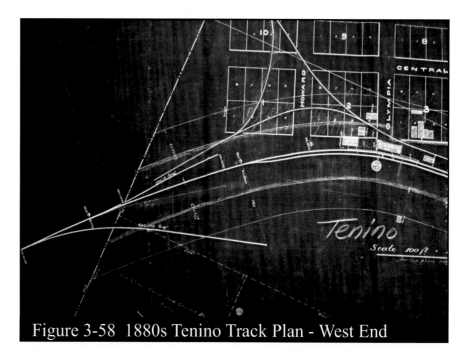

Figure 3-58 1880s Tenino Track Plan - West End

Figure 3-59 1880s Tenino Track Plan - East End

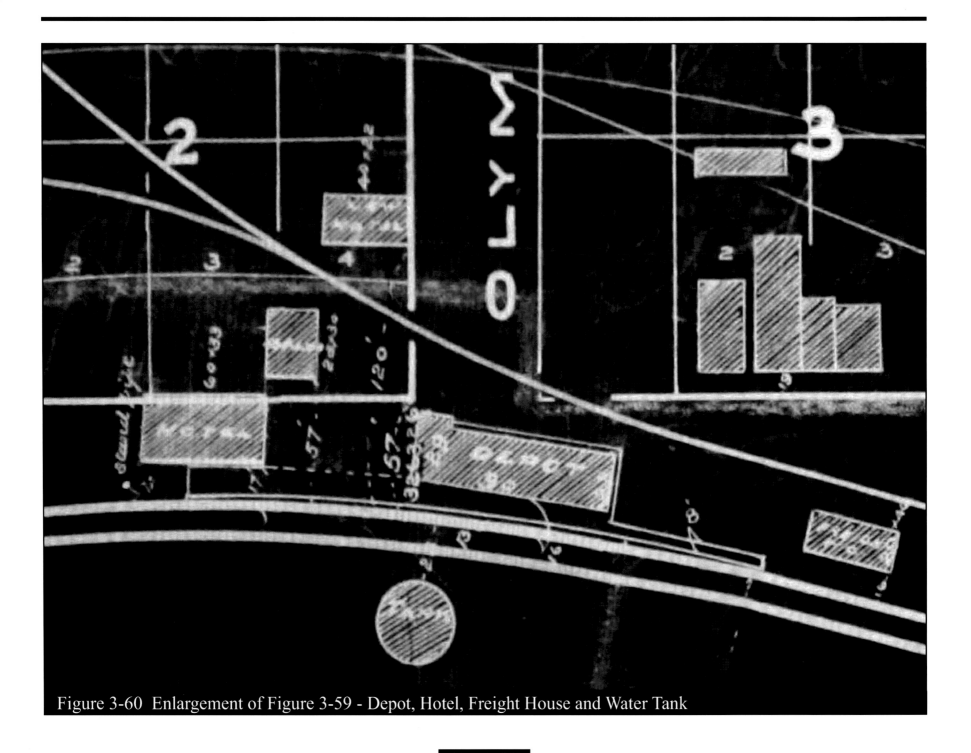
Figure 3-60 Enlargement of Figure 3-59 - Depot, Hotel, Freight House and Water Tank

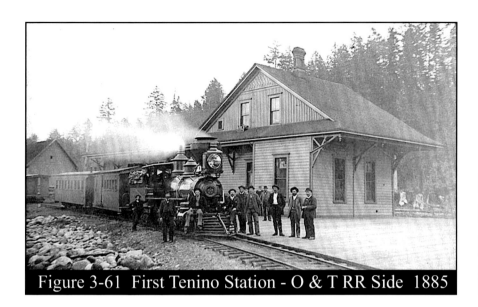
Figure 3-61 First Tenino Station - O & T RR Side 1885

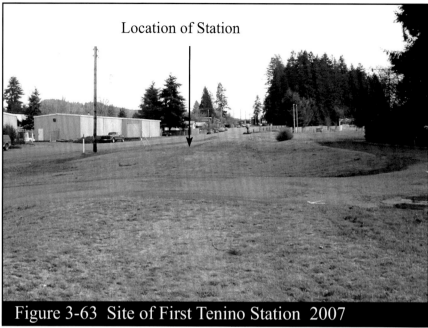
Figure 3-63 Site of First Tenino Station 2007

Figure 3-62 Site of First Tenino Station 1928

Figure 3-64 Former Huston Hotel 2007

B.", which stands for "Head Block" and denotes a switch. This track represented the planned northern terminal of the Tenino & Hanaford Valley Railroad. Although there is no evidence that any of this railroad was actually built, the line was incorporated 16 October 1883. Its handwritten incorporation papers are difficult to read. When indexed at the Washington State Archives, "Hanaford" was entered as "Hourford". The company proposed to construct a standard gauge railroad "from some point near the junction of the Tenino and Olympia Railroad with the Northern Pacific Railroad in the County of Thurston . . . thence in a southeasterly direction to the junction of Thompson Creek with the Skookum Chuck, thence crossing a divide between [it] and Hanaford Creek, thence following the base of a hill on the southwest side of Hanaford Creek to the crossing of the Northern Pacific Railroad in Section 25, Township 14 North, Range 2 West."

In 1890 the Port Townsend Southern Railroad widened the right of way between Olympia and Tenino to standard gauge. For the first time freight cars could be interchanged with the Northern Pacific at Tenino. Together, the two railroads constructed a new junction point, West Tenino, southwest of the first Tenino Station. The Northern Pacific built its second Tenino passenger station there and named it West Tenino. This station was also used by the Port Townsend Southern. The Huston Hotel was moved to West Tenino, but did not prosper there. That building was eventually moved yet again, this time to 148 East Sussex Street. Today it is part of the Tenino Ace Hardware store as it appears in Figure 3-64.

In order to use the West Tenino Station, the Port Townsend Southern had to construct a new entrance into Tenino. It began northwest of Tenino and came almost directly south to the new station. The track leading to the first Tenino Station, which passed through downtown Tenino, was abandoned. Figure 3-65 is part of a Northern Pacific Railroad Valuation Map which demonstrates both the old and new grades. Figure 3-66 is courtesy of Brian Ferris. The photograph shows the West Tenino Station in a view which looks west across the Northern Pacific's Prairie Line. The Port Townsend Southern track was located behind this building, and a small segment of it can be seen at the far left. Figure 3-67 is an additional photograph of the station and comes from the Roger Easton collection.

Norman Montgomery recalls that the West Tenino Station was being used for storage in 1941 when a wildfire threatened the structure. He and other young men were paid $1.00 each to carry water to fight the fire. The building was saved but has since been mostly removed. The only part of the station which remained in the year 2000 was a small piece of the loading platform, which was originally located at the

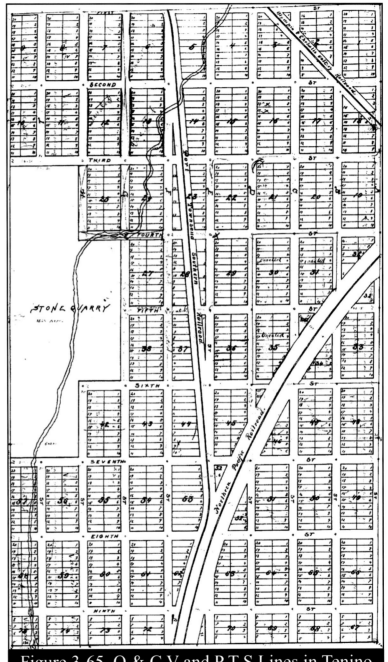

Figure 3-65 O & C V and P T S Lines in Tenino

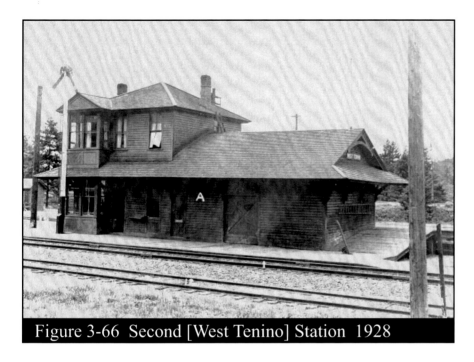

Figure 3-66 Second [West Tenino] Station 1928

Figure 3-68 Second Tenino Station 2000

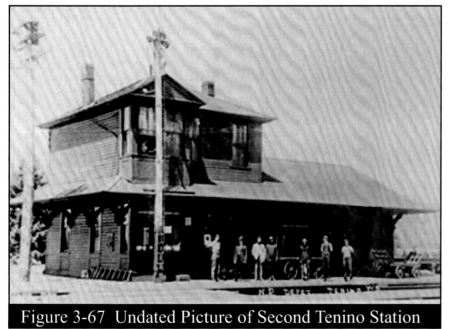

Figure 3-67 Undated Picture of Second Tenino Station

back of the building. The platform can be seen in Figure 3-68, a photograph from 2000 which was taken looking northeast. The building itself is gone, but would have been at the right side of the platform.

The ensuing chapter is devoted to the customers served by the Olympia & Tenino Railroad.

4

Customers of the Railroad - 1878 to 1916

Chapter 4 will visit places where several of the businesses on the Olympia & Tenino Railroad were located. The journey begins in Olympia and concludes in Tenino. Along the way, we'll examine some localities where the right of way can still be found in 2008.

The railroad reached its farthest point north of Olympia in 1891. At the close of that year, track ended near Butler Cove, immediately south of the community known today as Oldport. Although some logging probably took place along this three mile extension, before most of it was removed in 1894, no record of such activity has been found. Please see Chapter 2 for a closer look at this segment of the railroad.

The extension did secure one customer which continued to do business with the railroad for years to come. The Westside Mill was a going concern even before the railroad connected with it in 1891. When most of the Butler Cove extension was abandoned, the Port Townsend Southern continued to operate on the extension as far north as the Westside Mill. Figure 4-1 comes from an 1891 map of Olympia Harbor and demonstrates the relationship between the sawmill and the railroad.

Figure 2-1 shows the mill as it appeared in a 1936 aerial photograph. Over the last century successive businesses have used this site for a variety of industrial activities. The current building at that location is vacant and will likely be removed when plans for rejuvenation of the west side of Budd Inlet are finalized.

In 1905 the Westside Mill was bought by the Olympia Lumber Company. Although this company bought most of its logs from other suppliers, it did purchase and log a tract of its own timberland in 1907. The property was located next to the Port Townsend Southern Railroad in Section 7 of Township 16 North, Range 1 West. Undoubtedly, logs from this property went to the mill by rail. The Olympia Lumber Company applied to the Port Townsend Southern for a new spur to the Westside Mill in 1906. Figure 4-2, courtesy of the Minnesota Historical Society, was part of the application. The desired new track is seen in orange. The north end of the Port Townsend Southern track, as it existed in 1906, can be found at the far left side of the map.

The Henry McCleary Timber Company bought the Westside Mill in 1913 after it had been idle for some time. In 1914 McCleary requested and received a new spur

(500 feet in length) into the mill. In October, 1928 the Tumwater Lumber Mills Company leased the site and began conducting some of its business there. That company requested yet another new mill spur. It can be seen Figure 4-3, which comes from a Northern Pacific Railroad map.

North of the Westside Mill, at approximately the location of today's West Bay Marina, Orsal H. Hartson added another early twentieth century business to the Olympia waterfront. Hartson arrived in Olympia in 1906 and immediately began planning a new sawmill. His first attempt to secure a spur from the Port Townsend Southern Railroad was unsuccessful. Figure 4-4, from the Minnesota Historical Society, reproduces part of the map included with Hartson's initial application. Although this spur was not built, the document provides a detailed assessment of the topography in that region. The new track was supposed to start at the north end of the Westside Mill and follow, at first, the course of the 1891 extension toward Butler

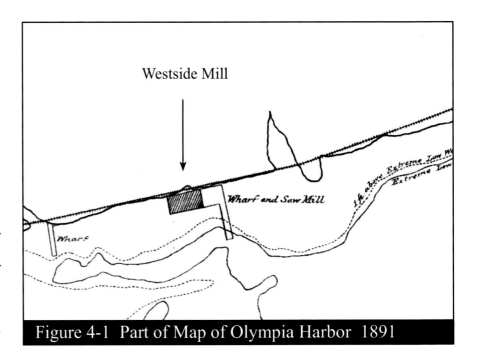

Figure 4-1 Part of Map of Olympia Harbor 1891

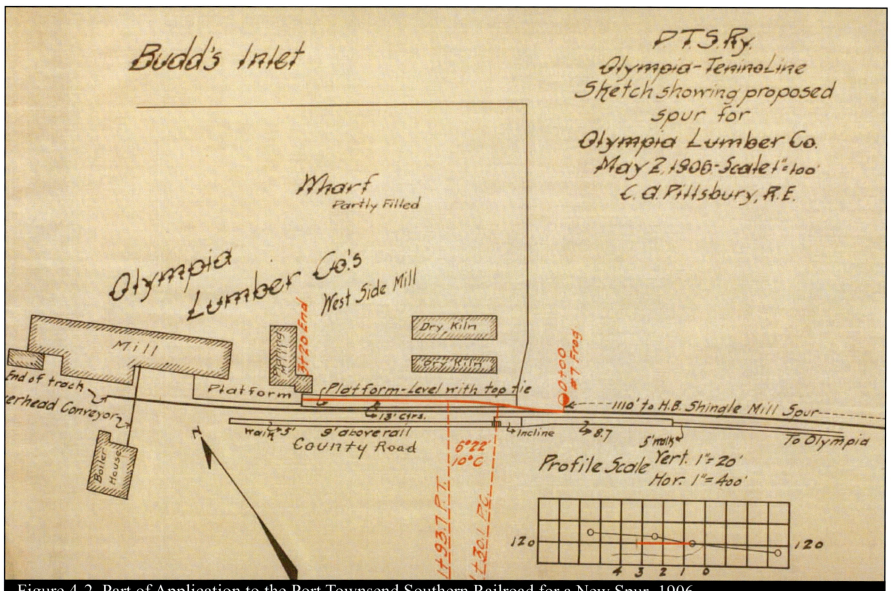

Figure 4-2 Part of Application to the Port Townsend Southern Railroad for a New Spur 1906

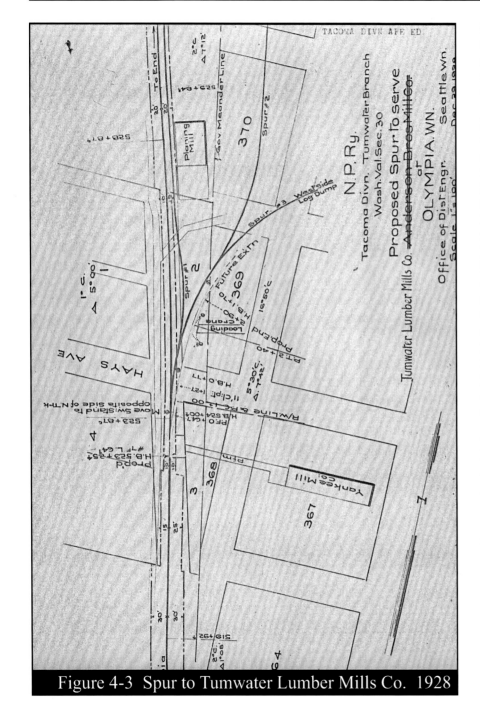

Figure 4-3 Spur to Tumwater Lumber Mills Co. 1928

Cove. Therefore, the initial 2000 feet would have been on a 1% upgrade. The final 600 feet of the spur descended a 1.4% downgrade into the mill. Figure 4-5 is an enlargement of part of Figure 4-4. It provides a view of those elevations. From an operational standpoint these were undesirable grades and may have been a reason why this spur was not built.

Late in 1906 Hartson attracted new investors and renamed his enterprise the Capitol City Lumber Company. In 1907 another unsuccessful attempt was made to secure a rail connection to the mill site. That year the company also bought timber on the South half of the Southeast quarter of Section 10, Township 17 North, Range 2 West. Logs were to be loaded at "Hartson Spur" on the nearby Port Townsend Southern Railroad. This siding was actually built and was located at the place where Henderson Boulevard now ends at Old Highway 99. A third request for a spur at the mill was submitted in 1911. By that time the business had become the Johns Lumber Company. When rail to the mill was finally installed in 1912, the enterprise had reorganized yet again as the Pacific Export Mill Company. Figures 4-6 through 4-8 are courtesy of the Minnesota Historical Society. They reproduce a 1911 map submitted with the application of the Johns Lumber Company. Figure 4-6 represents the south end of the spur, which began at the north side of the Westside Mill. Figure 4-7 describes an area farther north and includes the region where modern West Bay Drive and Harbor View Drive diverge. Note that in this proposal, track remained level through this part of the spur. This was accomplished by removing part of the hill that had been ascended by the 1891 extension to Butler Cove, and placing the spur on the east side of the road that led to the mill. Rail can still be found at this spot in 2007. Figure 4-8 displays the mill itself, at the north end of the spur.

Moving south toward Olympia, Figure 4-9 displays the segment of track between the Westside Mill and the Port Townsend Southern's Olympia Station. The map was made in 1904 and comes from the Minnesota Historical Society. It was part of an application for a spur submitted by the Olympia Manufacturing and Building Company. At that time the Capitol City Shingle Mill was already operating on that segment of track. The log dump used by the Mason County Logging Company was not included in the map, although it had been present since 1899. The dump was situated immediately north of the Olympia Station and can be seen in Figure 3-15.

Farther south, the Port Townsend Southern maintained a log dump at Warren's Point. It was located approximately where Deschutes Parkway and Lakeridge Drive now intersect. Please see the Appendix for an account of "A horrible disaster" that occurred there in May, 1892.

After coming back to land at Warren's Point, the roadbed began to climb before reaching Tumwater. A section of that part of the right of way remains visible today

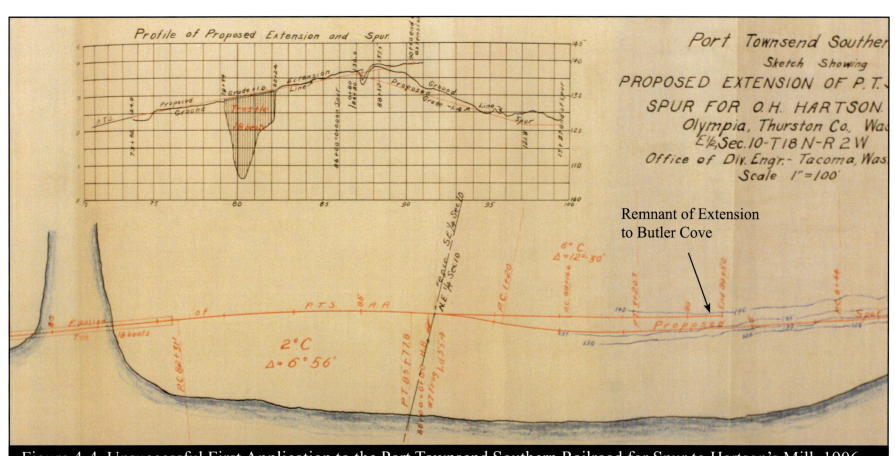
Figure 4-4 Unsuccessful First Application to the Port Townsend Southern Railroad for Spur to Hartson's Mill 1906

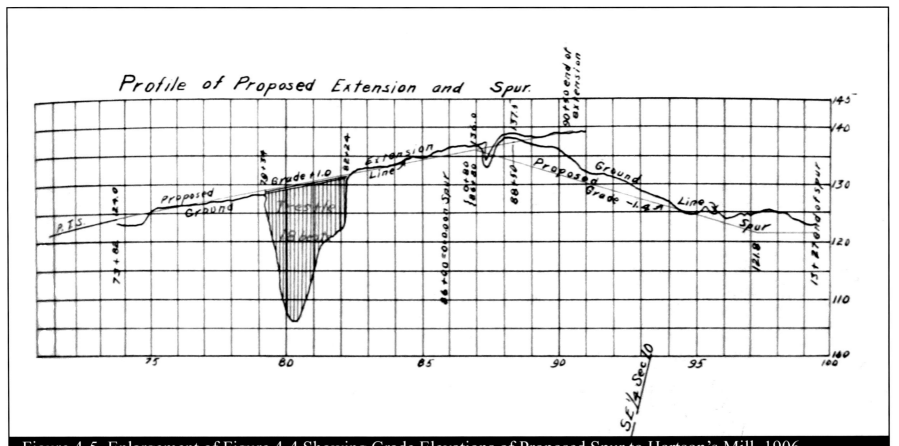

Figure 4-5 Enlargement of Figure 4-4 Showing Grade Elevations of Proposed Spur to Hartson's Mill 1906

Figure 4-6 South End of Johns Lumber Co. Spur 1911

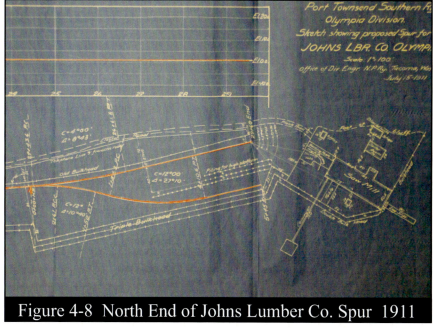

Figure 4-8 North End of Johns Lumber Co. Spur 1911

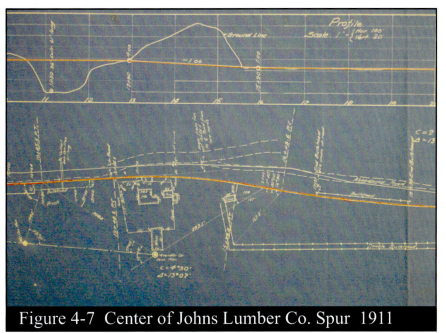

Figure 4-7 Center of Johns Lumber Co. Spur 1911

on the hill next to Deschutes Parkway. Figure 4-10 is a 2001 photograph taken looking southwest from the Capitol Interpretive Center. Figure 4-11 comes from a Northern Pacific Railroad Valuation Map. The area encompassed by the map begins (upper left corner) at approximately the place displayed in Figure 4-10 and extends south through Tumwater. Many of the businesses described in the following paragraphs were located in the area covered by this map.

In July, 1906 the Port Townsend Southern Railroad began service to the Olympia Brewery in Tumwater. Previously the trolley system of the Olympia Light and Power Company had been used to handle most of the brewery's transportation requirements. The brewery built a bridge across the Deschutes River to connect with a spur belonging to the railroad. These relationships are shown in the Northern Pacific Railroad Valuation Map reproduced in Figure 4-12. Figure 4-13, from the Minnesota Historical Society, is a Port Townsend Southern map dated 20 November 1906. It contained specifications for the bridge and track serving the brewery.

Figure 4-14, courtesy of the Washington State Historical Society, is a photograph looking west at the brewery spur as it descended from the mainline in Tumwater. It probably was taken from the east bank of the Deschutes River. The Crosby House, a 2007 landmark in Old Tumwater, can be used for orientation with modern

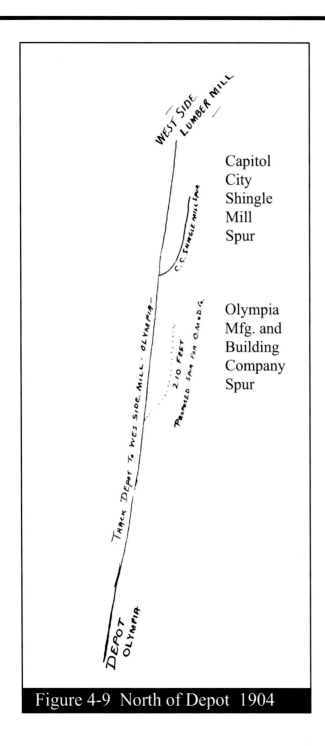

Capitol City Shingle Mill Spur

Olympia Mfg. and Building Company Spur

Figure 4-9 North of Depot 1904

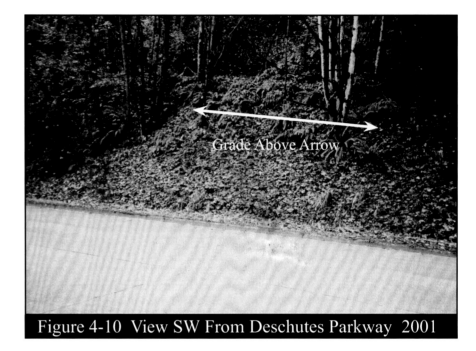

Figure 4-10 View SW From Deschutes Parkway 2001

topography. Begin by locating ties in the track in the lower left side of the picture. Follow the grade to a white house in the middle of the right side of the photograph. Behind this house, the rails bend to the left and then seem to be going directly up the hill. More distant still, the track veers right in front of a large log as it nears the mainline. At that point the mainline is oriented horizontally, immediately above the log. The illustration on page iii is a bird's eye view of Port Townsend Southern Engine #858 on the brewery spur.

One small branch was added to the brewery spur about 1908. It led to a structure built that year by the Olympia Brewery. Located on the west side of the Deschutes River, the building was used to manufacture gas from coal brought by rail from mines near Tenino. Figure 4-15 and the following two figures are photographs from the Henderson House Museum. Figure 4-15 was taken looking south during construction of the gas plant. Examination of the background reveals the Olympia Light & Power Company building which was located at the Lower Falls. The vertical tower of its water supply flume is visible above. The river cannot be seen in this view but was located on the left side of the photograph. In the foreground, the track passed over a small trestle. The trestle was also visible in the lower right corner of Figure 4-16. This view looked south toward the coal gasification plant and trestle.

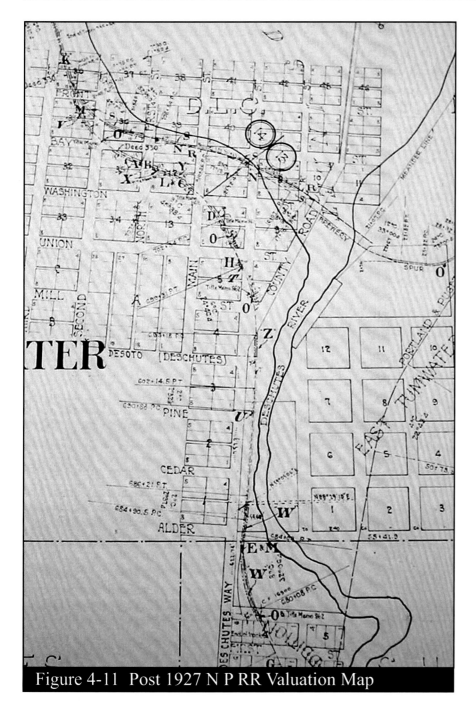

Figure 4-11 Post 1927 N P RR Valuation Map

Unfortunately, none of these figures show the origin of the gas plant branch from the brewery spur. It diverged from the brewery spur at a point immediately west of the Deschutes River, and traveled south for a short distance to the plant. Figure 4-17 comes from the Olympia Tumwater Foundation. The view looks northeast over the Deschutes River. The picture reveals a conduit for gas which crossed the river from the plant to the main part of the brewery. Figure 4-18 is a modern photograph of the plant's concrete foundation.

Between the place where the brewery spur originated and Tumwater Station, the mainline crossed Reserve Street, which is now Tumwater's Deschutes Way. Roger Easton provided the picture reproduced in Figure 4-19. The view is to the east and only a small part of Reserve Street (then unpaved) is visible at the bottom. The residence was the Franco house, which stood until 2004. The fence on the right side of the house was along Simmons Road. Compare this view of the house with that seen in Figure 4-17, in the lower left side of that picture. There, the mainline of the railroad can also be discerned, just above the bottom of the entire picture. Franco house may also be seen in Figure 4-28, situated immediately below the structure that is now the Henderson House Museum.

Two original plat maps from the Southwest Washington Regional Archives are helpful in understanding the industrial history of the south end of Old Tumwater. Figure 4-20 is the original plat of Tumwater filed by Clanrick Crosby. It includes the area where the Olympia Brewery would later be built, and extends south as far as a bridge located where the contemporary Boston Street Bridge crosses the Deschutes River. Figure 4-21 is a plat of the First Mill Addition to Tumwater. It recorded a survey which included 1st Street and the property immediately south of it. The northern part of this plat represents the area bordering the south end of Figure 4-20. Both documents were created in 1869. There is some discrepancy between the maps regarding two buildings and a bridge found at the bottom of Figure 4-20 and near the top of Figure 4-21. It seems likely that both drawings represent the same structures located at the Upper Falls of the Deschutes River. The sawmill that appears in Figure 4-21 was likely the building erected in 1852 by Ira Ward and Smith Hayes, at the northern edge of Hayes' Donation Land Claim.

After Ward & Hayes, a succession of proprietors operated the sawmill at the Upper Falls. Ward and his new partner, William Mitchell, owned it in 1868. When the Olympia & Tenino Railroad opened in 1878, the mill was able to count on a steady supply of raw material from remote timberland south of Tumwater. By 1889 the business was known as Mitchell & Johns Mill when it was sold to three partners: J. P. Allison, John W. Graff and Willis Townsend. They called their organization the Tumwater Lumber Company and still used the Upper Falls to power their mill.

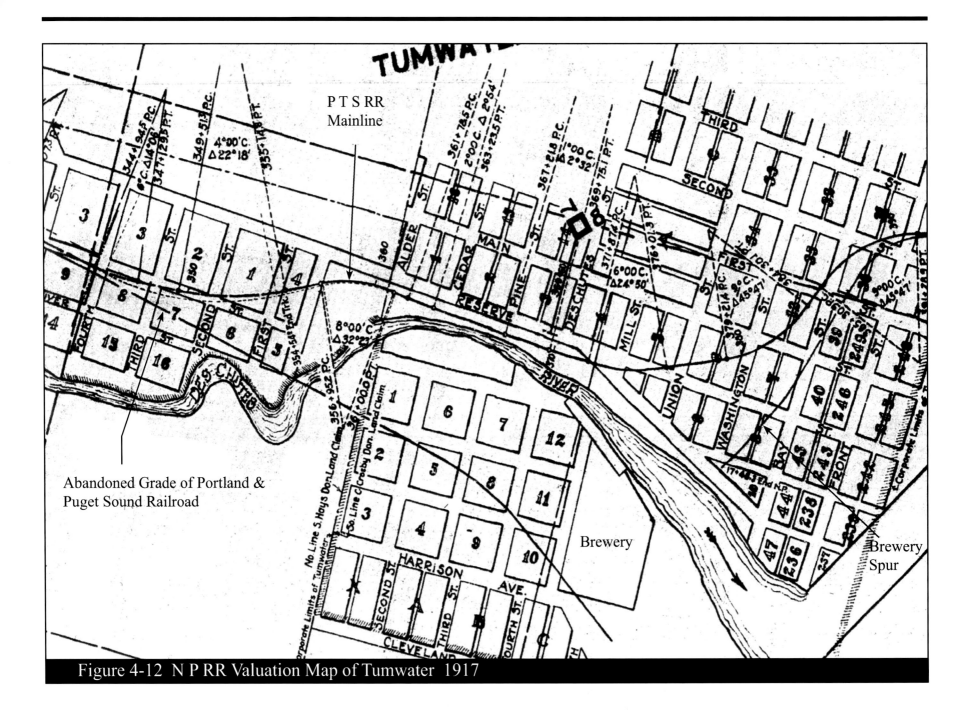

Figure 4-12 N P RR Valuation Map of Tumwater 1917

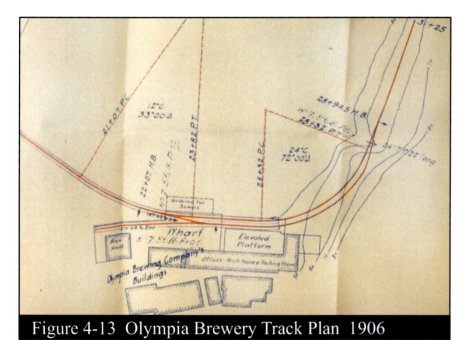
Figure 4-13 Olympia Brewery Track Plan 1906

Figure 4-15 Building the Brewery's Gas Plant 1908

Figure 4-14 Post-1906 View West Toward Tumwater Hill

Figure 4-16 Post-1908 View South Toward Tumwater and the Trestle to the Brewery's Gas Plant

Figure 4-17 Gas Plant, Brewery and Franco House

Figure 4-19 Mainline at Reserve St. (Deschutes Way)

Figure 4-18 Gas Plant Foundation 2007

The business was known as J. P. Allison & Company when it and several other Tumwater businesses were destroyed by fire in 1891.

In 1903 the Lea Lumber Company of Tacoma bought land for construction of a new sawmill near the Upper Falls in Tumwater. The property was located immediately south of the place where the J. P. Allison & Company Mill burned in 1891. The real estate included Lot 1 in Block 1 of the First Mill Addition to Tumwater (see Figure 4-21) plus land immediately east of Lot 1, between it and the river. Water power would not be used to operate the new mill. The site was selected because it straddled the Port Townsend Southern Railroad and was also on the Deschutes River. Even before acquiring land for the mill, the lumber company bought extensive timberland in Thurston County. Most of it, purchased in 1902, was in close proximity to the Deschutes.

The river was used to transport logs to the sawmill from the company's logging operation. The mill could also receive logs from other suppliers via the Port Townsend Southern. Equally important was the fact that the company was able to ship finished products by rail.

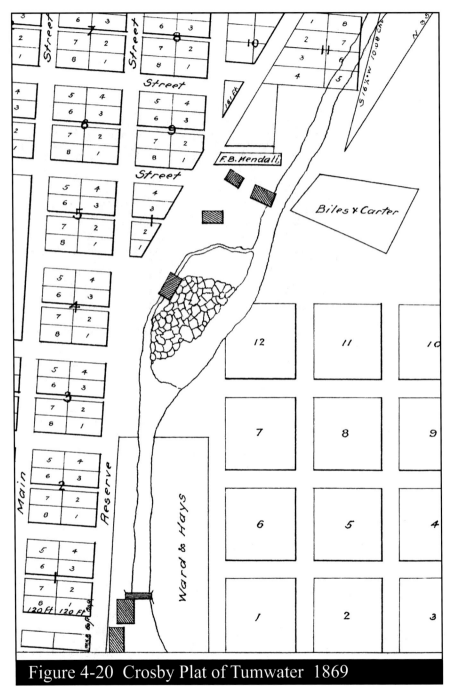

Figure 4-20 Crosby Plat of Tumwater 1869

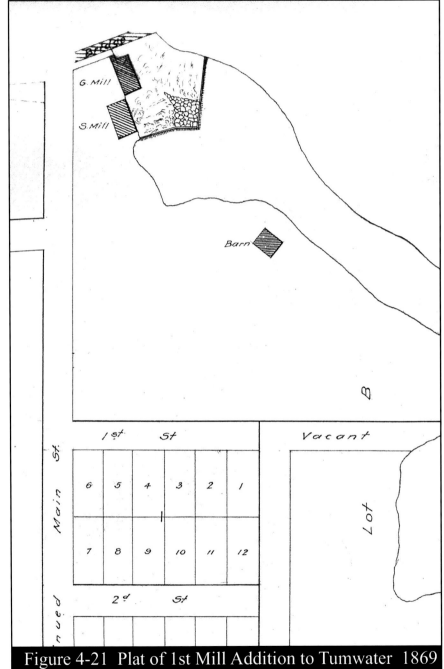

Figure 4-21 Plat of 1st Mill Addition to Tumwater 1869

Figure 4-22 Post-1919 View East Toward Tumwater Lumber Mills Company and Tumwater Spur of the N P RR

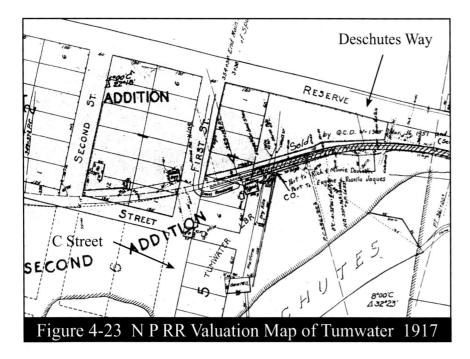
Figure 4-23 N P RR Valuation Map of Tumwater 1917

Figure 4-24 C Street and Deschutes Way 2007

The illustration on page iv depicts a 1910 scene in Tumwater. The vantage point is from the east side of the Deschutes River, immediately north of the Upper Falls. The view is toward the northwest. The visible wooden bridge was replaced in 1915 by the concrete structure which remains in use today as the Boston Street Bridge. In the illustration, Port Townsend Southern Engine #6 heads south from Olympia to pick up carloads of lumber at the Lea Lumber Company.

Reorganization occurred in July, 1912 when William F. Lea, Mabel O. Lea and A. L. Young incorporated the Tumwater Lumber Company. The new corporation owned the mill and also purchased rights (from the Deschutes River Boom Company) to transport logs to the mill, via the river. Charles W. Lea, a trustee of the Lea Lumber Company when it was incorporated in 1902, was the president of the boom company in 1912.

Ownership of the Tumwater Lumber Company evolved over the next several years such that in 1919, when it was sold to the Anderson Brothers of Seattle, its officers already included Arthur Anderson, Edward Anderson, E. M. Anderson and Mabel O. Lea. Later in 1919 the property was incorporated once again, this time as Tumwater Lumber Mills Company. By that time the Port Townsend Southern Railroad no longer existed, but the mill continued to be serviced by the Tumwater Spur of the Northern Pacific Railroad, which then was the only remaining segment of the original Olympia & Tenino Railroad. Cropping of Figure 4-23 cut off some of the labels found on the original map. At the top of the figure the full text read "End Main Trk" and immediately to the right, "(End) of Spur". This terminology may seem confusing, because in this case, the "(End) of spur" meant the sidetrack to the lumber company, while "End Main Trk" designated the southern terminal of the Tumwater Spur. Although the sidetrack stretched a little farther south than the end of the old mainline, both stopped immediately north of First (now C) Street in Tumwater. Figure 4-22 is a photograph from the collection of Kurt and Kit Anderson. It was taken in Tumwater looking east along what is now C Street from an elevated position, west of the street known now as Deschutes Way. Two boxcars are spotted for loading at a place which nowadays would be part of the parking lot of Tumwater Falls Park. Figure 4-24 is a similar view taken in 2007, looking east from the intersection of C Street and Deschutes Way.

In the late 1920s Tumwater Lumber Mills Company needed additional manufacturing capacity. It leased the Westside Mill on Budd Inlet from the Henry McCleary Timber Company in October, 1928. When the 1936 aerial photograph presented in Figure 2-3B was made, the lumber company had expanded its original plant into the area now occupied by the parking area for Tumwater Falls Park. By then, the track to the mill was used infrequently and the abandoned roadbed south of the mill, between C Street and E Street, had become a motor vehicle road. In

Figure 4-25 Circa 1912-1919 View of the Lea Lumber Company and Upper Falls of the Deschutes River

Figure 4-26 Upper Falls of the Deschutes River 2007

Figure 4-27 Employees of the Lea Lumber Company

1938 the state highway linking Olympia, Tumwater and Tenino was rerouted. A new bridge, which thereafter carried Capitol Boulevard over the Deschutes River, was constructed south of Custer Way. It was necessary to locate the south approach of the bridge at the place previously used by the lumber mill. Forced to vacate this property, the company renewed its lease of the Westside Mill and shifted all operations there in 1938. After 84 years, wood products were no longer produced at the Upper Falls of the Deschutes River.

Figures 4-25 and 4-27 were provided by the Henderson House Museum. Figure 4-25 was probably made between 1912 and 1919 and taken from the west end of the bridge at the location of the present Boston Street Bridge. The photograph looks southeast toward the Lea Lumber Company. On the left, an inclined conveyer is visible. This was used to extract logs from a storage pond in the Deschutes River. The building where logs were sawed can be seen next to the river in the middle portion of Figure 4-22. Today the presence of the Falls Terrace Restaurant makes it impossible to obtain a photograph from the precise vantage point where Figure 4-25 was taken. Accordingly, Figure 4-26 was taken within that restaurant at a place directly above the former railroad. The position was somewhat south of that used to make Figure 4-25. Figure 4-27 captured millworkers in a glimpse east between the sawmill and dry kiln (structures also visible in Figure 4-25). Figure 4-28 is a 1946 aerial photograph courtesy of the Port of Olympia and Southwest Washington Regional Archives. The view is north, with the Boston Street Bridge in the very center of the picture. The Capitol Boulevard Bridge is seen in the lower right quadrant as it crosses the Deschutes River. The railroad right of way remained visible two years after its rails were removed. The old grade passed through an empty area where the lumber mill had been, and then continued south to cross C Street.

The Tumwater Shingle Company operated near the Upper Falls of the Deschutes during the first half of the second decade of the twentieth century. James W. Cannon managed this business located on the west side of the Port Townsend Southern mainline, opposite the Tumwater Lumber Company. A spur to the shingle company can be recognized in Figure 4-29, which is an enlargement of part of the Valuation Map comprising Figure 4-11. Finished shingles were milled from cedar bolts brought in over the Port Townsend Southern. One supplier hauled bolts by wagon to Gilmore Station where they were transferred to boxcars. In 1916, when the Port Townsend Southern Railroad south of Tumwater was removed, transportation costs for raw material made the shingle company less profitable. When the photograph presented in Figure 4-22 was made, the shingle mill was gone from the open field in the foreground.

South of the Upper Falls the railroad traveled along the west side of the Deschutes

Figure 4-28 Aerial View Toward the North in Tumwater 1946

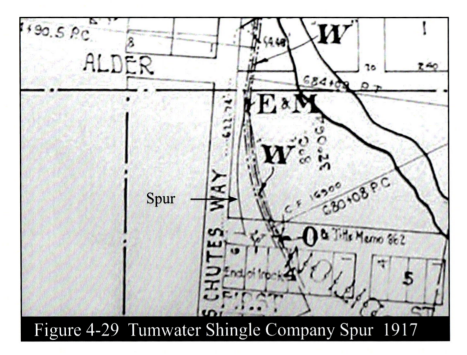
Figure 4-29 Tumwater Shingle Company Spur 1917

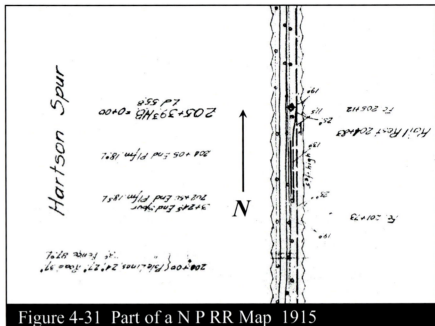
Figure 4-31 Part of a N P RR Map 1915

Figure 4-30 View NE From State Farm Office 2007

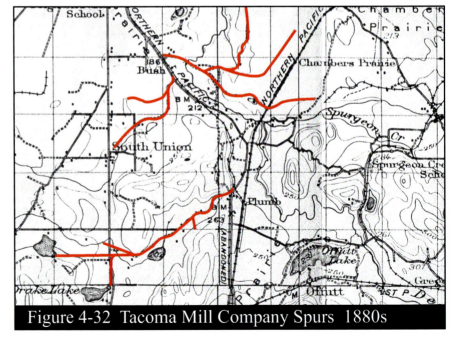
Figure 4-32 Tacoma Mill Company Spurs 1880s

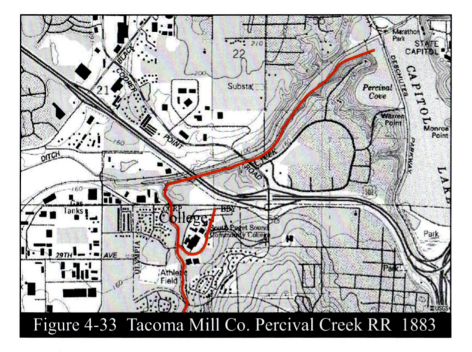

Figure 4-33 Tacoma Mill Co. Percival Creek RR 1883

Figure 4-34 Imprint of Percival Creek RR Spur 1936

River valley. Maps and photographs of the right of way in this region can be found in South Puget Sound Railroad Mania on pages 119 through 122. In that book, Figure 6-10 on page 122 looks southwest along the grade, with the State Farm office at 4780 Capitol Boulevard seen in the distance. In this book, Figure 4-30 was taken at the north end of the State Farm office, looking northeast along the same segment of right of way.

While under construction in 1890, the Portland & Puget Sound Railroad dug a cut under the Olympia & Chehalis Valley Railroad. The latter line was obliged to place a bridge across the cut. Although the Portland & Puget Sound was abandoned before reaching completion, the cut was not refilled. The bridge remained in place until that part of the Port Townsend Southern was abandoned in 1916. Figure 7-1, from that year, shows the bridge between miles 5-6 and 6-7. Construction of Interstate 5 and Capitol Boulevard destroyed all trace of the intersection of the two railroads. Today, that point would lie between those two roads, directly west of M Street in Tumwater.

South of M Street the railroad lay on the east side of the county road that has become Capitol Boulevard. Farther south, where Capitol Boulevard veers right (to begin running directly south) at Gerth Street, the railroad continued in a southeasterly direction through what has become a residential neighborhood. After crossing Dennis Street, the grade is currently occupied by Bonniewood Drive until it again meets Old Highway 99. Subsequently, the right of way was situated immediately east of the Olympia-Tenino Road (now Old Highway 99).

From time to time the Thacker Wood Company appeared in Port Townsend Southern records. John T. "Boss" Thacker was a colorful Olympian who was known better for his back room politics than for his forest products business. In 1898 his company contracted to sell ties and engine wood to the railroad. The 11 January 1901 issue of the Washington Standard reported that the Thacker Wood Company was preparing to ship shingle bolts (approximately 4½ feet lengths of cedar wood) from a tract of cedar timber sited along the Port Townsend Southern Railroad near Olympia. Although a spur was to be built into this tract, its location remains undiscovered.

In 1907 a spur for loading logs was built for Orsal H. Hartson's Capitol City Lumber Company. It was located in the vicinity of the intersection of today's Henderson Boulevard and Old Highway 99. The 1914 Northern Pacific Railroad Timetable called this spur "Hartson." Figure 4-31 was provided by Brian Ferris. It is part of a 28 September 1915 map of the Northern Pacific Railroad's Tumwater Branch. In addition to the spur on the west side of the mainline, a platform 155 feet long can be identified between the spur and the Olympia-Tenino Road.

South of Hartson Spur is an area named after the pioneer Bush family and known as Bush Prairie. In the region of today's Olympia Airport the grade remained on the east side of the Olympia-Tenino Road as far south as Heritage Lane SE. At that point the railroad crossed to the west side of the old county road and the two rights of way began to diverge. Several businesses were located along the stretch of track between Henderson Boulevard (Hartson Spur) and Heritage Lane. Unfortunately, traces of some of those enterprises, located on the west side of the railroad, have been erased by construction of the airport.

This is a good place to pause and consider the history of the Tacoma Mill Company in the 1880s, during the advent of railroad logging in Thurston County. The company was founded in 1868 at Tacoma's "Old Town" by Charles Hanson and J. W. Ackerman. Ackerman retired in 1878, leaving Hanson the sole proprietor. In the 1870s most large Puget Sound sawmills obtained raw material by rafting logs from other parts of the Sound, where timber could still be cut within one or two miles of salt water. By 1880, Hanson recognized that this source of logs was becoming exhausted. He began buying inland timber, in areas that could be reached by rail. Thurston County, with the Olympia & Tenino Railroad already in place, provided Hanson's company with an opportunity to secure a steady supply of raw material. Logs could be brought to tidewater in Olympia and then rafted to his mill in Tacoma. During the 1880s, the company harvested logs using no less than three separate spurs and one siding, all of which originated on the Olympia & Tenino Railroad. Figure 4-32 locates these connections.

It's important to note that these spurs were not built and used in the same way that logging railroads were utilized later, in the twentieth century. The steam shovel was not yet available. Grades were constructed manually, and it was not practical to push the rails right into a region of active logging. Oxen working on skid roads were still used to bring logs to the railroad. Viewed from this perspective, logging lines in the 1880s were merely an extension of Puget Sound into the hinterlands.

The Tacoma Mill Company also used a short railroad to harvest timber along Percival Creek. This land was cut under a contract with George H. Foster. Although that right of way ended on the west side of what is now Capitol Lake, it did not make a direct connection with the Olympia & Tenino Railroad. Later in this chapter, all of the Tacoma Mill Company spurs will be described in detail.

In the early 1880s Benjamin Buckman Turner was logging at Bush Prairie. A few years later, his main operation was at Black Lake and George H. Foster replaced him as the predominant logger at Bush Prairie. Figures 2-5A and 2-5B provide an overview of Bush Prairie. The imprint of a spur can be found in the upper left corner of both figures. Although research has not revealed when this track was active, or its exact purpose, it probably was used for logging. Farther southeast, at the junction of 79th Avenue and Old Highway 99, a farmhouse driveway appears likely to have been built over an old skid road or railroad spur.

A complex relationship existed between Turner, Foster, and other pioneers of railroad logging in Thurston County. William O. Bush, George Gaston and Charles Hanson of the Tacoma Mill Company were other innovators who played a significant role in developing the county's timber resource. In 1880 Benjamin B. Turner purchased all timber standing on the portion of the George Bush Donation Claim situated west of the Deschutes River. At the same time he bought more timber immediately to the north, which was also on the west side of the river, in Section 12 of Township 17 North, Range 2 West. A second tract of timberland in Section 24 was acquired in 1881. The 1881 purchase was approximately one mile south of the timber bought in 1880 and was located southwest of the junction of today's 93rd Avenue and Sheldon Road. In August, 1881 Turner sold his timber rights in all these areas to Charles Hanson of the Tacoma Mill Company. Included in the sale were four logging cars, suggesting that Turner had begun harvesting these holdings before the sale.

After 1881 Turner logged in other parts of Thurston County. In 1885 he began construction of the Black Lake & Sherman Valley Railroad, which stretched from a log dump at Percival's Point on the west side of Capitol Lake (then part of Budd Inlet) to Black Lake. The venture was partly financed by the Port Blakely Mill Company. Between Budd Inlet and South Puget Sound Community College, Turner utilized the roadbed of a logging railroad built in 1883 by George H. Foster on the south side of Percival Creek. That segment of Foster's line was built on land controlled by the Tacoma Mill Company. Figure 4-33 shows the path of this right of way as it followed Percival Creek through what is now the community college. Figure 4-34 is a 1936 aerial photograph of the place occupied now by the college. The imprint of a spur, constructed in the 1880s, can still be found.

Several documents made it possible to pinpoint Foster's 1883 railroad along Percival Creek and to explore additional business activities connecting him with William O. Bush, Charles Hanson and the Tacoma Mill Company. The papers include Thurston County Deed Book 14, pages 740-748, and Thurston County Miscellaneous Book 1, pages 405 and 552. These records make it clear that in 1883, Foster operated a second, substantial logging railroad at Bush Prairie. As at the Percival Creek location, it was used to harvest timberland controlled by the Tacoma Mill Company.

In July, 1883 Foster's Bush Prairie Camp #1 was located in the southwest quarter of the northwest quarter of Section 18 in Township 17 North, Range 1 West. Ten rail cars were used to transport logs from the camp to Olympia. Oxen toiled on a skid road 1.5 miles long which terminated at Camp #1. Loaded log cars traveled from the camp to a junction (located near the residence of William O. Bush) with the mainline of the Olympia & Chehalis Valley Railroad. In April, 1884 the logging line was 1.875 miles long and the end of track had been pushed east into Section 17. Figure 4-35 comes from an 1894 survey housed at the Thurston County Roads & Transportation Services. Foster's logging railroad had been removed, but the map indicates that William O. Bush resided at the same place where his pioneer father, George Bush, made his home (see Figure 3-32).

Foster's railroad is represented by a red line in Figure 4-37 which is another part of the 1916 Geologic Survey map presented previously in Figure 3-10. The position of the camp in 1884 is indicated by a blue dot. Figure 4-36 is a 2005 aerial photograph of areas where Tacoma Mill Company rights of way existed. Figure 4-38 is a 2000 aerial view which shows a trace of the old railroad as it approached the mainline.

In the early 1880s, while working in the Foster logging camp at Bush Prairie, George Gaston became an acquaintance of William O. Bush. Gaston and Bush developed a much closer relationship in 1882 when Gaston married Bush's daughter Belle. After logging was completed on the Bush property, the two men began a partnership known as Bush & Gaston and carried on the timber business elsewhere. Prairies & Quarries notes that "By the spring of 1886, Bush & Gaston were logging two miles south of Tenino." In the same year Bush bought timberland straddling the Olympia & Chehalis Valley Railroad. The land was northeast of Gilmore Station, in the northwest quarter of the southwest quarter of Section 7, Township 16 North, Range 1 West. The purchase also included the southwest quarter of the section immediately west of that tract and provided a supply of timber to be harvested and brought to the railroad for transport.

No record has been found which would identify precisely the path followed by the Tacoma Mill Company spur to South Union. The most likely hypothesis is that it came off the mainline at the approximate place where today's 88th Avenue SE meets Old Highway 99. A 1916 Geological Survey Map supports this notion. Part of that map is reproduced in Figure 4-39. In 1916 a trail passed toward South Union from the approximate location of the intersection noted above. Most of the trail passed through land owned and logged by the Tacoma Mill Company. The right of way can still be discerned in a 1933 aerial photograph (not included here) which suggests that the South Union spur also included a secondary branch leading to company owned timber in the southwest quarter of Section 14 in Township 17 North, Range 2 West. In 2007 the grade used by the South Union spur could still be found at the bottom of a bluff, approximately 200 feet northwest of the garage for the residence at 1043 93rd Avenue SE.

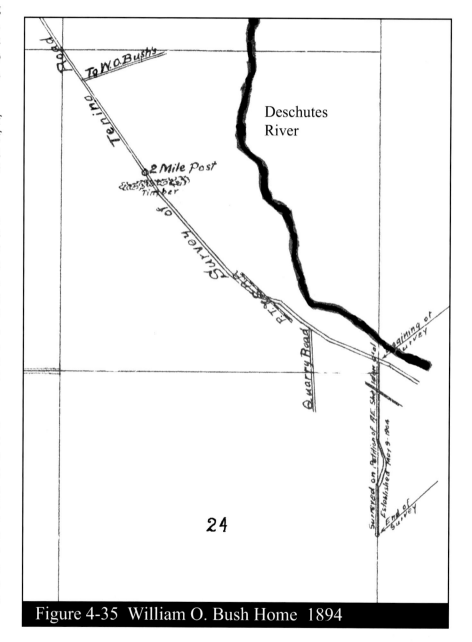

Figure 4-35 William O. Bush Home 1894

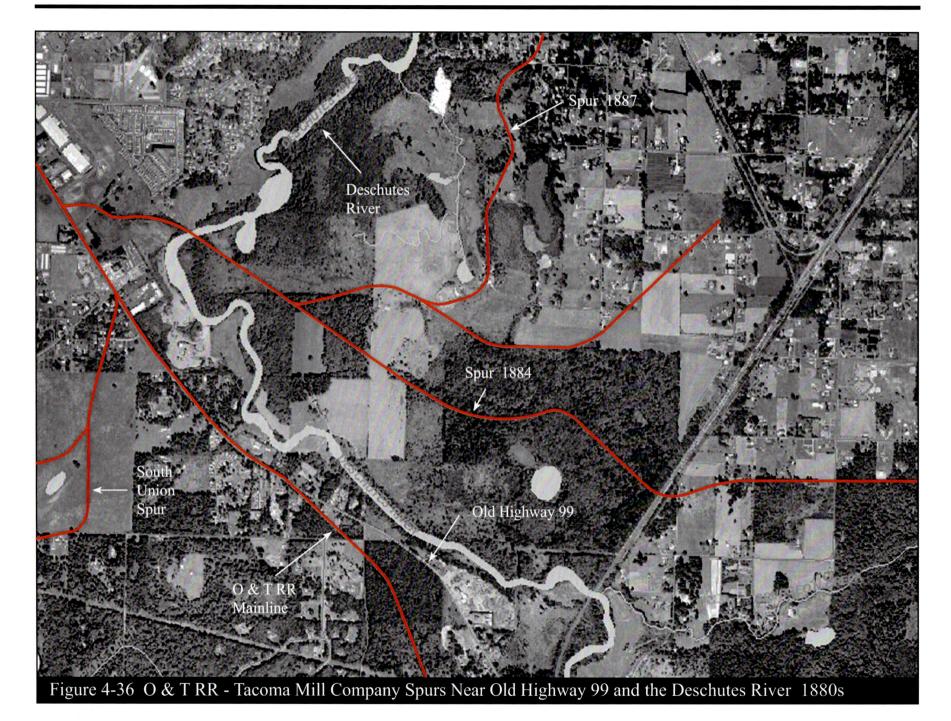
Figure 4-36 O & T RR - Tacoma Mill Company Spurs Near Old Highway 99 and the Deschutes River 1880s

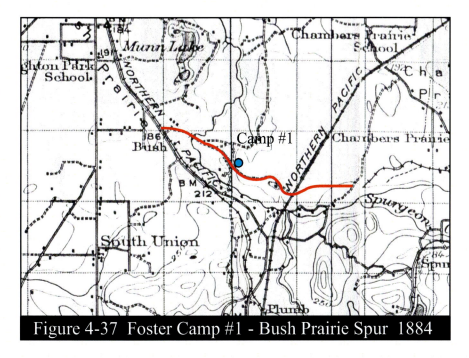

Figure 4-37 Foster Camp #1 - Bush Prairie Spur 1884

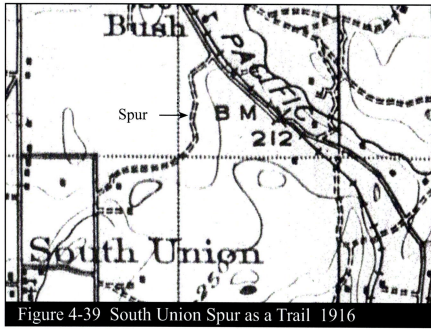

Figure 4-39 South Union Spur as a Trail 1916

Figure 4-38 White Arrows Locate T M Co. Spur 2000

The Morris Brothers (George W., Philip Guy, Robert James, and Frank M.) were in charge of logging on the South Union spur. Frank's obituary in the 22 March 1938 edition of the *Olympian* mentioned that "Mr. Morris was with the Tacoma Mill Company in its operations at South Union." Other articles of interest can be found in the Appendix of newspaper articles dated 11 June 1886 and 20 February 1903. Robert Morris was sometimes called "James" or "R. J." His obituary appeared in the 17 March 1950 issue of the *Olympian*. Aged 94 years, he had come to Olympia from Oregon 78 years before, and concluded his career as an employee of the Mason County Logging Company.

In 1904 a stone quarry was located on Bush property not far south of the William O. Bush home. The site remains a source for gravel in 2007 and is operated by Lakeside Industries, at 8840 Old Highway 99. Figure 4-40 looks east from the highway toward the entrance to this business. The driveway was built over the old spur to the Stone Quarry. At a position approximately 150 yards east of Old Highway 99, the current driveway diverges from the spur. Ten yards farther east, Figure 4-41 was taken while standing on the driveway and looking south toward the spur, which at that point lies within forest.

Figure 4-40 View East Along Stone Quarry Spur 2007

Figure 4-41 View South - Stone Quarry Spur 2007

Figure 4-42 Olympia Logging Company Spur 1903

Two hundred feet north of the position where the photograph presented in Figure 4-40 was made, the railroad's mainline can be found with some difficulty. It lies in dense brush in a cut approximately twenty feet east of Old Highway 99.

Farther south along Old Highway 99, evidence suggests that the driveway between 8925 and 8931 Old Highway 99 coincides with the spot where the Olympia Logging Company originated a spur in 1903. The spur led to a tract of timber in the west half of Section 24 in Township 17 North, Range 2 West. It is identified in Figure 4-42. The northern part of this spur is probably represented by a road seen in Figure 4-43, which is part of a 1974 map of the region. When the spur was in use, 93rd Avenue had not yet been built. Only one remnant of this spur could be identified in 2007. The spot where Figure 4-44 was photographed is identified in Figure 4-42. The picture looks north along a cut approximately 20 feet east of Brooks Lane. The cut can be found approximately 130 feet south of the origin for the driveway at 9433 Brooks Lane.

The Olympia Logging Company also harvested two additional areas. Both were farther south and likewise were located along the Port Townsend Southern Railroad. That activity will be discussed on page 103.

Figure 4-44 East of Brooks Lane - View North 2007

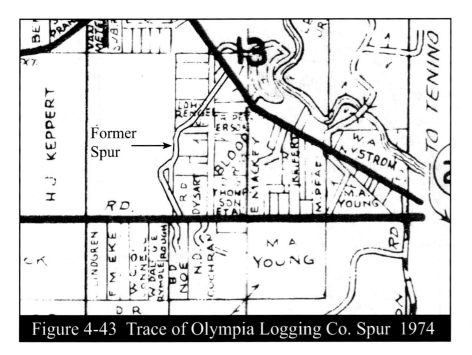
Figure 4-43 Trace of Olympia Logging Co. Spur 1974

Figure 4-45 View South at 8989 Old Highway 99 2007

Immediately south of 8931 Old Highway 99 the railroad remained on the east side of the road from Olympia to Tenino. It is easy to find it as an elevation running parallel to the highway at 8939 Old Highway 99. Figure 4-45 looks south at that address, from the driveway for the structure known as River House. The grade itself is difficult to see from the highway due to the wooden fence at the western edge of the property.

Near the upper end of Figure 3-52 (a 1909 road map of Thurston County) a wagon road, the Olympia-Tenino Road, can be seen crossing the railroad. This took place in the middle of the west half of the southeast quarter of Section 13 in Township 17 North, Range 2 West. Modifications to the road (now Old Highway 99) make it difficult to find the precise place where the two rights of way intersected. Figure 4-46 is a modern aerial view of that locale. The intersection was located approximately 90 yards northwest of the origin of the driveway at 9123 Old Highway 99.

Between the grade crossing at the Olympia-Tenino Road and what is now 93rd Avenue, the railroad lay on an elevated fill. It is readily visible today in Figure 4-47, a photograph taken looking west immediately south of the residence at 9215 Old Highway 99. The region south of 93rd Avenue is presented in Figure 4-48. This recent aerial photograph indicates the position of a siding that logically would have been used to harvest timber from the eastern half of Section 24 in Township 17 North, Range 2 West. This particular timberland (see page 81) was bought by Benjamin B. Turner in 1881 and resold later the same year to Charles Hanson of the Tacoma Mill Company. The Olympia & Tenino Railroad cut across the northeast corner of this tract (bounded by 93rd Avenue and Sheldon Road) allowing that part of the property easy access to the railroad. Because the topography in that area would have made it impractical to build a spur into the majority of this timberland, oxen and skid roads were likely used to bring logs to the siding. Figure 4-35 suggests that this property was used later as a gravel quarry. In 1894, 93rd Avenue did not yet exist. Figure 4-49 reveals features from a 1936 aerial photograph that may have originated as a skid road. While no mining was evident in 1936, a 1953 aerial photograph (not reproduced here) again showed active quarrying. With the disturbance made here by mining, it's understandable that no sign of either the railroad or a siding can be found nowadays in the field bounded by 93rd Avenue on the north, and Sheldon Road on the east. However, a ramp can still be seen in Figure 4-50, a 2007 photograph taken looking southeast from the field. It may have been used to lower logs from a skid road to the level of the siding. The visible house is located at 9410 Springer Lake Lane. Southeast of this siding, the mainline crossed today's Sheldon Road, as seen in Figure 4-51. This recent photograph looks southeast along the grade after it crossed Sheldon Road.

Figure 4-46 Grade Crossing - Old Highway 99

Figure 4-47 Elevated Grade West of Old Highway 99

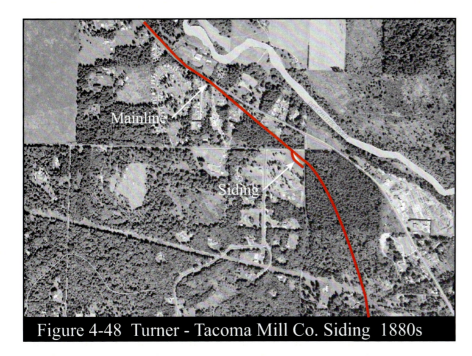

Figure 4-48 Turner - Tacoma Mill Co. Siding 1880s

Figure 4-50 View South at 9410 Springer Lake Road

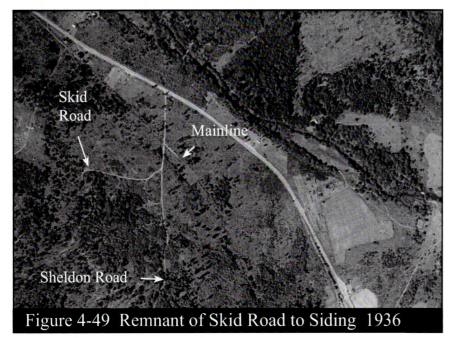

Figure 4-49 Remnant of Skid Road to Siding 1936

Figure 4-51 View SE Across Sheldon Road 2000

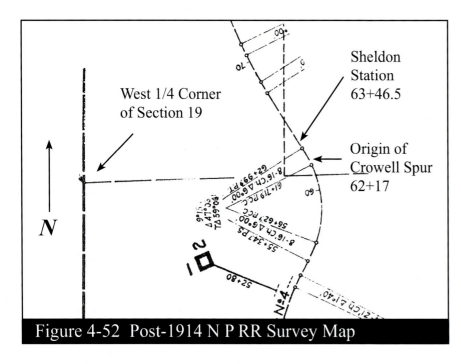

Figure 4-52 Post-1914 N P RR Survey Map

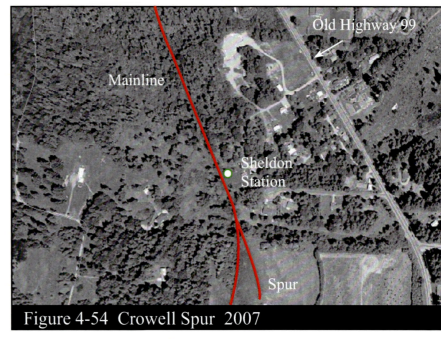

Figure 4-54 Crowell Spur 2007

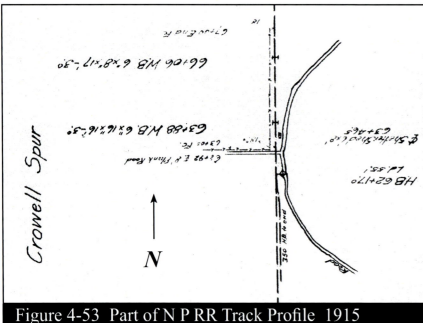

Figure 4-53 Part of N P RR Track Profile 1915

Crowell was the name given to a spur which originated 130 feet south of Sheldon Station. It achieved station status in maps issued by the Washington Railroad Commission between 1908 and 1914. Crowell Spur was 350 feet long and was the rail connection used by the Crowell Lumber Company Mill. This business was incorporated in 1904 by H. W. Crowell and John Graff. Their sawmill was situated on the south side of the Deschutes River in the northwest quarter of the northeast quarter of Section 19 in Township 17 North, Range 1 West. Crowell and Graff purchased nearby timberland in Sections 19, 20, 29 and 30. Most of the logs milled by the company were floated to the mill via the Deschutes. Finished lumber was carried by wagon across what is now Old Highway 99 and loaded on rail cars at Crowell Spur. The exact route of the wagon road between mill and spur can no longer be found. This is due largely to construction (and later rerouting in 2003) of a pipeline across the approximate place where the spur connected with the mainline of the Port Townsend Southern Railroad. Figures 3-43A and 3-43B are from the same 1933 aerial photograph. Two structures can be seen where the spur previously existed. These appear to have been substantial buildings and their presence suggests the possibility that some milling was done here, as well as at the primary mill on the Deschutes River.

Figures 3-38 and 7-1 are useful in understanding Figure 4-52, a survey map made by the Northern Pacific Railroad after it acquired the Port Townsend Southern. Distances noted on this map were measured from the second Plumb Station, toward Olympia, and correspond to data presented in Figure 7-1. Arrows indicating the location of Sheldon Station and the origin of Crowell Spur have been added by the author.

Figure 4-53 is part of a track profile of the Tumwater Branch of the Northern Pacific Railroad. Dated 28 September 1915, it was provided by Brian Ferris. All traces of the wagon roads leading northeast, and west from the spur have been destroyed by pipeline construction. The road to the southeast was probably used as the driveway for the modern house at 2908 99th Lane SE. Greg Richmond, who lives at that address, found two railroad spikes and some broken pottery while preparing the foundation for a new barn in 2005. The construction was north and slightly west of his residence and was on the site of Crowell Spur. In addition, Mr. Richmond was able to identify an elevated grade, oriented in a north-south direction, about 150 feet west of the place where the spikes were found. That grade is a remnant of the mainline of the Olympia & Tenino Railroad. Figure 4-54 is a modern aerial photograph showing where many of these features were located.

Farther south, much of McCorkle Road occupies the right of way of the most extensive spur built for the Tacoma Mill Company. The current roadway has been used for a variety of purposes over the last one hundred twenty five years. Now it functions as a county road. In the early 1880s it began as narrow gauge railroad track used to service the Tacoma Mill Company. After the rails were taken up in 1889, it became a county wagon road. Subsequently it was abandoned as a county road, and later was utilized again as a railroad spur. Eventually it became the automobile road which exists today.

McCorkle Road was named for James Fleming McCorkle. In 1963 Jessie Hartsuck Scott reported that "The McCorkles came to South Union about 1890 and lived on the Surveyor Brown homestead across from the Pittman farm, then [called] the Tollner Ranch." McCorkle himself homesteaded property which was entered in his name on 23 May 1903 (homestead #2206). In 1897 James and several neighbors petitioned the Board of Thurston County Commissioners for a road "40 feet in width, commencing at a point on the Olympia and Tenino Road 100 yards northeast of Plumb Station, thence in a southwest course… following the old Tacoma Mill Company Railroad grade which has been abandoned for 7 years, intersecting the road running from Spurlocks to South Union." A survey of the proposed road was included with the petition and is displayed in Figure 4-55. The "end of road" at the bottom of the map identified the west end of the new road. It terminated at

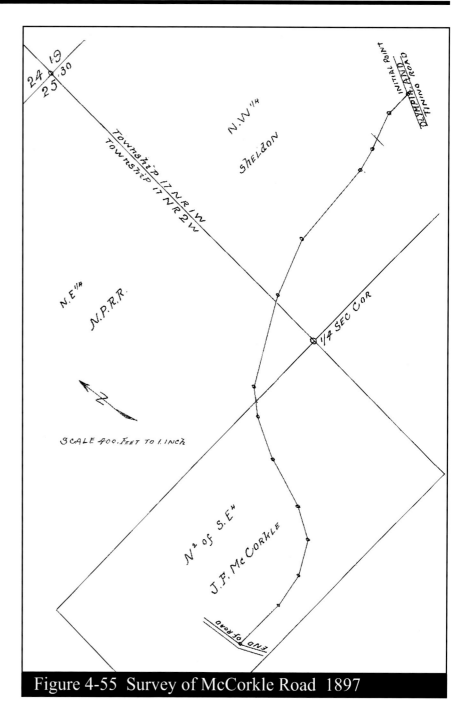

Figure 4-55 Survey of McCorkle Road 1897

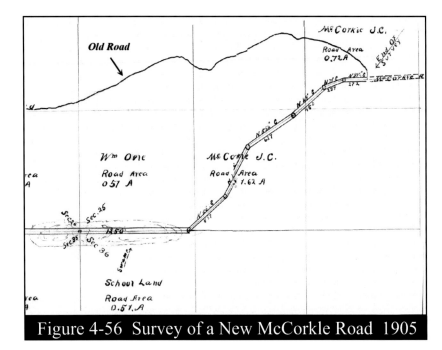

Figure 4-56 Survey of a New McCorkle Road 1905

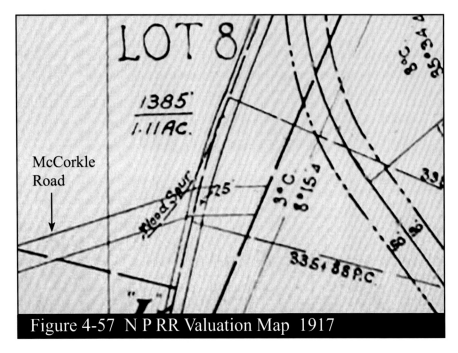

Figure 4-57 N P RR Valuation Map 1917

McCorkle's residence and was also the place of intersection with the Spurlock-South Union Road.

In 1905 McCorkle asked the Commissioners to abandon the original road to his house and to replace it with a new one coming from the west, which would originate from what is now Tilley Road. Figure 4-56 reproduces the survey for that proposal. The "Old Road" is the Spurlock-South Union Road, which apparently was abandoned between 1905 and 1909. By 1909 the original McCorkle Road was no longer being maintained by the county. It appeared in Figure 3-52 as the trail immediately above the word "Plum".

Records at the Minnesota Historical Society indicate that on 3 April 1909 the Port Townsend Southern Railroad agreed to build a spur to "the Ogle Lake Shingle Mill." It seems likely that track was merely placed on the abandoned right of way of the original McCorkle Road (former Tacoma Mill Company Spur). A small piece of this rebuilt spur remained in place for several years. It was a "Wood Spur" located at the junction of McCorkle Road and the Olympia-Tenino Road. Used for loading locomotive fuel, it is seen in Figure 4-57. This figure is an enlarged portion of Figure 4-69.

In addition to the property identified in Figure 4-56, William Ogle owned land in the northeast quarter of Section 35 in Township 17 North, Range 2 West. During the years Ogle owned that property, the small lake located there was known as "Ogle Lake". It was the site of his shingle mill. Later, when W. E. Pittman bought the property, the lake became "Pittman Lake." Figure 4-58 locates the lake with its latter name.

The Tacoma Mill Company spur along McCorkle Road was used in the 1880s to log a large area of timber. As noted in Chapter 2, the Olympia & Chehalis Valley Railroad was said to have seven miles of logging spurs in 1890. Although some of those miles may be accounted for by residual portions of the Tacoma Mill Company spurs at Bush Prairie and South Union, it seems likely that the majority of the seven miles was accessed by the spur currently under consideration. Figure 4-59 identifies parts of the spur that have been confirmed in person. Figures 4-60A and 4-60B show the western part of the spur on a 1933 aerial photograph. At least four branches originated from this spur. The first began at a place not far southwest of the James McCorkle residence, on what is now McCorkle Road. The second one loaded logs from Tacoma Mill Company property north of 113th Avenue. Both of the last two branches of the spur terminated at lakes. After felling, timber was placed in Scott Lake and Deep Lake, which were both used as temporary holding ponds. As needed, logs were retrieved and loaded on rail cars for the trip to Budd Inlet.

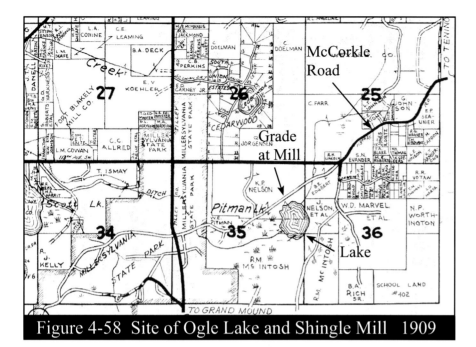
Figure 4-58 Site of Ogle Lake and Shingle Mill   1909

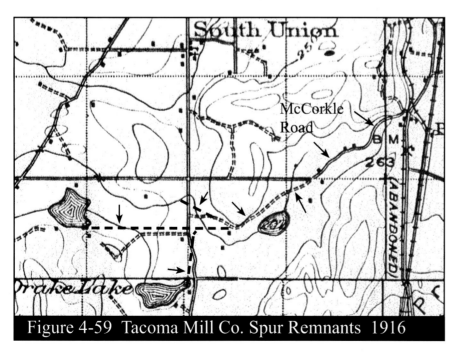
Figure 4-59 Tacoma Mill Co. Spur Remnants   1916

The origin of the main Tacoma Mill Company spur is shown on page v. This illustration imagines a scene in the late 1880s. The view is north near the place where today's McCorkle Road ends at Old Highway 99. Olympia & Chehalis Valley Railroad Engine #2 has just left the mainline and is starting onto the spur with empty log cars. Figure 4-61 is a glimpse of the same place in 2007. The home is at 2830 McCorkle Road. An imprint of the first branch of the spur can be seen in Figure 4-62, part of a 1933 aerial photograph. The unmistakable smooth curvature of an old railroad grade is readily visible where the branch separated from what is now McCorkle Road. The southern part of this right of way is at a significant elevation. That portion was probably a skid road when the spur was being operated. Ogle Lake (now Pittman Lake) can also be seen. Southwest of the takeoff point of the first branch, the spur followed today's McCorkle Road to the place where that road meets Patsy Drive. Figure 4-63 looks southwest at that intersection, where the railroad stretched across the field in the distance. That portion of the old spur is readily seen in Figure 4-62. The second branch from the spur pointed northwest toward 113th Avenue. It is challenging to locate today. After diverging from the primary spur on the east side of Bloom's Ditch, it headed northwest before crossing the ditch. In 2007 Tilley Road cuts across the remnant of this branch 0.27 mile south of 113th Avenue. The two rights of way intersect diagonally, approximately twenty feet south of a 35 MPH traffic sign.

The right of way that led to Scott Lake and Deep Lake can be found on the west side of Bloom's Ditch, immediately north of the maintenance buildings at Millersylvania State Park. Figure 4-64 looks southeast over the grade, with a park building visible on the right. The primary spur passed due west from that point before dividing into branches to the two lakes. The branch to Deep Lake curved south before crossing Tilley Road. The branch to Scott Lake continued directly west and crossed Tilley Road.

Although two modern roads meet Tilley Road at the point where the branch to Scott Lake crossed Tilley Road, neither occupy the old railroad grade. West of Tilley Road the branch lay in a cut on the north side of the current park road. The grade was elevated, after reaching a point 235 yards west of Tilley Road. Viewed from the park road, a large log lay upon it in 2007, when the picture in Figure 4-65 was taken. Terrain between that point and Scott Lake is relatively flat, making it difficult to find any of the western part of that branch. However, the right of way was readily visible in 1933 as a motor roadway (see Figures 4-60A and 4-60B).

Figure 4-66 preserves a faint imprint of the curving path followed by the branch to Deep Lake after it separated from the branch to Scott Lake. The majority of the northern two thirds of this grade has been covered by Tilley Road. The southern part is easily visible as a deep cut west of Tilley Road. The cut begins approximately 370

Figure 4-60A 1880s Tacoma Mill Company Logging Grades Near Deep Lake and Scott Lake

Figure 4-60B Aerial Photograph 1933

Figure 4-61 View North at 2830 McCorkle Road 2007

Figure 4-63 View SW at McCorkle Rd. and Patsy Dr.

Figure 4-62 First Branch of Spur 1933

Figure 4-64 View SE - Spur West of Bloom's Ditch

yards north of the main entrance to Millersylvania State Park and is 8-10 feet deep. Figure 4-67 was taken looking north in the cut, approximately 150 yards north of the park entrance.

Allan Haase has lived at Deep Lake for most of his adult life. Years ago he was told by older residents that a railroad had loaded logs at the north end of the lake. A wooden form, or crib, was made of logs and floated into position at the end of the line. Then the crib was sunk by filling open spaces with rocks, and track placed on it. Empty cars were backed into the lake and logs pulled aboard with a steam donkey engine. Immediately west of the track, the donkey sat on a platform at lake's edge. One piling from the platform was still upright in 2007 when Figure 4-68 was taken. The picture looks southeast from the east end of the lake's north shore. Mr. Haase mentioned that the crib was about 100 yards long and can still be seen from boats passing nearby.

Returning attention to the junction of McCorkle Road and Old Highway 99, an additional customer of the railroad must be mentioned before examining businesses farther south. In 1889 Chester W. Manville operated a sandstone quarry at precisely the place where the Tacoma Mill Company spur separated from the mainline of the Olympia & Chehalis Valley Railroad. This general area is visible in Figure 4-61 (also see 7 June 1935 in the Appendix).

Progressing south along the mainline, the next enterprise to be encountered was owned by Allen E. White. He was called A. E. White to distinguish himself from a fellow logger who was also his uncle, Allen White. A. E. White began a new enterprise in Thurston County in 1911. The business was called A. E. White Inc. and was independent of the White Brothers Logging Company, an earlier Black Lake venture with his brother, Henry W. White. White acquired extensive timber rights in the region of the first Plumb Station. Late in 1911 he applied to the Washington Public Service Commission (case #500 of records archived as part of the Washington Utilities and Transportation Commission) for permission to cross what is now Old Highway 99 with a logging railroad. The crossing was to be approximately 250 feet south of the first Plumb Station, and would only be used for about 90 days. Figure 4-69 is part of page 7 of a Northern Pacific Railroad Valuation Map from the Jim Fredrickson collection. White's railroad can be found near the bottom of the map. In this figure "Plumb" denotes the second Plumb Station. The Point Defiance Line of the Northern Pacific Railroad was built a few years after construction of White's railroad, and cut across it. The timberland harvested by White is shown within the red lines in Figure 4-70.

South of Waldrick Road the mainline of the Olympia & Tenino Railroad can still be observed on the west side of Old Highway 99. At the place where the highway

Figure 4-65 View North Toward Elevated Grade 2007

Figure 4-66 Trace of Branch to Deep Lake 1933

Figure 4-67 View North in Cut North of Deep Lake

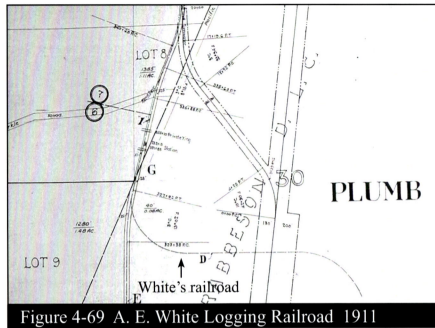
Figure 4-69 A. E. White Logging Railroad 1911

Figure 4-68 View SE from North Shore of Deep Lake

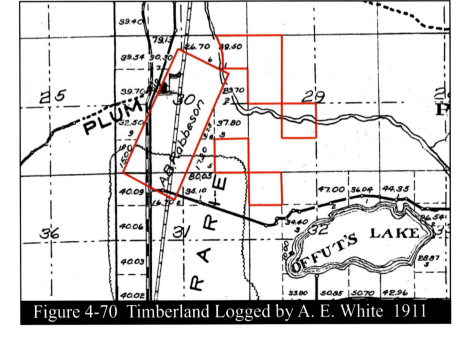
Figure 4-70 Timberland Logged by A. E. White 1911

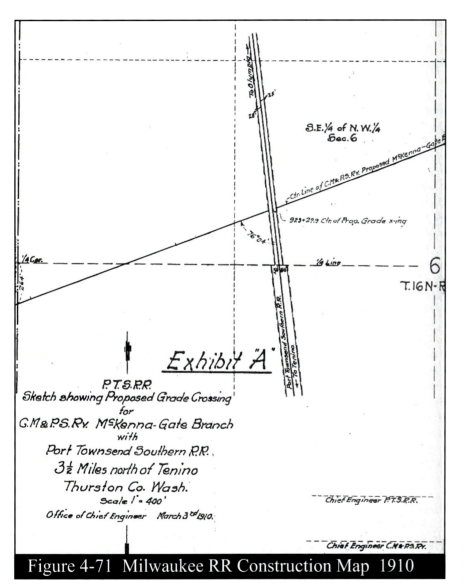

Figure 4-71 Milwaukee RR Construction Map 1910

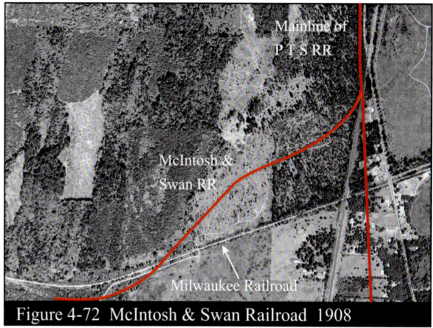

Figure 4-72 McIntosh & Swan Railroad 1908

Figure 4-73 View South From Angus Drive 2007

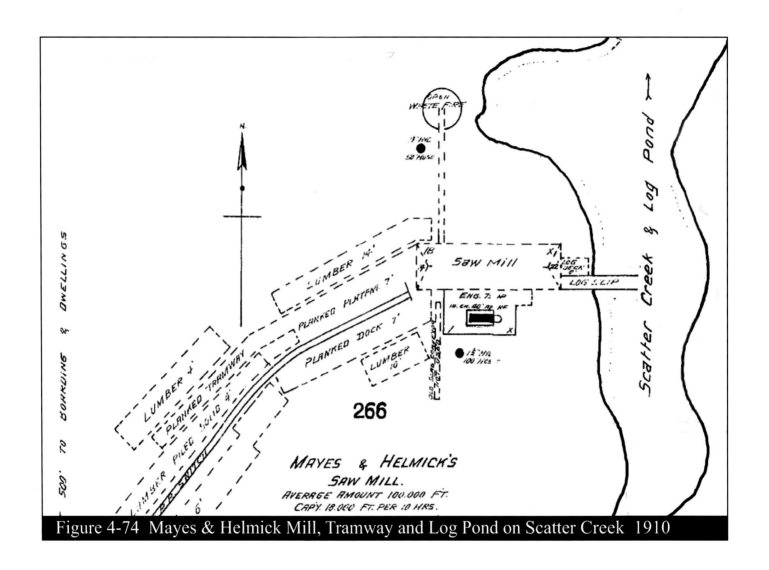

Figure 4-74 Mayes & Helmick Mill, Tramway and Log Pond on Scatter Creek 1910

curves left, to pass under the current Burlington Northern-Santa Fe Railway, the right of way of the older line continued south in a straight line. Eventually it reached a point where it became covered by fill placed when the Point Defiance Line was constructed. This portion of the Point Defiance Line was built from south to north, beginning at Tenino. When work reached this point, it was necessary to make a temporary connection between the newly finished double track mainline, coming up from Tenino, and the remaining right of way of the Port Townsend Southern, which continued on to Olympia. A remnant of that link can still be found in 2007.

In this same region, evidence of the origin of the logging railroad built by the McIntosh & Swan Logging Company (see below) has been destroyed by construction of the Point Defiance Line. Port Townsend Southern records show that the railroad made an agreement on 23 March 1908 with R. B. McIntosh and James Swan. It allowed the logging company to connect with the Port Townsend Southern mainline approximately 1.5 miles south of Plumb Station. The Port Townsend Southern was to provide logging cars and operate its locomotives over the McIntosh & Swan track.

The junction of the McIntosh & Swan logging railroad with the Port Townsend Southern can be found in the portion of the 1909 Thurston County map reproduced in Figure 3-52. Figure 2-10A indicates that the intersection was the site of Camp #5. The camp also appears in Figures 3-7 and 3-8 from 1909 and 1910.

Logically, the presence of Camp #5 implies the prior existence of Camps 1 through 4. Camp #3 is the only one that has been located. It will be discussed in the next paragraph. The evolution of these camps was a complicated process which began late in 1902 when Eugene Williamson, Frank G. Blake and Allen White (the uncle of Allen E. White) incorporated the White Logging Company. In December, 1902 and through 1903 the company purchased timberland along the Port Townsend Southern Railroad in southern Thurston County. This included a sizable part of Section 36 in Township 17 North, Range 2 West, and almost all of Section 17 in Township 16 north, Range 1 West.

Prior to the formation of the White Logging Company, Allen White owned and operated White's Mill at the village of Whites in Grays Harbor County. Although a forest fire destroyed his mill in September, 1902, Allen White recovered from that catastrophe. He formed the White Star Lumber Company and was back in business at the same location by August, 1903. As his business in Grays Harbor County rebounded, White sold his interest in timberland north of Tenino. The buyer was an organization incorporated 5 June 1903 as the Olympia Logging Company. The sale occurred on 12 June 1903 and included all properties in that area which had previously been owned by the White Logging Company. A document recorded 12 August 1903 (Thurston County Miscellaneous Book #6, page 238) indicates that the Olympia Logging Company was planning to build a logging camp (Camp #3) on two acres in the northeast corner of the Stephen Hogden Donation Claim. George and Ellen Sumption, who owned this property, also granted the logging company permission to cross their land with a logging railroad.

At its inception the Olympia Logging Company was controlled by Sol Simpson, Frank Williamson, and Frank's son, Eugene Williamson. Frank was in charge of logging operations. Later, Mark Draham and Thomas Bordeaux became directors of the company. In February, 1906, when R. B. McIntosh and W. A. Weller bought most of the Olympia Logging Company's land north of Tenino, the deed noted that a Camp #3 was located in Section 17 of Township 16 North, Range 1 West. Included in the purchase was a two mile logging railroad located in Sections 17 and 18. McIntosh & Weller also received the White Logging Company property in Section 36 of Township 17 North, Range 2 West.

A letter preserved in the Weyerhaeuser Archive (Box 35, Ma-Mc, 1906) specified some of the logging activity carried out by McIntosh & Weller. Dated 13 May 1906, it was written by Weller to the Weyerhaeuser Company. It implied that McIntosh & Weller had previously signed a note agreeing to pay Weyerhaeuser $925 for the privilege of cutting the latter company's timber in Sections 2 through 17 in Township 16 North, Range 2 West. The letter mentioned that McIntosh & Weller were starting that week to haul out timber being cut on the Lemuel Whittaker property, immediately south of the described Weyerhaeuser land. Weller requested to defer payment of the $925 for one month, as it was not anticipated that McIntosh & Weller could start on the Weyerhaeuser timber before 15 June 1906.

Weller sold his interest in the partnership to McIntosh in July, 1908. Prior to that time McIntosh had taken on James Swan as a new partner. As noted above, it was not until March, 1908 when the Port Townsend Southern Railroad agreed to connect with the McIntosh & Swan logging railroad. Camp #5 was located at the point of that junction. It seems likely that the railroad shown in Figure 3-50 represents the eastern portion of a larger line used to harvest the Weyerhaeuser timberland mentioned above. Exactly how far, in the direction of Section 17, McIntosh & Swan's railroad reached is an unanswered question.

Figure 4-72 is a modern aerial photograph which locates McIntosh & Swan's railroad in relationship to other rights of way. In 1910 the Chicago, Milwaukee & Puget Sound Railroad, a part of the Milwaukee Road, constructed a new line from McKenna, which crossed the Port Townsend Southern. The construction map reproduced in Figure 4-71 suggests that this part of the Milwaukee Road was intended initially to terminate at Gate. After this map was made, the actual construction led to a connection with the Union Pacific Railroad at Helsing Junction.

Continuing south, the Olympia & Tenino Railroad grade can be found today in the region north and south of Angus Drive. Figure 4-73 looks south along the right of way, which currently is in use as the driveway for the residence at 2905 Angus Drive. Farther south the railroad skirted the east side of Mud Lake and then curved gently to the southwest to cross what is now McDuff Road. In 1886 a logging camp operated by Bush & Gaston was located between Mud Lake and McDuff Road.

In 1907 George W. Mayes acquired timberland near Gilmore Station. By 1910 the Mayes & Helmick Lumber Company operated a sawmill at the place where the residence at 2737 143rd Avenue is currently located. Figure 4-74 shows the layout of the mill and a quarter-mile tramway that connected to the Port Townsend Southern Railroad. Figure 4-75 is part of a Northern Pacific Railroad Valuation Map which included the southwest corner of Section 7 in Township 16 North, Range 1 West. This region was immediately north of the Mayes & Helmick mill. An "Old Skid Road" can be seen crossing the right of way of the Olympia & Tenino Railroad. This skid road may have led to the Mayes & Helmick mill.

After fire destroyed his mill, George Mayes reorganized the business in 1913 as the Chain Hill Lumber Company. However, the sawmill was not rebuilt. The tramway later became Baldassin Road until it was abandoned as a county road in 1966.

While the Point Defiance Line was under construction, a siding for the Chain Hill Lumber Company was installed per AFE 310-14. It was placed at approximately the position where a previous side track had serviced the loading platform at the southwest end of the Mayes & Helmick tramway. These relationships are seen in Figure 4-76. In 1916 the Northern Pacific Railroad installed a derail on this siding (AFE 2446-16). A diagram of the new installation is shown in Figure 4-77. The "County Road" is McDuff Road. Figure 4-78 is courtesy of Jim Fredrickson and Brian Ferris. The image comes from Northern Pacific Railroad Joint Facilities Book #4. The view looks south over the McDuff Road grade crossing as it appeared in 1927. Although the lumber company itself was no longer in operation, the siding (designated by the number "3") was still identified as "Chain Hill Lumber Company". The letter "D" represented the original loading platform at the siding. The platform was leased to the Tenino Manufacturing Company beginning in July, 1919. Figure 4-79 is a glimpse of the same area in 2007. Figure 4-80 is a view looking northeast across the present day railroad. The origin of the Chain Hill siding was at the far left side of the picture. The barn in the distance is on McDuff

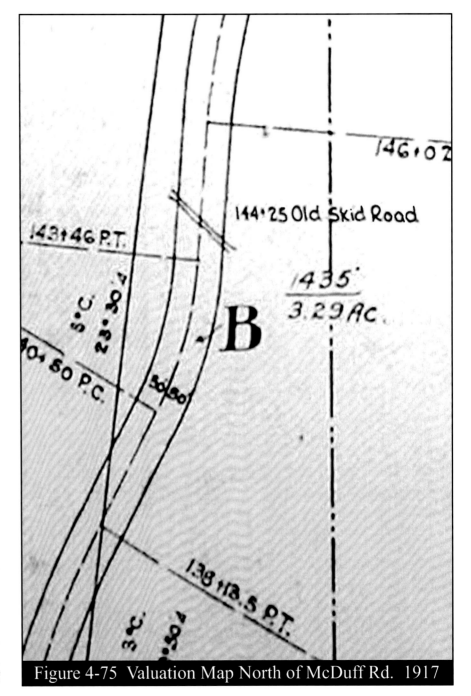

Figure 4-75 Valuation Map North of McDuff Rd. 1917

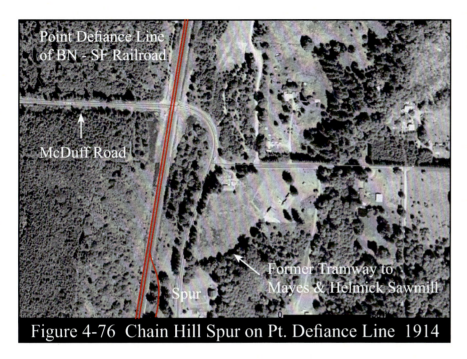

Figure 4-76 Chain Hill Spur on Pt. Defiance Line 1914

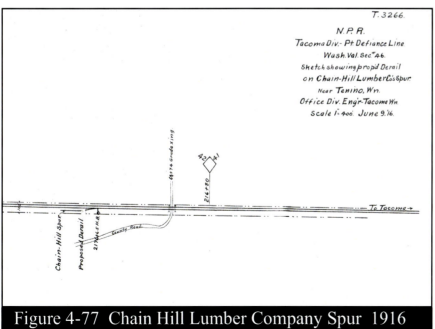

Figure 4-77 Chain Hill Lumber Company Spur 1916

Figure 4-78 View South at McDuff Road 1927

Figure 4-79 View South at McDuff Road 2007

Figure 4-81 View West From 2929 McDuff Rd. 2000

Figure 4-80 Location of Chain Hill Spur 2007

Road. The Chain Hill Spur was 401 feet long and was removed about 1942 per Northern Pacific Railroad AFE 74-42.

Closer to Tenino, a remnant of the Olympia & Tenino Railroad is still visible opposite 2929 McDuff Road. Figure 4-81 looks west from that address.

Northwest of Fenton Avenue in Tenino is the place where the Olympia Logging Company's railroad connected with the Port Townsend Southern. In August, 1903 the logging company purchased a right of way for their line from Alfred Webster, Peter Currie, Albert Nelson and George Sumption. The grade nearest the Port Townsend Southern utilized an abandoned part of the Olympia & Tenino Railroad. This segment of right of way had been unused since 1890 when the Olympia & Chehalis Valley Railroad, recently transformed into the Port Townsend Southern, was rerouted to the second Tenino Station. A 1905 survey of McDuff Road, reproduced in Figure 4-82, reveals that a "switch" crossed the wagon road. This switch was the origin of the Olympia Logging Company's railroad. It was part of the original right of way built in 1878 for the Olympia & Tenino Railroad, and was not used between 1890 and 1903.

Immediately southeast of the switch, the logging railroad diverged from the 1878 grade and curved in a long arc, eventually heading northeast. Figure 4-83 is a recent photograph taken looking north at the junction of Wichman Street and Fenton Avenue. Now used as a farm road, the old railroad grade remains visible. Figure 4-84 is a modern aerial photograph showing the location of these features.

The red line in Figure 4-85 indicates the path of the Olympia Logging Company Railroad immediately north of Tenino. A short length of track built in 1910 by the Hartson-Otis Lumber Company is represented by a yellow line. The two rights of way diverged at the location of Camp #3.

Assessing the location and builder of various trails, roads and railroads north of Tenino is challenging. Native Americans were using a path through this region long before European immigrants widened it to form the part of the Oregon Trail known as the Cowlitz Trail. A series of maps and aerial photographs were useful in determining which features found here represented trails or roads, and which began as railroad grades. Figure 4-86 comes from an 1894 survey of Nelson (now Hyatt) Road. It establishes the fact that in 1894, the road from Olympia to Tenino passed over the junction between Sections 7, 8, 17 and 18 in Township 16 North, Range 1 West. The Olympia-Tenino Road followed the Cowlitz Trail. Part of the 1909 road map of Thurston County is reproduced in Figure 4-87. Note that the Olympia-Tenino Road still passed through the junction of the same four sections. South of that point, the road pointed precisely southwest until it made a 60 degree turn to the south. Figure 4-88 is part of a 1916 Geological Survey Map of the area north of Tenino. Two roads are seen in the northeast corner of Section 18. Both continued north into the southeast corner of Section 7. Finally, Figure 4-89 is part of sheet 11 of the construction plans for a 1920 rebuilding of Pacific Highway. A previous position of Pacific Highway is shown with two dotted lines in the upper right hand corner of the figure, and this feature corresponds to the 1894-1909 Olympia-Tenino Road that passed through the junction of Sections 7, 8, 17 and 18. In the lower half of the map there is an unidentified grade, also represented by dotted lines, over which the new Pacific Highway would be built. Notably, this unidentified grade

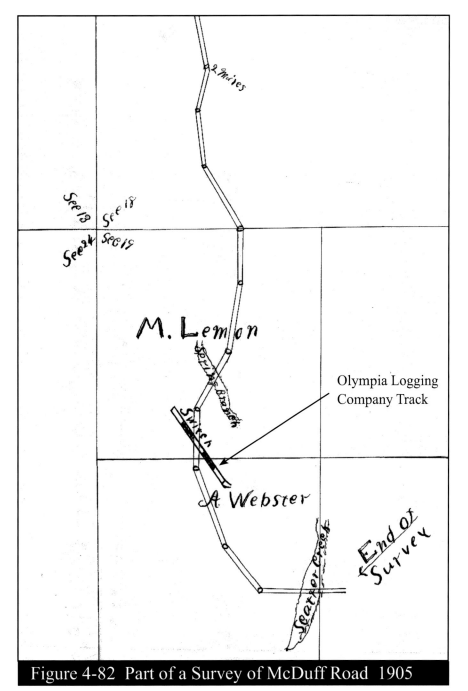

Figure 4-82 Part of a Survey of McDuff Road 1905

Figure 4-83 View North From Fenton Avenue 2007

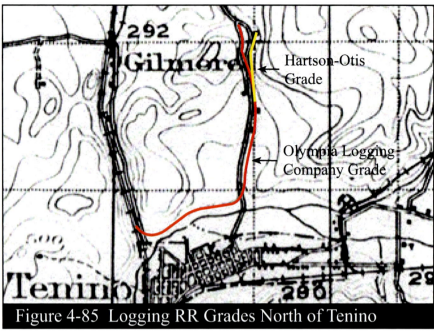

Figure 4-85 Logging RR Grades North of Tenino

Figure 4-84 Aerial Photo of Northern Tenino 2007

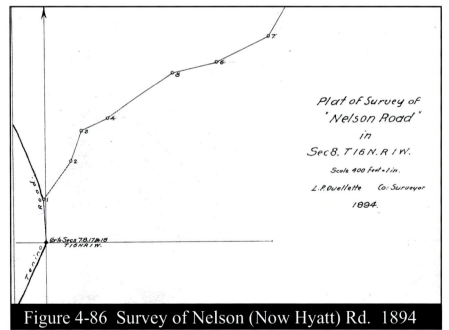

Figure 4-86 Survey of Nelson (Now Hyatt) Rd. 1894

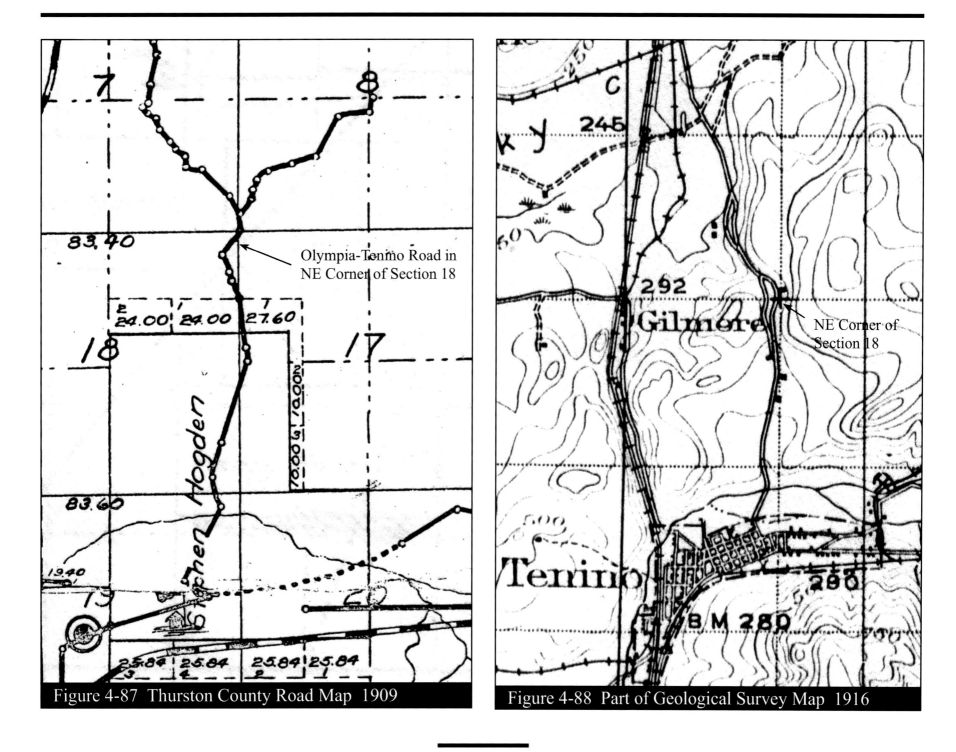

Figure 4-87 Thurston County Road Map 1909

Figure 4-88 Part of Geological Survey Map 1916

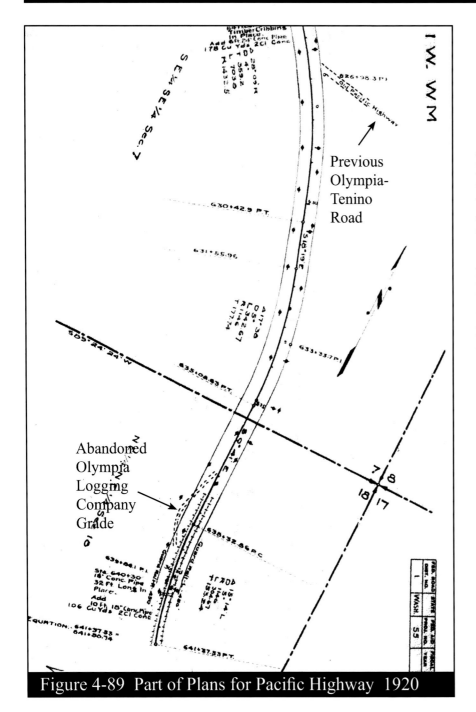

Figure 4-89 Part of Plans for Pacific Highway 1920

does not point toward the northeast corner of Section 18. Thus it is not likely to have been the old Cowlitz Trail. On the other hand, it was in use as a wagon road (see Figure 4-88) in 1916. Logic suggests that this grade was the one constructed by the Olympia Logging Company in 1903. After logging was finished in the southeast quarter of Section 7, rails were removed and local residents began using the right of way as a wagon road.

Another old grade can be found in this region. Additional information about the Hartson-Otis Lumber Company will be found on pages 109, 110, and 112. In 1910 this company began operating in Tenino. The owners purchased the timber rights to the southwest quarter of Section 8 (same Township and Range mentioned in the preceding paragraph) from the Olympia Logging Company. A new segment of railroad was built south from the southwest corner of Section 8. It passed over the junction of the previously enumerated four sections, as had the Cowlitz Trail. Farther south it headed south-southwest and then made a 30 degree turn, such that it then led almost directly south. It joined the original Olympia Logging Company grade at the place where Camp #3 had been located in 1903.

Figure 4-90B is a 1936 aerial photograph of the Chaen Hill (often spelled Chain Hill) region north of Tenino. Figure 4-90A is the same picture with various features superimposed. Look again at Figure 4-88. Between Sections 7 and 18 the Olympia-Tenino Road split into two segments. Both the eastern and the western segments were in use as a wagon road in 1916. The northern portion of the western segment was built originally by the Olympia Logging Company as a railroad grade. The southern part of that segment was a combination of the Cowlitz Trail and the logging company grade. The northern part of the eastern segment was part of the Cowlitz Trail originally, while the southern section was constructed in 1910 by the Hartson-

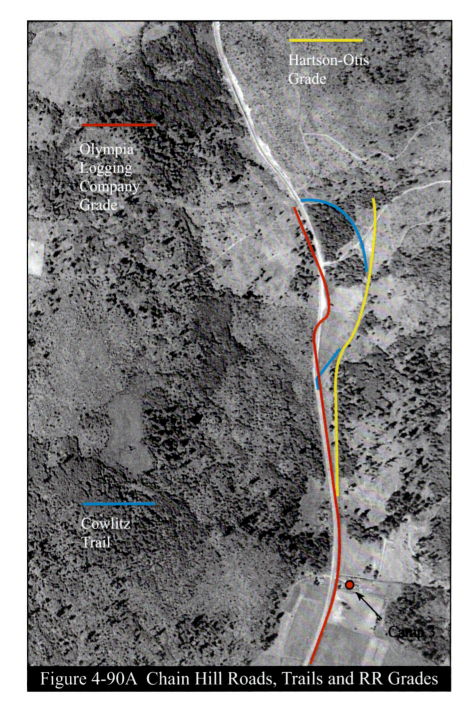

Figure 4-90A Chain Hill Roads, Trails and RR Grades

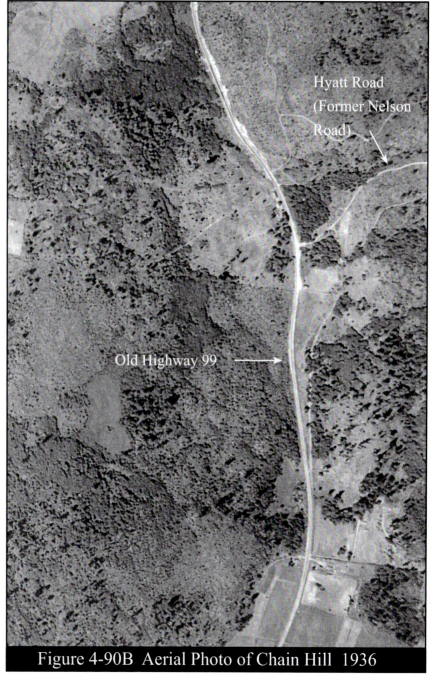

Figure 4-90B Aerial Photo of Chain Hill 1936

Figure 4-91 Modern Aerial Photo of Chain Hill

Otis Lumber Company as their new railroad grade. Figure 4-91 is a modern aerial photograph of the area.

In the early 1900s the Jonis Spar and Lumber Company operated at Jonis Spur, which was sited approximately one mile south of Tenino on the Northern Pacific Railroad. In January, 1906, the company moved to a spot northwest of Tenino, on the mainline of the Port Townsend Southern. The railroad constructed a trestle for access to the relocated mill. A blueprint used in that construction, reproduced courtesy of Jim Fredrickson, appears in Figure 4-92. The trestle is visible on the left side of Figure 4-93, a photograph from the Tenino Depot Museum collection. Dated 24 June 1909, the picture was taken looking east from the Hercules Sandstone Company. The Jonis mill itself is not visible, but was located immediately beyond the left end of the photograph. Figure 4-94 is a 1910 diagram showing the relationship of the mill to Scatter Creek, the loading docks north of the trestle, and the Port Townsend Southern Railroad.

Figure 4-95, courtesy of the Tenino Depot Museum, is a view which looks north from a place now occupied by the Point Defiance Line of the Burlington Northern-Santa Fe Railway. The Jonis mill appears in the far left part of the picture, while the trestle leading to it can be seen immediately below the mill. From the mill, the trestle rises to the height of the mainline of the Port Townsend Southern. Only a small portion of that railroad can be seen on the right side of a large fir tree in the foreground. Figure 4-96 enlarges part of Figure 4-95. It displays the railroad's mainline as it crossed a long trestle over Scatter Creek. Figure 4-97 is a modern view from approximately the same place where Figure 4-95 was obtained.

The Jonis Spar and Lumber Company was bankrupt in 1910 when its mill was sold to the Hartson-Otis Lumber Company. The latter company was incorporated 29 August 1910 by Orsal H. Hartson and John T. Otis. Hartson's Olympia businesses

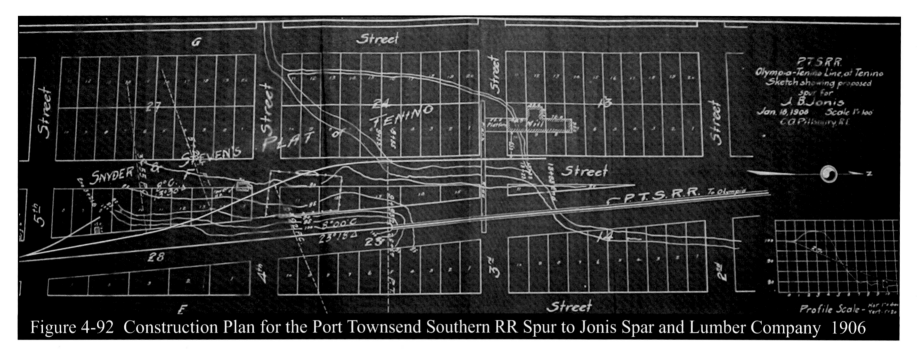

Figure 4-92 Construction Plan for the Port Townsend Southern RR Spur to Jonis Spar and Lumber Company 1906

were described earlier in this chapter. The Hartson-Otis Lumber Company built a small logging railroad which originated at the south side of its mill. That right of way will be described with the Hercules Sandstone Company, on page 112. The lumber company also reactivated the grade constructed in 1903 by the Olympia Logging Company, as described four paragraphs above. The Hartson-Otis mill was only in operation for about two years. Construction of the Point Defiance Line of the Northern Pacific Railroad obliterated the rail connection between the mill and the Port Townsend Southern. Possibly the cost of establishing a connection with the Point Defiance Line was too great, or available timber ran out. At any rate, the mill closed after its rail link was severed.

A legacy of the Hercules Sandstone Company remains in the rectangular rock on Lemon Hill, still visible from almost anywhere in Tenino. Located directly west of downtown Tenino, the quarry began in 1904 as the Tenino Sandstone Company. Initially, a tramway running directly east led to the west side of the Port Townsend Southern Railroad. There, blocks of stone were hoisted up to the level of the railroad for loading on rail cars. The termination of the tramway and the hoist next to the railroad is visible on the right side of Figure 4-93. The business reorganized as the Hercules Sandstone Company in 1907. Plans for a railroad spur to the quarry were created in 1907 and appear in Figure 4-98, from the Jim Fredrickson collection. In 1908 the Port Townsend Southern began service on the spur. Figure 4-99 is courtesy of the Tenino Depot Museum. The view is to the east soon after the quarry spur was finished. The old tramway still had its rails when the picture was taken. The

Figure 4-93 View East From Hercules Quarry Toward Port Townsend Southern Mainline and Jonis Spur 1909

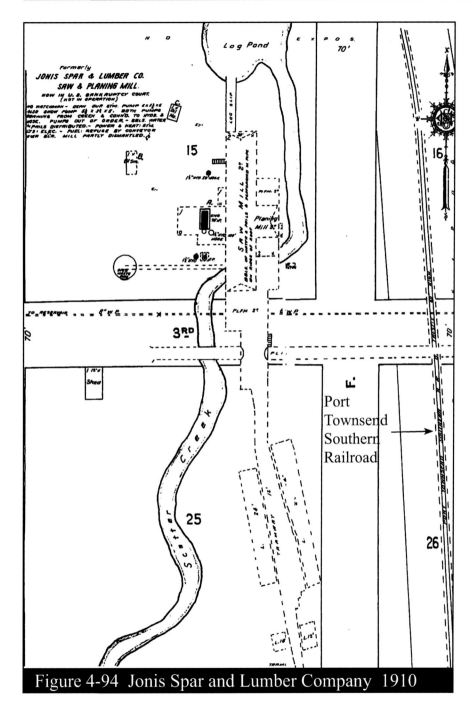

Figure 4-94 Jonis Spar and Lumber Company 1910

illustration on page vi imagines the same structures as they would have appeared from a vantage point east of the quarry. Port Townsend Southern locomotive #858 pushes two flat cars into position for loading.

When the Point Defiance Line was constructed, a few years after the Hercules spur was installed, the spur had to be modified. It was reengineered to allow it to connect with the new double track mainline. These relationships are demonstrated in Figure 4-100, part of a Northern Pacific Railroad Valuation Map. The most distant part of the reconfigured Hercules spur was removed in 1920 per Northern Pacific Railroad AFE 1019-20. Later, when the business reopened as the Western Quarry Company, the entire spur was reactivated. All of the spur was removed permanently in 1943 per Northern Pacific Railroad AFE 504-43.

Clearly, a great deal of railroad construction and revision was occurring on the west side of Tenino between 1905 and 1915. With that in mind, the short logging railroad built by the Hartson-Otis Lumber Company can now be addressed. This track is shown with a yellow line in Figure 2-13A. A newspaper article from 6 April 1911 reported that the Hartson-Otis grade used a culvert to travel under the Hercules quarry spur (which had been built in 1908). On a recent trip to this area, a depression along the quarry spur could still be found. It marks the spot excavated in 1911 to allow the Hartson-Otis track to pass underneath. West of Tenino the Hartson-Otis grade is visible along Old Highway 99. Figure 4-102 was taken looking north approximately 200 yards west of the residence at 16343 Old Highway 99. Arrows locate a visible trace of the Hartson-Otis right of way.

Figure 4-95 Post 1906 View North - Port Townsend Southern RR (Center) - Jonis Spar and Lumber Company (Left)

Figure 4-96 Enlargement of Part of Figure 4-95

Figure 4-97 View North Toward Jonis Mill Site 2007

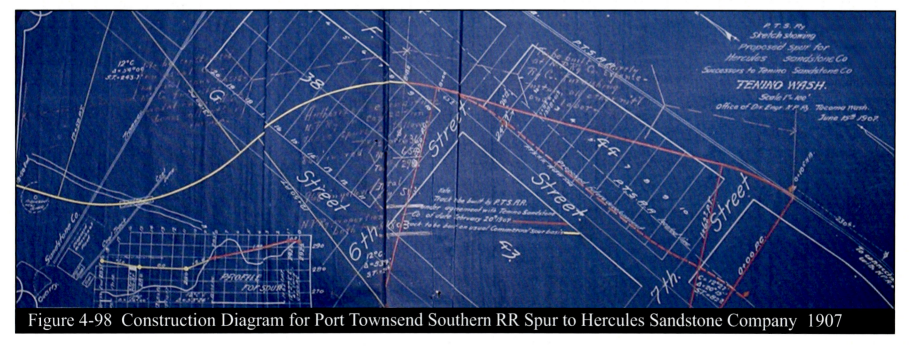
Figure 4-98 Construction Diagram for Port Townsend Southern RR Spur to Hercules Sandstone Company 1907

Figure 4-99 View East From Hercules Sandstone Company 1908

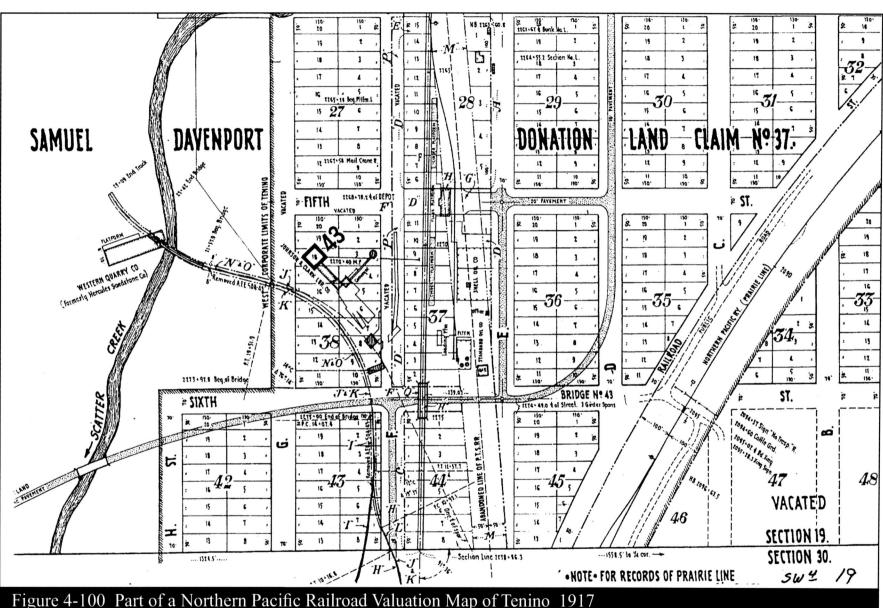

Figure 4-100 Part of a Northern Pacific Railroad Valuation Map of Tenino 1917

Figure 4-101 View Southeast From Hercules Sandstone Company Quarry 1930

Figure 4-102 View North From Old Highway 99 2007

At about the time the Hartson-Otis mill closed in 1913, Delbert A. and J. Frank Clark founded the Tenino Mill Company. Their mill was located immediately northeast of the original spur built to the Hercules Sandstone Company in 1908. It occupied the land immediately north of the place where the Hartson-Otis rails passed under the Hercules spur. By 1921, J. T. Johnson had acquired an interest in this mill which operated thereafter as the Johnson and Clark Mill.

Figure 4-101 is a 1930 panoramic view of Tenino taken from the Hercules Sandstone quarry. It is part of the Tenino Depot Museum collection. Several features can be identified in this photograph. The tramway from the quarry has been removed. The rebuilt second spur from the Northern Pacific Railroad to the Western Quarry Company is visible. A waste wood burner used by the Johnson and Clark Lumber Company (see pages 196-199 of Gone But Not Forgotten, Abandoned Railroads of Thurston County, Washington) is still standing. Figure 4-103 enlarges part of Figure 4-101. A trace of the Hartson-Otis grade can still be seen, southwest of the Hercules spur.

Chapter 5 will take a closer look at the motive power that serviced the industries described in this chapter.

Figure 4-103 Enlargement of Part of Figure 4-101

5

Locomotive Roster - 1878 to 1916

Ships and Narrow Gauge Rails, the Story of the Pacific Coast Company contains a nearly complete catalog of the locomotives which operated on the Olympia & Tenino Railroad between 1878 and 1916. It is reproduced in Figure 5-1. Missing from the list is Engine #858, which started its working career on the Northern Pacific Railroad as #119. It had a 4-4-0 wheel arrangement and 62 inch drive wheels. Volume 2 of Encyclopedia of Western Railroad History reports that it was one of seven similar Baldwin locomotives delivered to the Northern Pacific in March and April of 1882. Later it was renumbered to become #858 on the Northern Pacific roster. In 1902, when the Port Townsend Southern was leased by the Northwestern Improvement Company, the railroad came under indirect control of the Northern Pacific. The roadbed between Olympia and Tenino was upgraded in early 1903. Subsequently, Northern Pacific Engine #858 was transferred to the Port Townsend Southern, where it retained the same number. The cab was repainted with "P. T. S. R. R." Figure 2-27, courtesy of the Tenino Depot Museum, captured the image of the locomotive at Tenino. The same engine (with a different smokestack and tender) was recorded at Port Townsend in Figure 5-2, courtesy of Peter J. Replinger and Bert Kellogg. Sketches of Port Townsend Southern #858 appear in the illustrations on pages iii and vi.

Turning to the motive power used prior to the era of the Port Townsend Southern, Engine #1 was built in 1878 by Baldwin specifically for the Olympia & Tenino Railroad. It was memorialized with the name "E. N. Ouimette" in honor of Esdras N. Ouimette, a former two term mayor of Olympia. He was also a primary organizer of the Thurston County Railroad Construction Company.

Engine #1 arrived in Olympia by boat and was put to work immediately, laying rail for the new line. The E. N. Ouimette appears in the illustration on page ii as well as Figure 3-61. In May, 1891, after the railroad was converted to standard gauge, the engine was sold to the Columbia & Puget Sound Railroad, where it operated as #10. Figure 5-3, courtesy of the California State Railroad Museum, captured the locomotive in Seattle after 1891.

Ships and Narrow Gauge Rails, the Story of the Pacific Coast Company suggests that there must have been a second locomotive on the Olympia & Tenino Railroad between 1879 and 1880, as company reports list two engines during those years. No information about this second engine could be found. An additional locomotive, the Wallula, was bought in December, 1881. It carried the number 2 from its previous owner, the Walla Walla & Columbia River Railroad. The new owner retained that same number for the engine. Built by Porter-Bell in 1872, the Wallula carried water in a saddle tank and had a 0-4-0T wheel arrangement. The illustration on page v is an artist's conception of a scene immediately north of the junction of modern McCorkle Road and Old Highway 99. The view is to the north as the Wallula leaves the mainline with empty log cars to be loaded along the Tacoma Mill Company spur. This engine was destroyed in June, 1889, when a suspected arson fire burned the Tenino roundhouse as well as a newly built passenger car. The perpetrator was never apprehended.

Engine #3 of the Olympia & Chehalis Valley Railroad was named the Olympia. Baldwin Locomotive Works built it in 1884 with a 2-6-0 wheel arrangement. It appears in the photograph on the front cover of this book, and is described further in Figure 5-1. Along with #1, it was sold to the Columbia & Puget Sound Railroad in May, 1891.

After the Olympia & Tenino Railroad became part of the Port Townsend Southern, not all of the new railroad's engines operated on its Southern Division (between Olympia & Tenino). However, the first standard gauge locomotive to do so was aptly designated #1. Built by the New York Locomotive Works in July, 1890, it was a classic "American" design, with a 4-4-0 wheel arrangement. It appears in the illustration on page i. It was sold to the Columbia & Puget Sound Railroad in 1897, where it carried the #5.

Engine #2 was identical to #1. Ships and Narrow Gauge Rails, the Story of the Pacific Coast Company reports that it spent time on both the Northern and Southern Divisions of the Port Townsend Southern. It was also sold to the Columbia & Puget Sound Railroad in 1897.

According to Ships and Narrow Gauge Rails, the Story of the Pacific Coast Company, Engines #3 and #4 operated only on the Northern Division of the Port Townsend Southern. Both were built in October, 1890 by Baldwin Locomotive Works. The book suggests that #3 went on the Northern Pacific roster in 1902. However Figure 5-4, which is an enlargement of a portion of Figure 6-1, clearly shows Engine #3 hauling a passenger train, north of Tenino, in 1912. Figure 5-5

OLYMPIA & CHEHALIS VALLEY (3 ft. gauge)
Locomotives

No.	Type	Builder	Constr. No.	Date Blt.	Drivers	Cyls.	Total Weight
1	4-4-0	Baldwin	4294	3/1878	42	12x16	43300
2	Unknown						
2	0-4-0T	Porter-Bell	124	2/1872	—	8x16	15000
3	2-6-0	Baldwin	7298	5/1884	37	12x16	38000

Notes:

No. 1 Left Baldwin lettered "Olympia & Tenino," name E. N. QUIMETTE. To Columbia & Puget Sound No. 10, 5/1891.

No. 2 Nothing is known of this engine except 1879 and 1880 reports list two locomotives on the line. Apparently sold by 12/1881.

2nd No. 2 From Walla Walla & Columbia River No. 2, WALLULA. Acq. 12/1881. Destroyed by fire at Tenino roundhouse 6/10/1889.

No. 3 Bought new. Named OLYMPIA. Delivered to Columbia & Puget Sound 5/1891. Further history unknown.

PORT TOWNSEND SOUTHERN (Standard gauge)
Locomotives

No.	Type	Builder	Constr. No.	Date Blt.	Drivers	Cyls.	Total Weight
1	4-4-0	New York	628	7/1890	62	17x24	78000
2	4-4-0	New York	629	7/1890	62	17x24	78000
3	4-6-0	Baldwin	11280	10/1890	54	17x24	80000
4	4-6-0	Baldwin	11265	10/1890	54	17x24	80000
5	4-4-0	See note					
6	2-4-2T	Porter	1784	10/1897	40	10x16	41000

Notes:

No. 1 on Olympia Division until 1897. To Columbia & Puget Sound No. 5 - 1897. To Seattle & Northern, 1898-1901. To Columbia & Puget Sound No. 5, 1901. Probably not on Port Townsend Southern as No. 5.

No. 2 ran on both Olympia and Port Townsend Divisions. To Columbia & Puget Sound No. 9 in 1897.

No. 3 On Port Townsend Division. Became Northern Pacific No. 369 in 1902.

No. 4 On Port Townsend Division until 1897. To Columbia & Puget Sound No. 4, 1897.

No. 5 Doubtful if this engine ever ran on the Port Townsend Southern as No. 5.

No. 6 On Olympia Division. Went with the road to the N.P. in 1902. Later sold to Rogue River Valley No. 6. Became Portland & Oregon City No. 6 in 1915.

Figure 5-1 Locomotive Roster - From *Ships and Narrow Gauge Rails* - 1878 to 1916

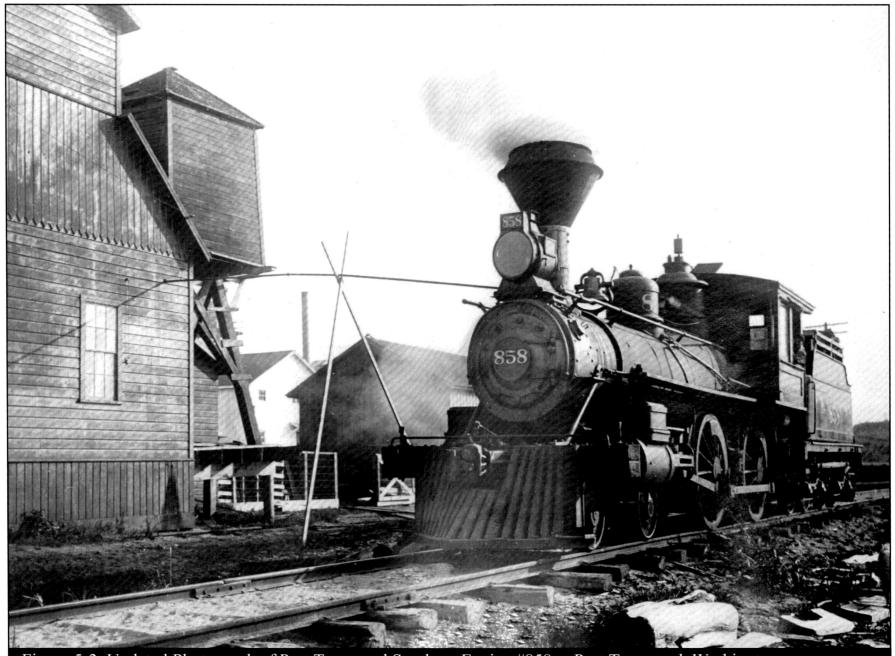
Figure 5-2 Undated Photograph of Port Townsend Southern Engine #858 at Port Townsend, Washington

Figure 5-3 Post - 1891 Photograph of the E. N. Ouimette in Seattle as Columbia & Puget Sound Railroad Engine #10

Figure 5-4 P T S Engine #3 at the Summit Slide 1912

appeared on page 37 of the fall, 1987 edition of *Columbia* magazine, and came from the personal collection of Arthur Dwelley. It is another photograph of #3, also taken north of Tenino about 1912. The train was headed south, immediately north of the summit slide (see Chapter 6). A document supplied by Allen Stanley of Greer, South Carolina, resolved these conflicting notions. Figure 5-6 is the engine diagram created 14 October 1914 by the Northern Pacific Railroad, when Port Townsend Southern Engine #3 was transferred to the parent railroad's roster. In the records of the Northern Pacific, the locomotive became #369.

A hand written note on the diagram adds that the Union Lumber Company (which was located at Union Mills in Thurston County, Washington) purchased Northern Pacific #369 in October, 1918. Issue Number 6 (Spring, 1994) of *Timber Times* published Part 3 in a series of articles about the Union Lumber Company. Page 25 included a photograph of this locomotive after it became Union Lumber Company # 4. The picture is from the personal collection of Steven R. Gatke and is reproduced in Figure 5-7. However, when the Union Lumber Company closed down in 1925, #4 no longer appeared on its equipment roster. It seems likely that it was one of the company's engines involved in a collision 4 May 1922 in the Hanaford Valley of Lewis County (see the Appendix). Given the degree of damage to the locomotives involved, a scrap yard was probably the last stop for Port Townsend Southern Engine #3. Finally, it must be mentioned that the literature contains references suggesting that this engine was sold to the Alaska Northern Railroad in 1917, where it operated as #3. Figure 5-6 adequately refutes that suggestion.

Engine #3 spent some time on the Northern (Port Townsend) Division of the Port Townsend Southern Railroad, in addition to its career on the Southern Division between Olympia and Tenino. Figure 5-8 is courtesy of Peter J. Replinger. It captured #3 on an outing near Quilcene. Engine #4 had a diamond shaped, spark arrester smokestack. Engine #4 was otherwise similar to #3, but there is no evidence of operation by #4 on the Southern Division.

Engine #6 worked exclusively on the Southern Division between Olympia and Tenino. Figure 3-14 captured the locomotive preparing to leave Olympia Station. It was built in October, 1897 by Porter as a 2-4-2T (Saddle Tank) locomotive. At that time the Port Townsend Southern used fairly light rail and it seems likely that engine weight was causing excessive track wear. Engine #6 weighed significantly less than Engine #1, which it replaced.

Sometime after 1902, when the railroad started using heavier rail, #6 was sold to the Rogue River Valley Railroad. Subsequently it was resold to the Portland & Oregon City Railroad in 1915. The engine is also displayed in Figure 5-9, a picture obtained by John Labbe from the University of Oregon Collection. At the time the photograph was taken in 1918, the locomotive was owned by the Warren Spruce Company at Willapa Bay. It still carried the number 6. Army trainmen operated that railroad, which hauled spruce logs for airplane construction.

After the Northern Pacific obtained a controlling interest in the Port Townsend Southern in 1902, Engine #858 was used as the primary road engine for the line. Sadly, none of these locomotives survive today.

Figure 5-5 P T S Engine #3 North of the Summit Slide With Southbound Passenger Train 1912

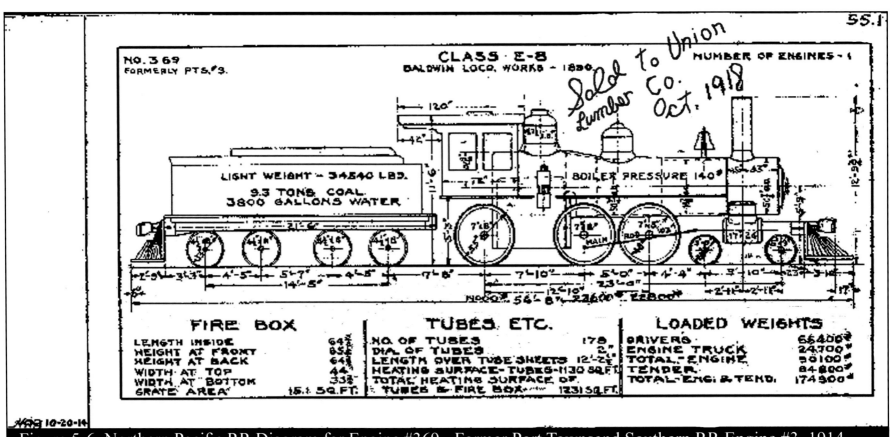

Figure 5-6 Northern Pacific RR Diagram for Engine #369 - Former Port Townsend Southern RR Engine #3 1914

Figure 5-7 Post-1918 Photograph of Union Lumber Company RR #4 - Former P T S RR #3 and N P RR #369

Figure 5-8 Undated Photograph of Engine #3 Near Quilcine (Northern Division of the Port Townsend Southern RR)

Figure 5-9 Warren Spruce Company #6 Near Willapa Bay - Formerly Port Townsend Southern RR #6 1918

Railroad Operation and Decline - 1910 to 1915

In retrospect, the decline of the Olympia & Tenino Railroad began on 1 January 1910 when the Union Pacific Railroad gained access to the Puget Sound region. On that date the Northern Pacific began allowing Union Pacific trains to operate over its mainline between Portland and Tacoma. Almost immediately there was a spike in traffic between the two cities, although trains of both railroads had to run over a single existing track. Soon, planning began for a new double track mainline linking Tacoma and Portland. The Northern Pacific's Point Defiance Line, between Tenino and Tacoma, would create an entirely new right of way as part of the solution for this problem. It was designed to bypass an unfavorable grade, south of Tacoma, on the original Prairie Line. In addition, the mainline between Portland and Tenino was to be widened from one to two tracks.

The decision to build the Point Defiance Line doomed the Olympia & Tenino Railroad. Most of that older railroad, from West Tenino to Plumb Station, was obliterated by construction of the Point Defiance Line. The remainder, between Plumb Station and Tumwater, held little prospect of generating enough traffic to justify its existence. Virtually no harvestable timber remained along that right of way. On the other hand, when the Point Defiance Line was built, it included a repositioned (second) Plumb Station. Clearly, initial plans did call for keeping the old line open from the new Plumb Station to West Olympia. Subsequently, late in 1913, it was reported that the Union Pacific Railroad would build its own branch line into downtown Olympia. This meant that passenger traffic on the Olympia & Tenino Railroad, which had never been heavy, would soon be reduced further. For those who were aware of these facts it was little surprise when the Northern Pacific announced suspension of rail service on the line, south of Tumwater, on 16 January 1916.

On 16 February 1912, the Porter Brothers Company of Portland, Oregon was awarded the contract for construction of the Point Defiance Line between Tenino and a tunnel that was to be dug under Point Defiance. The company was tasked with the complex problem of keeping traffic flowing between Olympia and Tenino while reengineering and double tracking the portion of the Olympia & Tenino Railroad between Plumb Station and Tenino. The most problematic area in this segment was a place called Summit, approximately one mile north of Tenino. There, excavation exposed underground springs which caused recurring slides of unstable earth. After the first of these events, the *Morning Olympian* reported 21 May 1912 that for the time being, passengers between Tenino and Olympia would have to travel by stagecoach between Tenino and the area north of the slide.

A glimpse of the Summit slide can be found in Figure 6-1, which is a collection of photographs assembled in 1914 and provided by the Tenino Depot Museum. Three of the locomotives seen in these pictures belonged to Grant Smith & Company of St. Paul, Minnesota, a subcontractor for this portion of the Point Defiance Line. Two distinct locomotives carry the number 3. The one pulling a passenger train would have been Port Townsend Southern Engine #3. Figure 5-4 is an enlargement of part of Figure 6-1 and shows the engine halted at the north end of the slide.

The following information from Northern Pacific Railroad Timetables was provided by Brian Ferris. The Timetable of 22 November 1914 was issued in the year the Port Townsend Southern was absorbed into the Northern Pacific system. Appearing in the railroad's Pacific Division, on the Grays Harbor Line, was "Tumwater Branch Crossing & Track Connection 0.07 mile west of Olympia [meaning the Water Street Station]". The line from Olympia to Tenino was shown separately as the 14th Subdivision of the Pacific Division. It used the original Olympia & Tenino Railroad right of way between the diamond on the west side of Budd Inlet (Capitol Lake did not yet exist) and the new Plumb Station. From that station trains operated on a completed part of the Point Defiance Line to Tenino. Mileage on the 14th Subdivision was measured from the Water Street Station, across the trestle to the west side of Budd Inlet, and then south to Tenino. Stations and commercial sidings located at each milepost were: "0.0 Olympia – 1.7 Olympia Brewing Company – 2.0 Tumwater – 2.0 Lea Lumber Company – 3.0 Hartson – 6.0 Bush – 8.0 Crowell – 9.0 Plumb – 12.2 Chain Hill Lumber Company – 13.0 Gilmore – 15.0 Tenino."

Figure 7-1, on page 132, is a map prepared in 1916 for the purpose of abandoning the remaining Olympia & Tenino Railroad right of way between the second Plumb Station and Tumwater. It provides a glimpse of the railroad at the conclusion of 1915, just before the end of its operating life.

Figure 6-1 Building the Point Defiance Line - North of Tenino in the Vicinity of the Summit Slide 1914

7

Abandonment of the Railroad - 1916 to the Present

At the beginning of 1916, all that was left of the Olympia & Tenino Railroad was the portion between West Olympia and the recently built second Plumb Station. The lion's share of that track was to be removed in 1916. Figure 7-1 is a schematic drawing provided by Jim Fredrickson. This image was part of AFE 2338-16, which authorized removal of rails from the second Plumb Station to Tumwater. After that track was taken up, the remaining rail between Tumwater and West Olympia became known as the Tumwater Spur of the Northern Pacific Railroad. The Tumwater Spur began at the Tumwater Lumber Mills Company plant in Tumwater, crossed the diamond on the west side of what is now Capitol Lake, and extended to the mills located north of the 4th Avenue Bridge.

Timetables from 1917 through 19 June 1932 include a designation for the "Tumwater Spur Crossing – Track Connection." That notation disappeared in the Timetable issued 9 July 1933, suggesting that after that date, there was no longer any regularly scheduled service to Tumwater.

Between 1916 and 1952 the right of way between Tumwater and West Olympia underwent a gradual process of attrition. Several factors led to the eventual demise of the south end of the Tumwater Spur. Prohibition, which started earlier in Washington than in the rest of the country, meant that no beer was made at the old Olympia Brewery after 1915. The brewing company tried to remain profitable by reorganizing itself as the Northwest Fruit Products Company. After producing carbonated fruit drinks for a few years, that business failed.

In 1916 the Union Pacific Railroad began operating over its right of way between downtown Olympia and the Point Defiance Line at East Olympia. That same year it constructed its own spur to the old brick Olympia Brewery building. The existing spur from the Northern Pacific Railroad, including a bridge over the Deschutes River (the bridge was owned by the brewery) was in need of costly repairs. Just then the owners of the brewery were in a weakened financial position and found it prudent to accept the new spur offered by the Union Pacific. Thereafter the Northern Pacific's brewery spur was not only unusable but also unneeded. Figure 7-2 is courtesy of Jim Fredrickson. It displays the map which accompanied AFE 1580-20, the document which authorized removal of the brewery spur in late 1920.

Between 1920 and 1926 the only business at the south end of the Tumwater Spur was the Tumwater Lumber Mills Company. A short-lived resurgence of traffic occurred in 1927 when the Tumwater Paper Mills Company opened a plant in a small building located between the old Olympia Brewery building and the Deschutes Basin. The Northern Pacific constructed a new rail bridge over the Deschutes River, immediately north of the older, larger original bridge. It also re-laid rail on the old brewery spur leading to the new bridge. The position of both bridges can be seen in Figure 7-3, which enlarges part of the Northern Pacific Railroad Valuation Map presented in Figure 4-11. The 1933 aerial photograph presented in Figure 7-4 indicates the location of the paper mill, its spur, and the original and new bridges over the Deschutes. Unfortunately, this mill was unprofitable and closed after approximately one year.

Track from the reestablished brewery spur and new bridge were removed per Northern Pacific Railroad AFE 71-43. Figure 7-5 is a map that accompanied the AFE and is courtesy James Dick. It comes from the collection of the Northern Pacific Railway Historical Association Archive in St. Paul, Minnesota.

Text associated with the map mentioned that "There has not been any business handled either to or from the southerly portion of the Tumwater Spur for several years. The U.P. R.R. has removed its connection to the private tracks of the Tumwater Paper Company, and the Paper Company tracks have been removed by independent contractors."

"Accordingly, it is recommended that the southerly 4086 feet of the Tumwater Spur, including the 504 foot spur at the present end [the Tumwater Lumber Mills Company spur] and the 1811 foot connection to the former Paper Company tracks, be removed and the rail and other track materials recovered for sale as scrap and for use in repairing other tracks in active service."

An additional document filed with the AFE indicates that track removal began in April, 1944, and was completed on the 28th of that month.

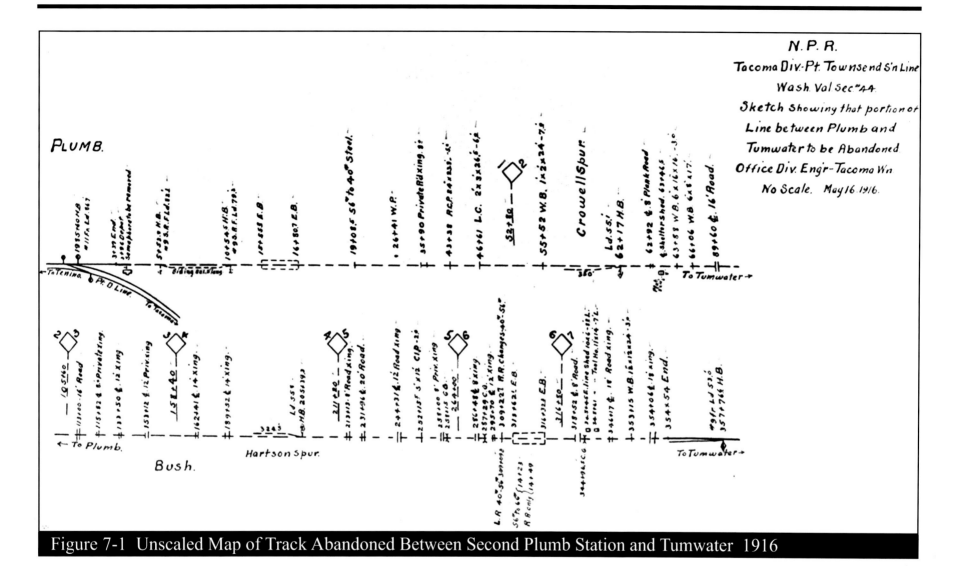
Figure 7-1 Unscaled Map of Track Abandoned Between Second Plumb Station and Tumwater 1916

It seems unlikely that any significant freight business was generated in Tumwater after 1938. The timetables mentioned above imply that regularly scheduled service to the Tumwater Lumber Mills Company probably ended between 1932 and 1933. Figure 7-6, an aerial photograph from 1933, does not suggest that any weed control was being done on the railroad grade north and south of the Boston Street Bridge. A circa 1937 photograph on page 180 of Olympia, Tumwater, and Lacey, A Pictorial History (not reproduced here) suggests that track under the Boston Street Bridge was mostly obscured by vegetation when that picture was taken. Construction of a new bridge, which today carries Capitol Boulevard, required removing the main building of the Tumwater Lumber Mills Company in 1938.

As noted on page 131, track to the south end of the Tumwater Spur was removed in April, 1944. Tax records indicate that the land occupied by the spur, in Tumwater,

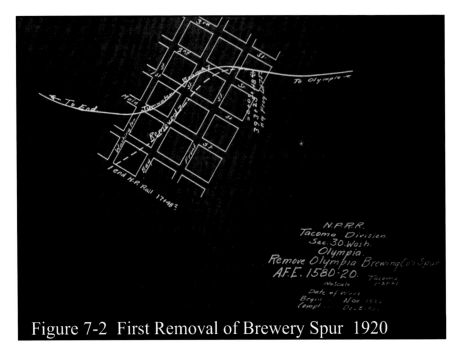
Figure 7-2 First Removal of Brewery Spur 1920

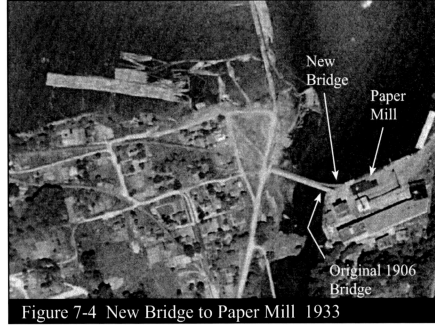
Figure 7-4 New Bridge to Paper Mill 1933

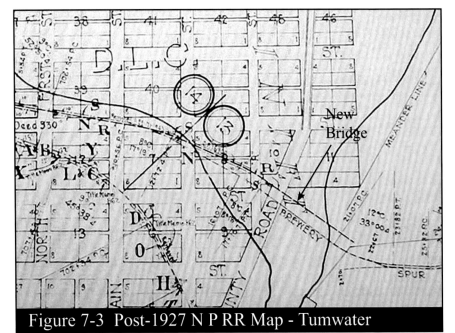
Figure 7-3 Post-1927 N P RR Map - Tumwater

was still owned by the Northern Pacific Railroad in 1945. That year the railroad paid $2,379.00 in property taxes for the right of way.

For the purpose of this book, it is convenient to divide the Tumwater Spur (or "Branch" as it was still occasionally called) on the west side of Capitol Lake into segments south and north of Percival Creek. Even after 1944 about 6150 feet of the southern segment still had rails. Sheet 3 of a map titled "Des Chutes Basin in the Cities of Olympia and Tumwater" is dated January, 1949. It is reproduced in Figure 7-7, courtesy of the Washington State General Administration. That year, track ended about 4250 feet south of Warren's Point. A Northern Pacific Railroad employee reported that as late as the early 1950s the southern segment was used to store temporarily idle log cars.

Another map from the Washington State General Administration (not reproduced here) is titled "Des Chutes Basin Project, Unit No. 3". This map was issued 25 November 1949 and revised in May, 1952. In the revised map, prepared for the Army Corps of Engineers, the connection between the northern and southern segments of the Tumwater Spur has been erased. The Corps built Capitol Lake and Deschutes Parkway during this time, and the project included construction of the

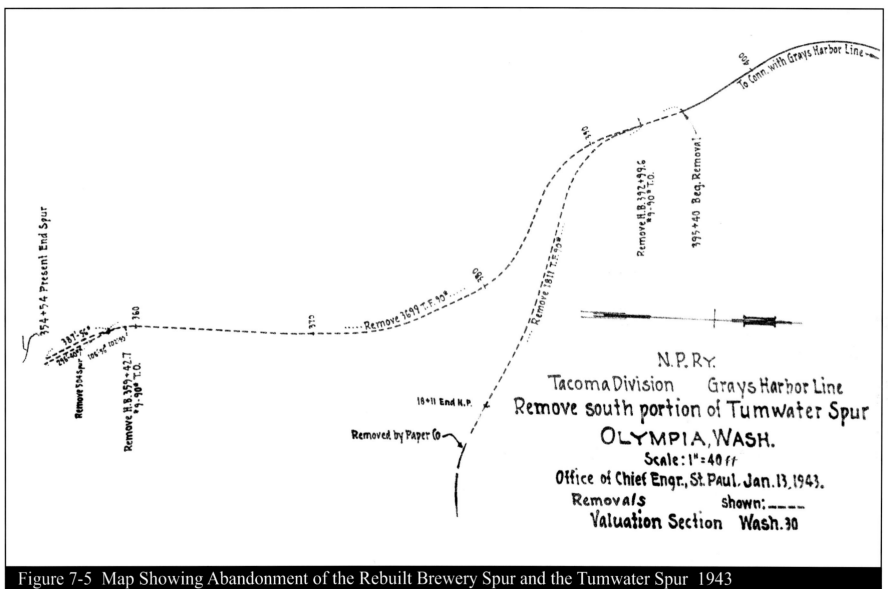
Figure 7-5 Map Showing Abandonment of the Rebuilt Brewery Spur and the Tumwater Spur 1943

Figure 7-6 Tumwater Spur in Tumwater 1933

Figure 7-7 South End of Tumwater Spur 1949

present dam on Fifth Avenue. The entire job was completed in 1952. The creation of Deschutes Parkway eliminated the southern segment of the Tumwater Spur.

Figure 3-22 is part of a Northern Pacific Valuation Map which first appeared about 1917. Updates added to the document indicate that some of the former Tumwater Spur was sold to a private owner as early as 1949. In 1955 the State of Washington purchased another part of the grade, farther north, over which Interstate 5 was constructed.

At the beginning of the twenty-first century none of the original Olympia & Tenino Railroad was in use as railroad. However, a segment of the portion rebuilt in 1886 still had its rails. Even in 2008 the line refuses to disappear entirely. A short stretch of the 1886 alignment remains in place, immediately north of the old Northern Pacific diamond.

The delusions of grandeur faded away years ago, but the memories persist.

Appendix
Newspaper Articles

Newspaper articles included in the appendix are all related to area railroads and the people associated with them. Publications represented include: the *Washington Standard*, *Olympia Transcript* and the *Olympian* from Olympia, the *Mason County Journal* from Shelton, and the *Daily Chronicle* from Centralia. Microfilm copies of most may be viewed at the Washington State Library.

Washington Standard
23 August 1873
Reception
Governor Salomon and Colonel Bee, agents of the Washington Coal and Transportation Company, arrived by special conveyance from Tenino last Wednesday evening and were received by our citizens with a cordiality that indicated the great interest they felt in the object of their mission. . . In the evening, the gentlemen were serenaded at the governor's residence, and both responded, briefly acknowledging the compliment.

30 August 1873
The Olympia Railroad
The agreement between the Citizens' Committee and the agents of the Olympia Railway & Mining Company, in the preliminary measures to secure connection between Olympia and the Northern Pacific Railroad, warrant us in the belief that we will have a railroad after all. The time for action is at hand, and as we understand it, this is the last and only chance to bring a road into Olympia. . . But we learn there are people here who are opposed to the building of railroads; others would like one, but do not wish to be taxed for it. Some want a wide gauge, others want a narrow gauge; some want it to run down the wharf, others on the east and others down on the west side. . . The extensive coalfields of the Olympia Railway & Mining Company are located about a mile south of Tenino. The company intends to begin work at the mines at once, and will soon ship coal by way of Kalama to Portland. If they cannot find an outlet for their coal at Olympia, they will be compelled to contract with the Northern Pacific Railroad Company for the shipment of coal to Tacoma. The Board of Directors have resolved to build or purchase two first-class propellers to transport the coal from Puget Sound to San Francisco. If these ships should make their regular trips to Tacoma instead of Olympia, it would do more to build up that town than the Northern Pacific Railroad can do, with all its shops, depots and offices. We are assured that these steamers will run to Olympia if the railroad is built, and this important consideration alone should be sufficient to make the proposition of the Olympia Railway & Mining Company acceptable to everyone.

Olympia Transcript
7 February 1874
O & T R.R. - Engineer's Report
At a meeting of the trustees of the Olympia & Tenino Railroad Union, on Wednesday evening, 4th instant, T. B. Morris, engineer, presented the following report:

The route surveyed may be generally described as follows: Leaves the constructed road of the Northern Pacific Company near the present station of Tenino, and runs almost north, crosses Scatter Creek and ascends from the valley of that stream, using a grade of 53 feet per mile for a distance of nine-tenths of a mile, to the summit of the low ridge dividing Mound and Rocky Prairie. The elevation above tide water at Tenino is 299 feet; at this summit the elevation is 340 feet. Descends from this summit using the same rate of grade for nine-tenths of a mile, reaching Rocky Prairie. Elevation of 270 feet. . . . The character of the work up to this point is relatively heavy. The grade lines are forced to the sidehills to find supporting ground, and the alignment conforms to the shape, which is curved. A summit cut of 20 feet for a distance of 700 feet is encountered. The line runs almost due north across Rocky Prairie entering it a few hundred feet west of the stage road; crosses that road, and passes just west of the house of Mr. Kratz, recrossing the road about opposite the house of Mr. Plummer. Near here it enters the timber again. Upon this portion the work is light, and the grades undulating, the prairie gradually rising from the south to the north. Elevation at north end is 288 feet. Distance to this point from Tenino is 5.7 miles.

After entering the timber, more uneven ground is encountered, and the line is broken up into short tangents and curves. For about a mile from Rocky Prairie the general direction continues as before-north. Here it turns to the northwest, which direction it follows until Bush Prairie is entered just east of the stage road. Distance from Tenino, 8.35 miles. The grades are chiefly descending between Rocky and Bush Prairies. Elevation of the latter about 210 feet--80 feet lower than Rocky Prairie. Crossing this prairie with the same general direction, light work and grades are obtained, and the alignment is very favorable. The ground is undulating, but has the same general elevation, viz: 210 feet.

From a point a short distance north of this prairie, the bench ends, and the ground falls rapidly to tidewater. Elevation of high tide being 32 feet. There are really two benches, or two steep descents; one descending from the bench on which Bush Prairie is situated to the valley of the Deschutes, above the falls, and the other descent from this valley, or, from Tumwater to tidewater. As these are very close together, it is best to treat them as one, overcoming all the elevation by one grade. To enable the road to overcome this descent, the line is laid on the west sidehill of the Deschutes Valley, and descends gradually, being in the valley bottom, near the sawmill of Messrs. Ward & Mitchell. Elevation here 130 feet. Passes through the town of Tumwater by following the main street, to the point where it descends abruptly. Here the line bears to the west and finds support ground by clinging to the steep slopes of the sidehills inclosing the upper portions of Budd's Inlet, and descends to tidewater which is reached near the first deep in the western shore. Distance from Tenino to head of grade is 11.69 miles; to Tumwater, 12.26 miles; to foot of grade 13.01 miles. Soon after leaving the sidehill the line crosses Budd's inlet on a pile bridge 1,550 feet long, and follows closely the foot of the bluff on the eastern shore, near the Episcopal Church, when it crosses into Main Street, which it follows to the wharf at the end of that street. Distance from Tenino to Olympia Wharf is 14.83 miles [note that when the line was built, it did not cross the mud flats to Main Street, but terminated at a wharf located near the west end of the bridge connecting 4th Avenue and West Olympia].

The most difficult country is from the north end of Bush Prairie to Olympia, or more generally, to tidewater. Over this ground a number of lines have been run, having various terminal points. In the examinations and comparisons instituted for your company, the line to the eastern donation is discarded, because it is much more expensive, is longer, and ends at a point so far from the present town of Olympia, that in my judgment it will start a rival town rather than build up and improve the present one.

Washington Standard
30 January 1875
The Railroad Union - Statement
The following report upon the operations of the Olympia Railroad Union, since its organization a year ago, its condition and prospects, is respectfully submitted:

The company was incorporated January 5th, 1874, under the laws of Washington Territory, for the purpose of building and operating a railroad from Olympia, the capital of the Territory, to connect with the Northern Pacific Railroad at Tenino, a distance of 16 61-100 miles. The capital stock was fixed at $200,000, in 2,000 shares at $100 each. Subscription of lands, materials and labor, as well as cash, were invited. Mr. T. B. Morris, late Chief Engineer of the Northern Pacific Railroad, Pacific Division, made the preliminary survey and estimates, putting the cost of a three-foot gauge road as: Roadbed, $47,973 – Superstructure, $89,032 – Rolling Stock, $25,200 – Total, $162,205. [Morris was quoted as] estimating the probable business, or receipts, of the road, when built, at $28,522 per annum, an amount which he declares would more than pay the expense of operating a narrow-gauge road.

A small force of twenty Chinamen and twenty white men was engaged, tools and supplies were procured, and the people of Olympia, Tumwater and the country [side] were called upon to turn out en masse, with pick and shovel, and unite in the opening of work on the Olympia-Tenino Railroad at Warren's Point, on Tuesday morning, April 7th, 1874. It were needless to recount to you, the actors in the scene, how manfully the call was met-how, in the early morning hours, at the ringing of the bells, and roar of guns, the whole male population of Olympia, governors, judges, preachers, lawyers, doctors, farmers, printers, mechanics, and representatives from every vocation in life, formed a long column of sturdy laborers in workman's garb, armed with axes, picks and shovels; how headed by the Olympia Light Guard Band the column marched to the shore of the bay opposite Warren's Point, embarked and crossed in a fleet of boats waiting there to receive them and, debarking upon the ground, set manfully at work. The resounding blows of axes and the crash of falling trees soon attested the steady progress of the clearers, while close behind them the graders fell to work, and the road-bed gradually lengthened out under the steadfast strokes of pick and shovel. How the men of Tumwater cleared the track through the dense timber from their town until met by those of Olympia, and both parties labored zealously in friendly emulation, until the last beams of the setting sun rested upon a mile of heavy timber cleared and a quarter of a mile of road-bed graded; and how the ladies appeared on the ground, cheering on the work by their bright presence, and what a bountiful repast was spread by them at noon upon the rustic tables beneath the grand old forest trees; and, unprecedented as was this effort in the history of railroading, still more astonishing was the enthusiasm and earnestness with which the people turned out, again and again on "field day" during the summer until the greater part of the grading of the first five miles of road-bed was done by their spontaneous voluntary labors, enabling thereby the regular force, increased in strength, to be thrown upon the farther end of the line. Subscriptions aggregating over $50,000 were freely made, including bonds, lots, supplies of all kinds, and the labor of volunteers who joined the regular force and worked out their one or two months each, side by side with the hired laborers, until ten miles of road-bed was constructed. Great credit is due the Chief and Constructing Engineer, Peyton H. Brooks, Esq., for the skill and judgment evinced in the location of the road, and the management of the work, and to Benjamin Todd, Esq., the Foreman, for his energy and tact in working the incongruous force at his disposal, and the remarkable saving of cost of the road-bed, thirty percent, on the estimates, [which] is mainly due to their care and efficiency.

Olympia Transcript

13 July 1878

Railroad News – During the week, our railroad folks have been busy as bees pushing the work of building the road along. The iron has all been taken to Warren's Point by scows, towed up from the west side wharf by the Capital, and track-laying has been completed to Bush Prairie, about one-third of the distance to Tenino. The putting up of the locomotive was finished on Monday, and it was taken up that evening to the track. On Tuesday it was run up to Tumwater. Since then, it has been employed in taking out rails on the road. Yesterday the directors had a field day, and a large number of townsfolk went out to Bush Prairie to help carry iron, lay track, and have a good time generally. The ladies of the city and Tumwater went out with their lunch baskets to see that everything was done in proper order, and were taken out on the cars, by special trains, and accompanied by the Olympia Cornet band. The whole work is progressing vigorously, and in a few days we shall have the pleasure of announcing that the Olympia and Tenino railroad is completed and running regular trains.

20 July 1878

Railroad Work – The railroad work is progressing finely, and everybody is in good spirits over the manner in which it is being done. The track is laid to Rocky Prairie, two-thirds of the way to Tenino, and is being put down at a rate of about a mile a day. The railroad folks expect to complete laying it to Tenino on next Thursday evening. The placing of stringers on the trestle work, and the laying of rails on the same is being pushed forward from Warren's Point toward the [4th Avenue] bridge, and will soon be completed, one-half of the stringers already being in place. The locomotive, E. N. Ouimette, under the hands of Mr. Mason, is constantly employed in hauling iron to the front. The general superintendence of the work is under Engineer C. H. Hale. On Thursday a number of our citizens had another field day, and assisted in loading and unloading iron, carrying and laying ties, etc. The company has five truck cars and keep them constantly employed carrying materials to the front. The passenger car is about finished, and is got up in the finest order. Some of the woodwork is made out of our best curly maple and ash. It is built in the same style as wide gauge cars, and there does not appear to be the difference in the size of it as is generally supposed. In fact, the whole road is not diminutive by any means, and does not carry that character with it.

27 July 1878

Railroad Agent At Tenino – We are glad to learn that Mr. Charles L. Reed, the agent of the Northern Pacific Railroad at Tenino, has been selected as the agent of the Olympia and Tenino road at the same place. Mr. Reed is held in high esteem by his present employers; and is well qualified for the position. We also learn that Superintendent Black, of the former road, has proposed the use of the depot, water tanks and buildings at that point to our road, a convenience which our people will fully appreciate, and a favor which the former superintendent of that road would have been far from extending. This arrangement will ensure a perfect agreement between the two companies, and all at that point being under the charge of one person cannot but result in satisfactory transactions in business.

3 August 1878

Railroad Benefits – Notwithstanding the vexatious delays attending the building of the railroad between this city and Tenino, we are gratified to announce that the work is completed, and on the 1st [August] instant regular trains began running, carrying passengers, freight and mail. This has been a long wished for day with our citizens who have had the growth of our city and county at heart, and the happiness they feel in accomplishing so great an undertaking is not to be wondered at.

10 August 1878

How The Commissioners Had A Ride – As our county commissioners have to decide at this term about giving bonds to the railroad company, the railroad directors concluded to give the commissioners and their friends a ride over the road, so that they could see for themselves and judge whether or not they had complied with the terms entitling them to the subsidy. So on Tuesday afternoon, the commissioners, directors and quite a number of our citizens got aboard of the train for Tenino. At the start everything went well, Commissioner Swan mounting the tender, so that amid the smoke, dust and noise he could pay his whole attention to business. The train passed Tumwater all right but a little south of that place, on rounding the curve opposite Mr. Nelson Barnes' old place, one of the short rails, which had not been sufficiently fastened, gave away, and the wheels of the tender and one or two cars began thumping the ties. The brakes were brought down, and the train suddenly stopped, and very few passengers knew there was any harm done.

31 August 1878

Tumwater Items – The turntable for the O. & T. R. R. in this place is about completed. It is understood that it will be ready for use about the first of next week.

Washington Standard

7 September 1878

The new turntable at Tumwater is fast nearing completion. A few days longer and the engine will come over the trestle bridge "head on."

Olympia Transcript

6 August 1881

Railroad Officers Elected - The annual meeting of the stockholders of the Olympia and Tenino Railroad took place on Monday, at which the number of directors was reduced from nine to five, and the following elected: General J. W. Sprague, F. R. Brown, A. A. Phillips, Otis Sprague and Robert Wingate. The following are the officers elected for the ensuing year: General J. W. Sprague president, Robert Wingate vice president, F. R. Brown treasurer, and A. A. Phillips secretary. The name of the company [Thurston County Railroad Construction Company] was changed to the Olympia & Chehalis Valley Railroad Company. Notice was given for an increase of the capital stock from $250,000 to $500,000.

Large Sale of Timber and Logging Camps - We understand that Benjamin Turner sold on Thursday, to George H. Foster and the Tacoma Mill Company, all of his logging camps and timberlands and timber in this vicinity. The price paid is said to be $12,000. This includes several hundred acres of timber along the railroad, his camp, oxen and all logging fixtures, the four logging cars, his old camp and timberland east of Tumwater, and the Warbass tract. The new firm will enlarge and continue the business as formerly. Two new logging cars will be added to the railroad line, making six in all, when it is expected that fifty thousand feet of logs will be brought out daily to tidewater.

20 August 1881

New Conductor – The managers of the Olympia & Chehalis Valley Railroad Company have appointed Mr. A. D. Glover as conductor, to take the position on the first of next month, or soon thereafter. Mr. Glover was the first conductor on the road, and always filled the bill. Frank Mitchell, who is now holding that position, will go to California to attend studies in one of the universities in that state. Frank has filled various positions on the road, and always with great credit.

28 January 1882

That Locomotive – The diminutive, but nevertheless powerful locomotive, Wallula, of wheat fame, which was purchased and brought here for use by the Olympia and Chehalis Valley Railroad Company, is now in the machine shops of the Tacoma Iron Works, dismembered and undergoing a thorough overhauling. Although it was in service for a long time, having hauled an amount of wheat probably greater in value than its own weight in gold, its boiler, cylinders and other essential parts were found to be in good condition and capable of no end of work for the future. It will soon be in readiness for the track, and is expected to do valuable work in hauling logs.

4 February 1882

Railroad Logging Camps – Many of the large logging camps are adopting cars to haul their logs to the water, some of which we mention in another item. Oxen, horses and mules are used; only one steam engine besides the O. & T. road yet being employed. This one is by the Blackman Brothers, at Mukilteo, where it runs up a grade of 21 feet in every 100 feet for the distance of one mile and a quarter, to accomplish which the wheels and rails are made with cogs. Williamson, of Seattle, is also building another engine for level ground, for Eugene Smith of Snohomish, which will be in operation this summer. The Olympia and Tenino road brings out cars one and a half miles, from the Deschutes River to the road, and then runs to this bay, five miles further. This is the well known camp belonging to George Foster, who also employs a large force in cutting and barking the logs, and a number of teams in hauling the logs to the line of the railroad. Mr. Foster has a large body of fine timber in the region of his camp, sufficient to keep him for several years employed in the business. From the railroad depot, where they are put in a boom, they are towed by steam tugboat to the sawmills below. In a few years it is likely the principal logging camps will employ steam engines to run their logs to the water, as the distance will be too great to make it profitable to employ oxen or horses, just as skid roads are now getting too slow, except by camps close to the water's edge, ox and horse cars will have to give away to the locomotive.

18 March 1882

The O. & C. V. R. R. trains are bringing in daily, from Foster's camp, about fifty five thousand feet of logs. Five cars are used and three trips made each day.

30 December 1882

Sad Accident – One of those lamentable accidents which occasionally casts a gloom over the whole community, occurred on Saturday last. Mr. Austin James Brazel, a sawyer in the logging camp of George H. Foster, Esq., was suddenly killed while at work near Bush Prairie.

9 February 1884

New Coal Mines And Coal Road – We are reliably informed that the owners of the new coal mines, which were found and prospected last summer in the Hanneford Creek valley, have made arrangements not only to open them, but have contracted with the Northern Pacific and Olympia & Chehalis Valley railroads to transport their coal to salt water and the Columbia River. The Northern Pacific will put in a wide gauge branch, six miles from their railroad, near the Skookumchuck River, to carry the coal to Tacoma or to the Columbia. The Olympia & Chehalis Valley road will be extended from Tenino to the mines, ten miles; also, a new road from Bush Prairie to deep water on the west side of our harbor. We understand that a party of surveyors have been out for the past week engaged on this end of the line, which will run west of Tumwater and back on the hill on the west side [none of the proposed new Olympia & Chehalis Valley Railroad grades were built].

Washington Standard

16 January 1885
The Olympia & Chehalis Valley Railroad Company has just finished the construction of a new freight car at the depot; a fact which might be reasonably taken as a good business indication.

20 March 1885
A set of trucks for another car were received by the local railroad company a few days ago.

Mr. W. O. Bush was in the city, on Monday, in quest of supplies for his logging camp on the upper Deschutes. He reports everything prosperous and contemplates increasing his working force to meet a rapidly growing demand in the lumber trade.

15 May 1885
Mr. William Abrams had his right knee badly crushed between two logs, last Tuesday, in Bush's logging camp, a few miles south of this place.

12 June 1885 Reprinted from the Tacoma *News*
The Lumber Trade – An Estimate of the Product of Camps at the Head of the Sound. From a gentleman well versed in all the lumbering operations on the Sound, as well as familiar with the entire lumbering business at the present time, the News is furnished with the following information concerning the output at various points, embracing all the camps of any importance on the upper Sound.

I. Ellis, putting logs into the bay at Olympia, operates with cars drawn by mules and running on iron rails. He works about 50 men, and puts in some 55,000 feet daily. Logs come to Tacoma Mill Company.

Tacoma Mill Company's railroad camp employs 30 men; daily output 34,000.

Bush's camp on Bush Prairie, haul by rail to Olympia, employ 15 men; daily output 16,000. Sell to Tacoma Mill Company.

Ben Turner is running two camps putting logs into Black Lake, from which he will haul them to the bay by means of a steam railroad. Employs 30 men; output 40,000. Sells to [Port] Blakely Mill.

Bartwell, on Oyster Bay, employs 12 men; daily output 14,000. [Port] Gamble Mill.

Callow, on the same bay, employs 12 men; output 14,000. [Port] Gamble Mill.

Kennedy, on Little Skookum, employs 25 men; daily output 30,000. [Port] Blakely Mill.

Howard, on same bay, is building a tramway, will run 25 men; daily output 30,000. [Port] Blakely Mill.

McLoud, on Mud Bay, operates 10 men; daily output 12,000.

Smith & Byrd, on same bay, employs 8 men; daily output 10,000. Tacoma Mill [Company].

McLain, on Big Skookum, employs 14 men; daily output 17,000. [Port] Blakely Mill.

George Perry, on Big Skookum, employs 8 men; daily output 10,000. For himself.

Edward Miller, on Big Skookum, employs 10 men; daily output 13,000. [Port] Blakely Mill.

Currie & McDonald have just gone in with a crew to open another extensive camp on Big Skookum.

Sam Coulter, at the head of North Bay, operates 15 men; daily output 18,000. [Port] Gamble Mill.

Thomas Moyne, on Hartstein Island, employs 24 men; daily output 30,000. [Port] Gamble Mill.

Knap & Smith, on Henderson Bay, employs 10 men; daily output 13,000. [Port] Gamble Mill.

Carpenter, on same bay, employs 7 men; daily output 8,000.

David Barnard operates two camps, one on Henderson Bay, employing 20 men, daily output 28,000, and another on Vashon Island, employing 10 men, output 12,000. [Port] Gamble Mill.

5 February 1886
Mr. George Giddings, section boss on the Olympia and Chehalis railroad, was severely injured, early in the evening of Thursday by a collision between a hand car and platform car, near Bush Station. The platform car, with a load of freight for the logging camp, after being unloaded in the woods, was let loose to run down of itself to the main track. Just as it reached the main track at a high rate of speed, it met a

hand car coming in the opposite direction on which were Mr. Giddings and another man. Mr. Giddings was thrown forward and received a terrible blow on the head, completely crushing in the whole face below the eyes. . . The companion of Mr. Giddings was thrown the whole length of the platform car and alighted on the track beyond, receiving no other hurt than a few bruises.

1 May 1886
Mr. P. D. Forbes has been doing an excellent job of work on the new trestle for the railroad connecting Warren's Point with the beach grade at the mouth of Percival Creek. He will probably complete the work today.

11 June 1886
While the logging cars from Morris' camp were passing onto the siding [at] the south end of the trestle, Monday, one of the brakes gave away and five cars with the logs went over the end of the track into the bay. This accident occasioned a delay in the logging operation of the road of a couple of days, the cars being replaced on the tracks by Tuesday evening.

1 October 1886
Seatco Coal Mine – What is known as the Northwestern Coal Company composed of S. Coulter, J. R. David and F. R. Brown, the latter one of the proprietors of the O. & C. V. Railway, are now opening a new lead on the Seatco coal property, where they have about 40 men employed. They have run a tunnel in 500 feet, and are at work on a vein 7 feet in thickness. They expect soon to have coal in the market from the new mine. The coal is said to be the best in the Territory. There has been considerable talk by the owners of the said railroad company of extending their railroad from Tenino to the mines, and continuing their track at Olympia down the west side of the channel to deep water, with a view of erecting bunkers for the shipment of coal.

11 February 1887
Mr. George Gaston, of the Bush and Gaston logging camp, has been laying in a stock of supplies this week, and reports a favorable outlook for the opening.

Mason County Journal
4 November 1887
It is announced on excellent authority that the Olympia & Chehalis Valley Railroad will, next summer, build a road from Olympia to Gray's Harbor, or deep water navigation on the Chehalis. This is now being made a standard gauge road.

Washington Standard
27 July 1888
While handling a spar about 100 feet in length at Tacoma Mill Company's camp, nine miles from this city on the O. & C. V. R. R., the snub-line broke, letting the timber go tearing down the hill about 400 yards. During the transit it passed between the animals of a twelve ox team without touching one of them.

9 November 1888
Messrs. Bush and Gaston were in town this week, in the interest of their extensive logging business.

14 June 1889
This morning at a quarter to three o'clock, a fire broke out in the roundhouse of the Olympia and Chehalis Valley Railway Company at Tenino, consuming the roundhouse, a new passenger coach and an engine. About the time the fire broke out, two men were seen running from the place and the act is thought to be that of incendiaries. The new car burnt was one that the company was having built to accommodate the increased travel that will set in about the first of July, and was about completed. The loss to the company is between $8,000 and $10,000.

Mason County Journal
25 October 1889
The sale of the Olympia & Chehalis Valley Railroad, consummated last week, is of great importance to Olympia. The roadbed will be at once widened to standard gauge and extended to Kamilche, which will connect Olympia with Gray's Harbor, and put it on a through-transcontinental line.

Railroad Gazette
25 April 1890
Olympia & Chehalis Valley – It is stated that the Oregon Improvement Company has purchased this road and will extend it south six miles to Cherry Hill, Washington, and to other points, and also change the gauge to standard. The road extends from Olympia to Tenino, 15 ½ miles, and is 3 foot gauge.

Washington Standard
16 May 1890
One hundred men are working on the new grade of the Olympia and Chehalis Valley road. It will be completed in July, and broad-gauge trains will then run to Olympia.

Railroad Gazette

23 May 1890

Port Townsend Southern Railroad – The town of Olympia has raised $50,000 for the Oregon Improvement Company, to be used to complete the purchase of the Olympia & Chehalis Valley road, and to change the grade to standard. The road is also to be extended from Olympia north 20 miles to Union City, at the southern end of Hood's Canal. The present 15 miles from Olympia to Tenino is being changed to standard gauge. It will be operated in connection with the above road.

Washington Standard

30 May 1890

The Union Pacific began work on the grade at Moxlie Creek Thursday morning, on the Connoly block, just west of the pumping house of the water company. About a dozen scrapers were used and the hillside was soon excavated to the grade established by that company. This is the point where the Northern Pacific will cross its rival's track, and the work yesterday was to obtain precedence in fixing the height of the grade.

20 June 1890

The San Francisco Bridge Company has received the contract for building the Port Townsend Southern track from the present terminus of the narrow gauge to Butler's Cove. A large portion of the roadbed will be on piles. Work will begin in a few days.

The railroad improvements are making our city present a bustling appearance. Large forces of men are employed at several points, slashing, clearing and grading for the several tracks that will soon span our city in all directions. The Northern Pacific have a large amount of supplies stored in the Percival warehouse, and the Union Pacific have established a depot for their supplies on Fifth and Columbia streets.

A passenger for Portland, under the new schedule that went into effect last Sunday, can leave this city [on the Port Townsend Southern Railroad] at 6:30 AM and connect with the accommodation train at Tenino at 10:10; or at 11:00 AM and connect at that junction with the 1:30 through train; or if he prefers can leave here by the 4 PM train and connect with the through train at 1:30 past midnight. In going north the local train connects at Tenino in the morning at 7:30 AM and 1:30 and 6:10 PM.

4 July 1890

The [Union Pacific] railroad tunnel, near Tumwater, begins to look like a big hole in the ground.

11 July 1890

It seems, from a Tacoma dispatch of yesterday, that the Port Townsend Southern Railway Company has still another proposition to make to our people. Colonel Haines, its attorney, writes that if it is granted concessions, the company will build a line from this city to Tacoma, the route running between those of the Northern and Union Pacific roads. The "concessions" asked for are right-of-way and terminal facilities, and doubtless a douceur of coin will be acceptable, as "an evidence of good faith," you know. The Port Townsend Southern has, it is reported, already acquired the ownership of the Puget Sound & Gray's Harbor road [the Port Blakely Mill Company's railroad, operating from Kamilche to Montesano], but this is disputed, and it is confidently alleged that the Northern Pacific is the purchaser [a statement which proved to be correct].

18 July 1890

Piles for the Port Townsend Southern Railroad track are being driven along the waterfront of Westside. They will be used for a mile or more where when the route passes to the land and will be built on the beach with cribbing and fill. The roadbed will be fifteen feet wide.

5 September 1890

The Port Townsend Southern propose to make the transfer from narrow to a broad gauge on the Olympia-Tenino road next Sunday. They propose to put on enough men to accomplish the job in one day. This speedy movement will be in marked contrast with the building of the road a few years ago, when its progress largely depended upon the frequency of picnic parties. For the benefit of newcomers we state that almost the whole road was prepared for the ties by the individual labor of our citizens, who designated what were denominated field-days, generally one day in each week, when business was suspended and the whole community turned out to work on the grade.

Railroad Gazette

12 September 1890

Olympia & Chehalis Valley – To be widened to standard gauge and will connect with the Port Townsend Southern. In places where cuts and new grades have been made, the rails for the broad gauge are now being laid, but the other portion of the line will be widened by laying permanent track outside the present narrow track. When widened it will be turned over to the Port Townsend Southern.

Washington Standard

12 September 1890

The first train of broad gauge cars came in Wednesday, and Olympia is now connected by a standard gauge line with the "rest of humanity." The change was not made on Sunday, as was contemplated, as there was a delay in getting the new grade completed.

Mason County Journal

19 September 1890
The Olympia & Chehalis Valley railroad was officially transferred to the Port Townsend & Southern railroad on September 10. The purchase price was $300,000. $65,000 has been expended in improving the roadbed and widening the track to standard gauge.

Washington Standard

26 September 1890
Logging camps along the line of the railroad between Olympia and Tenino are closed down, waiting for new developments.

The Port Townsend and Southern railway track is nearly ready for the rails from the Long Bridge to the Westside sawmill.

Railroad Gazette

10 October 1890
Port Townsend Southern - About four miles have been graded north from Olympia toward Union City. The company will connect by boat with Quilcene. Trains are now running on a regular schedule between Port Townsend and Crocker Lake, ten miles from Quilcene. The right of way between Quilcene and Crocker Lake has been located and secured. Between Union City and Tenino a few right of way cases are not yet adjusted.

Washington Standard

17 October 1890
But a short time will elapse before the present passenger depot of the old Olympia and Tenino Railroad will exist no longer forever. The new depot at the end of Long Bridge is rapidly nearing completion, and when once in operation it will prove a great convenience to pedestrians and vehicles.

19 December 1890
Workmen are engaged in propping up the entrance of the Tumwater tunnel [Union Pacific project], presumably for the winter, as it is understood that forward work is for the present postponed.

9 January 1891
The Port Townsend and Southern railroad company are now running their freight and passenger trains into their new depot grounds near the west end of Long Bridge.

16 January 1891
A coal yard has been established on the new depot grounds of the Port Townsend and Southern railroad, an enterprise which will redound greatly to the convenience and comfort of Olympia's citizens.

Since the Union Pacific laborers have exchanged their time-checks for cash, there has been a sensible thinning out of unemployed men upon the streets of this city. A great number of them have accepted work under Northern Pacific contractors, while others have found employment in various ways about town and in the country.

10 April 1891
Messrs. Bush & Gaston are opening a large logging camp near Tenino, and the timber will reach tidewater by rail.

24 April 1891
Bids for grading the Port Townsend Southern between Olympia and Union City will be opened May 10.

Mason County Journal

28 May 1891
Trouble is threatened at Olympia between the Northern Pacific and the Port Townsend Southern, and the work of laying rails across the [Northern Pacific] trestle is stopped. The Port Townsend Southern road refuses to let the Northern Pacific pass until certain conditions are complied with. The Northern Pacific officials anticipated trouble, but worked ahead. A hitch in some of the track-laying machinery prevented them from reaching the mouth of Percival's Creek Saturday night, as was expected, but the last rail, which comes within two or three feet of the Port Townsend Southern track, was laid this morning. Further work was prevented by a big Port Townsend Southern engine, which stood on the company's track and guarded the crossing. No attempt was made to proceed but the Northern's men returned to their camp to await orders from their officials. The Port Townsend Southern people are mum as are the Northern. Some say the latter company refuses to sign an agreement to bear the expense of maintaining the crossing. There is a good deal of indignation around town against the Port Townsend Southern for indulging in obstructive tactics.

Washington Standard

12 June 1891
The Union Pacific railroad tunnel, near Tumwater, is being largely utilized by tramps as a lodging house. It affords a splendid shelter from the inclement weather.

Mason County Journal

4 September 1891
Within a few weeks it is said that construction work will be begun on the extension

of the Port Townsend Southern from Olympia to Union City, a distance of about twenty-five miles.

Washington Standard

30 October 1891
Next Sunday the new passenger schedule will go into effect on the Northern Pacific, and trains will run as follows:

Going north, train No. 10 leaves Chehalis at 7 AM, leaves Olympia at 8:37, connecting at Tacoma with the Seattle train. No. 6 leaves Portland at 10:45 AM, leaves Olympia at 4:50 PM and connects at Tacoma with a train for Seattle.

Going south, train No. 4 leaves Tacoma at 11:10 PM, leaves Olympia at 1 AM, and arrives at Portland at 7 AM. No. 7 leaves Tacoma at 8:10 AM, leaves Olympia at 9:32 and arrives at Montesano at 11:52. Returning from Montesano, a train leaves there at 2:25 PM, arrives at Gate City at 3:50 and connects with the train from Portland, leaving Gate City at 3:55, leaving Olympia at 4:50. Train No. 9 leaves Tacoma at 3:55 PM, arrives at Olympia at 5:20 and at Chehalis at 7 PM.

The Port Townsend Southern will likewise have a new schedule, taking effect the same day. The morning train leaves Olympia at 9:40 from the depot at the west end of Fourth Street bridge, arrives at Tenino at 10:30; leaves Tenino at 10:50 and arrives at Olympia at 11:50. The afternoon train leaves Olympia at 3:50, arrives at Tenino at 4:50. Returning, leaves Tenino at 5:05, arrives at Olympia at 5:55.

20 May 1892
A horrible disaster occurred Tuesday noon, at the log station at Warren's Point, where the logs hauled by the Port Townsend Southern Railroad are dumped into the bay. William Stewart, of Bucoda, was engaged in unloading a car. He had inserted a peavey between the logs to start them from the car, when it caught and the moving log fell upon it causing the handle to strike his chin with a severe blow as it flew into the air. His neck was broken and death must have been instantaneous.

17 June 1892
George Gaston, of Tenino, was in the city this week, and reported the logging business to be in a fair condition. He is paying the Port Townsend and Southern railroad $400 per month for services performed in bringing logs from his camp to tidewater.

Mason County Journal

28 April 1893 - Reprinted from the *Olympia Tribune*
Trial for divorce was called in Judge Irwin's court yesterday by Mrs. McLeod who wants to be severed from matrimonial bonds with Alexander McLeod, one of the best known loggers in this section of the country. The plaintiff alleges desertion and cruelty, and asks that a child which was born to them be placed in her care. They were married about five years ago. The plaintiff's name was Young, and her father [S. C. Young] was at one time an engineer on the narrow gauge road in this city.

Washington Standard

11 August 1893
The pile driver is steadily at work at the junction of the Northern Pacific and Port Townsend and Southern railways, and the Y connection will soon be finished.

6 July 1894
The Railroad Situation – The railroad service throughout the west is in a very uncertain condition. Few trains are run and those arrive and depart on anything but schedule time. At the United Stock Yards in Chicago, on the 4th, an incoming train containing five companies of U. S. Artillery was surrounded by strikers and two cars were uncoupled, and this in the presence of eight artillerymen on the engine and tender, with a pistol in one hand and a rifle in the other, and troops on the top of box cars with loaded rifles held in a threatening position. With this formidable showing the troops failed to intimidate the crowd, and when the cars were reattached, were again uncoupled. The troops were then ordered out of the cars, and by marching on each side, succeeded in getting the train to the depot.

The [local] railroad premises suggest the thought that there is some unpleasantness on foot.

There is music in the scream of a locomotive: that is, we mean, there was music in it in the olden days when locomotives used to run.

The railroad suspension has given steamboats a large business in carrying freight, and so exacting is this demand that schedule times of arrival and departure have been abandoned and the service fitted to the demand. The Aberdeen and Multnomah have come in loaded to the guards almost every day this week.

The suspension of train service has given steady and remunerative employment to everybody owning a team and rig.

7 December 1894
The stone for the Capitol foundation [Old Capitol Building on Washington Street] will be brought to Tumwater by the Port Townsend Southern, where the cars will be transferred to the track of the Light and Power Company and brought to the site over their track.

24 May 1895
The Port Townsend Southern brought in 30 passengers yesterday. The travel is steadily increasing over this line.

14 June 1895
Workmen have been engaged the past few days in hauling the wheels of the cars used on the old logging road owned by George Foster that terminated at the mouth of Moxlie Creek. When the camps that used this road closed, several years ago, the trucks used were dumped together, where they have laid until the wood work was destroyed by rot. The wheels, however, are still serviceable and will be used at Skookum Bay, for the camp to be opened soon by I. C. Ellis. Sam'l McClelland has a contract for construction of six of these logging trucks.

26 July 1895
The Port Townsend Southern is building a turntable near the site of the old depot. [Thurston County Lien Book #2, page 163, dated 17 December 1890, indicates that the Olympia Iron Works filed a Mechanic's Lien for $130 against the Port Townsend Southern Railroad for construction of a turntable " . . . at present depot of company on the west side in the City of Olympia"].

1 November 1895
Daniel Sully has cancelled his date for appearance at Olympia Theater, December 4, giving as a reason that he will not pay the exorbitant charge of $50, exacted by the Port Townsend Southern, for a special to carry his company fifteen miles to make connection with the Northern Pacific at Tenino.

12 June 1896
The track of the streetcar switch to the Capitol is being taken up to be used in a spur to the brewery at Tumwater. The car company doubtless regard the latter institution as much the best business certainty.

30 April 1897
In the case of [Alexander] McLeod vs. Horr, for recovery of damages for use of a logging camp and railroad, a verdict was rendered in favor of the plaintiff for $1,000. This suit is an old one. Last year, on a trial before Judge Reed, the jury disagreed after two days' consideration of the matter. The trial at this time occupied the court's attention a like period.

18 June 1897
It is not always safe to rely upon newspapers. The Olympian persists in the statement that the Port Townsend Southern train leaves for the junction daily at 1:45 PM when in fact the hour of departure is 11:35 AM. This is an instance in which if you rely on the daily paper you will "get left."

15 October 1897 - Reprinted from the Portland *Oregonian*
PORT TOWNSEND SOUTHERN – *A Scheme Said to Be on Foot to Finish the Road and Connect Portland With the Entreport on Puget Sound* – W. B Dennis, president of the Port Townsend, Washington Board of Trade, is at Portland. He has spent several days in the city, interviewing leading merchants, bankers and railroad men, concerning the prospect of building a railroad from Portland to Port Townsend. The Port Townsend Southern Railroad has been the subject of a good deal of recent newspaper gossip. This road is a part of the assets of the Oregon Improvement Company. The entire property of that company is advertised to be sold November 6, at Seattle.

A rumor emanated from San Francisco and asserted that the Southern Pacific was negotiating for the purchase of the Port Townsend Southern, the plan being to complete the line to Portland, thus giving the Southern Pacific an outlet to the Sound and enabling her to put on a line of steamers to Alaska to compete with the Pacific Coast Steamship Company. The rumor was credited in Seattle. The papers of that city came out in scared headlines, warning the merchants to wake up, lest Portland, by means of this line to Port Townsend, would give Seattle a sharp race for the Klondike business.

29 October 1897
The new equipments of the Port Townsend Southern are neat and clean, and an improvement for the public over the old in that respect at least, while the company finds that it is a decided improvement in the way of operation, lessening the expense of coal and wear of track.

3 December 1897
A Port Townsend dispatch of the 27th ult. [in the month preceding the present] states that a large force of men had arrived in that city to begin work on the Port Townsend Southern Railroad, straightening the track and repairing the road its entire length. It may be that this action means more than repairs, and that it will include construction of the gap between the terminal sections.

31 December 1897
A new trestle is being built from the Port Townsend Southern depot to the Westside Mill.

11 February 1898
Edmund Rice is now Superintendent, conductor, brakeman and ticket seller on the

Port Townsend Southern, in place of J. B. Copeland, who has been assigned to other duties. Mr. Copeland is a man of extended information, a positive nature, and accommodating spirit, and his marked individuality will be missed by those with whom he has associated. Mr. Rice needs no introduction; he is one of us.

1 March 1898
E. M. McClintock succeeds George Walcott as engineer on the Port Townsend Southern "dinky."

13 May 1898
The Port Townsend Southern train ran over a cow belonging to George W. Hopp, at Tumwater, on Saturday night, and in consequence it was an hour late in arriving at the depot on Westside.

24 March 1899
A Northern Pacific construction train passed through this city Monday for Little Rock, to engage in track laying for the new Mason County Logging Company, which is to have its output at the head of Budd's Inlet, via the Percival Creek Northern Pacific track.

7 April 1899
The trestle of the Olympia-Tenino road is being repaired by renewal of its piling.

For the first train-load of logs to arrive from the Black Hills and be dumped into the basin, above Long Bridge, is now only a matter of a very short time.

The dump of the Mason County Logging Company just north of Long Bridge, on Westside, will be enclosed with piles and include a space 400 by about 2000 feet.

The Port Townsend and Southern railway brought in the first load of logs yesterday from the camp recently opened adjacent to Bush Prairie. The logs are dumped into a basin surrounded by boom sticks just below the depot building.

14 July 1899
The Mason County Logging Company, whose output will be at a new boom on Westside, will begin the logging business proper soon as their cars arrive from the east, and they are now overdue. Their labors so far have been directed toward track-laying into their timber lands, pile-driving to secure a receptacle for their logs in tidewater, and securing every facility for transacting business on a large scale. About 90 men are now employed by the company. When logging begins the payroll will be increased to 200 or 300 men.

4 August 1899
Everything is on the move in Olympia. The Eastside and Westside sawmills, the Olympia Sash and Door Factory, the Richardson Shingle Mill, and the several other shingle mills adjacent to this city, are all running on full time. Hardly a day passes but a locomotive is seen hauling away carloads of lumber and shingles from the Eastside mills and three ships are loading at the Westside mill. The several logging camps near here are all running full blast and dumping into the bay on Westside carloads of logs every day.

25 August 1899
The Mason County Logging Company has five donkey engines in operation at their camp near Gate City. They bring into their Westside dump two trains of logs daily, aggregating 100,000 feet.

29 September 1899
James D. Spurlock, a pioneer of 1852, died at his farm at Plum Station, in this county, Wednesday at 4 PM. He was 84 years of age, and the immediate cause of his death was gangrene in the foot. Mr. Spurlock was a native of South Carolina. He came to the Coast in response to the gold excitement which half a century ago brought the western part of the hemisphere so prominently before the world as a gold producer. Mrs. Spurlock and three children survive – Mrs. L. S. Cogswell, Mrs. Andrew Nelson, and Miss Pearl Spurlock. The funeral was held this morning at 11 o'clock, at the family home, Plum Station.

26 January 1900
The Port Townsend Southern Railroad is undergoing extensive repairs between Long Bridge and Tumwater.

6 April 1900
The people of Tumwater have presented a petition to the County Commissioners to have the contemplated plan for repair of the lower Tumwater Bridge amended, so as to make the span 80 feet in width and raised above the water level at high tide at least 6 feet. This presages a like change in the Long Bridge on Fourth Street and the railroad bridge to Percival's Point, as well as opening a passageway in the never-used "Billings Bridge" just above it, the object being to open up the privilege of navigation to the [Olympia] brewery and other growing industries at the future Lowell of Washington.

20 April 1900
John Mills and J. F. McCorkle have started a logging camp, which will give employment to a score or more of men this summer, just beyond Bush Prairie. The logs will be brought in by the dinkie railroad.

2 November 1900
The train schedule of the Port Townsend Southern has made a slight change in arrivals and departures to connect with the through N. P. trains at Tenino. The train leaves at 1:35 PM and arrives at 6:55 in the evening.

11 January 1901
The Thacker Wood Company is making arrangements for the delivery of shingle bolts from a splendid tract of cedar timber which they own on the Port Townsend Southern near this city. A spur will be necessary to tap the tract.

18 January 1901
The Port Townsend Southern has been making Tumwater its northern terminus the past few days, while repairs were being made to the trestle across the arm of the bay.

12 July 1901
A general renovation of the Port Townsend Southern track and depot on Westside is being made, which leads to the impression that the "Short-Line" is still in it.

31 January 1902
Mr. George Gaston, employed on the Seventh Street tunnel repairs for the Northern Pacific, met with a painful accident Monday, whereby a fracture of the smaller bone of one of his legs and a severe strain of the ankle were sustained. He will be laid up for several weeks by the injury.

30 May 1902
A BIG TIMBER TRANSACTION - The Simpson Logging Company Buys 6,000 Acres in Jefferson County - The Sol Simpson Logging Company this week bought 6,000 acres of timberland from the Weyerhaeuser syndicate, including the old Port Discovery mill, for the sum of $125,000 cash. The transfer is said to include some of the best timberlands in Jefferson County. It is said that the purchase was made on inside information that Thomas F. Oakes, former President of the Northern Pacific Railway Company, has obtained control of the Port Angeles Eastern [railway] franchise and right of way, and that a line of railway will be immediately built to Olympia from Port Townsend and serve for carrier to and from the Simpson Company's reconstructed mill. The late purchase of that company gives it a continuous line of camps, from the Black Hills in this county, to the mouth of Puget Sound, and it is said to be the largest concern handling timber in the world, with a daily capacity of a million feet. The mill will be placed in order to cut 200,000 feet per day. [This railroad connection to Olympia was not built].

2 January 1903
As noted in a former issue of the *Standard* the railroad surveyors continue at work for discovery of a new route for the Northern Pacific main line, on less grades, by way of this city, despite the inclement weather. They seem to have encountered some difficulty in obtaining just such a grade as is desired.

9 January 1903
George Gaston has tendered his resignation as janitor of the court house and Ellery Eastman has been appointed to fill the place.

Port Townsend *Morning Leader*

22 January 1903
RAILROAD PRESIDENTS MEET – *Made Inspection Tour Over Port Townsend Southern Yesterday* – President I. A. Nedeau, of Port Townsend Southern Railroad, is in the city for a stay of several days. Yesterday, accompanied by C. A. Cushing, president of the projected Port Angeles Eastern Railway, who "happened" to be in the city also, President Nadeau made a careful inspection of the line as far as Quilcene. In conversation with the [Port Townsend] *Morning Leader*'s representative last evening Mr. Nadeau said he found the roadway and bridges in excellent condition, leaving but few repairs and renewals to be made. President Nadeau said he could not now speak of the future prospects for the completion of the road to a transcontinental connection. To all enquirers on this subject he was politely evasive. There are good reasons for believing, however, that the studied silence on this subject will soon be broken, and it will not surprise the well-informed to see work actively begun the coming season.

Washington Standard

6 February 1903
A surveying party of the Northern Pacific Railroad has been encamped at Priest's Point, a mile below this city, the past few days, making an examination for a new route for the through traffic via Olympia, as outlined in these columns some weeks ago.

Mason County Journal

20 February 1903 - Reprinted from the *Olympian*
Improving the P. T. S. – Under its new ownership the Port Townsend Southern is making many improvements in equipment, rolling stock and roadbed. Section crews have been at work for some time putting the railroad in shape for heavier rolling stock. The logging business now being done by the railroad is the largest in many years or since the Morris Brothers and Bush-Foster camps were in operation. To accommodate the increase a new standard engine will be sent from the Northern

Pacific shops in the near future along with sixteen new flat cars for logging purposes. The days of the "cannon ball express," as a butt of ridicule are passing as the road becomes an up-to-date branch of the Northern Pacific.

Washington Standard

15 May 1903
The Northern Pacific Railway Company has condemned the trestle on which their track is laid from the Port Townsend Southern depot to the sawmill, and this will cause a temporary suspension of the shingle mill, which ships exclusively by rail.

22 May 1903
A train of logs from the Williamson [Olympia Logging Company] camp was stalled on the Port Townsend Southern, Saturday afternoon, by spreading of the rails on a trestle about a mile and a half south of Tumwater. The cars were let down on the ties, but no damage except delay resulted.

A freight train was run into by a logging train at the N. P. station in this city, Monday, while backing out of the Seventh Street tunnel. Two flat cars were lifted from the track and one was run under a box car, doing considerable damage to them, but none of the crews were hurt.

29 May 1903
Workmen are engaged in placing the Block system of railroad signals in the track-yard of this city. The depot tower has been erected at the south end of the platform. W. B. McConnell, of Chicago, has charge of the work of installation, as the service is entirely new to this state, though used on the mainlines of railway in the East.

5 June 1903
The Northern Pacific has already started to construct a drawbridge across the Deschutes waterway, doubtless impelled by the prospect of large damages involved in the suit brought by the brewery company.

2 October 1903
The Olympia Logging Company has a contract to supply the Northern Pacific Railway Company with 8,000 piles during the year 1904 and are now ready to receive proposals for furnishing sticks from 26 to 90 feet in length in large or small numbers. Address: Frank Williamson, President of the Olympia Logging Company, Olympia, Washington.

30 October 1903
The Northern Pacific draw [bridge] is now completed and can be swung out of way whenever any watercraft wants to pass through its embankment.

4 December 1903
A number of logging cars left the track on the Port Townsend Southern, Wednesday, on the grade at Tumwater, and it took several days to repair the damages. An engine had to be sent from Lake View [Lakeview, south of Tacoma] to aid in placing the cars on the track.

11 December 1903
George Foster, the veteran logger and pioneer, died at Tenino Tuesday night, after a prolonged illness, aged 63 years. He was born in New Hampshire and came to this country in 1861, and engaged in logging, first as a teamster, and afterwards in partnership with I. C. Ellis, operating a number of camps near the head of the Sound. In 1885 he was engaged with A. E. Laberee in the livery business, and in 1890, they organized the Gurney Cab & Transfer Company, which is still maintained by the latter gentleman. Mr. Foster was at one time well to-do, and like many others, lost nearly everything in the prolonged season of business stagnation. In 1884 he married a daughter of Judge Henry, and he was living with his daughter Georgia and conducting a livery business at Tenino, when called hence.

15 January 1904
Frank Williamson is having some location lines run near Tenino by Surveyor Lemon, for roads to prosecute his extensive logging business in that district.

Shelton Journal

22 January 1904 - Reprinted from the *Olympia Standard*
Robert McIntosh, the logger, has bought the Whitemarsh sawmill, on the flats at Tumwater, and is installing a 40 horsepower boiler and machinery for a mill of considerable capacity. It is said that the Olympia Brewing Company are behind the enterprise, having use for a large quantity of lumber in present improvements and a steady supply thereafter for boxes used by the brewery. It is likewise reported that the Lea Lumber Company will in the spring begin the erection of their promised sawmill.

Washington Standard

11 March 1904
The Plum Station School, taught by Miss Alice Yantis, has closed from a prevalent disease among the pupils believed to be scarlet fever.

Six logging cars at the Williamson logging camp, south of the city, started down a steep grade, Monday, doubtless from the brakes being too loosely set, and ran a distance of about a mile, when they were stopped by a tree that had been blown over by the wind and laid partially on the track. The trucks were, of course, considerably crushed and the logs scattered, but fortunately nobody was hurt.

25 March 1904
The construction of an expensive draw on Long Bridge and the payment of the damages awarded in the Gallamore suit, bid fair, with the necessary incidental expenses of the city, to keep the taxpayers' nose pretty close to the grindstone for the next few years.

8 July 1904
Construction of the lift on Long Bridge will necessarily be postponed till [sic] next month, from inability to secure the iron at an earlier date.

Will Trosper's team shied off the bridge where the county road passes over the old Union Pacific grade, on the hill this side of Tumwater, yesterday afternoon and fell a distance of about fifteen feet. Neither wagon, horses, nor owner were materially injured by the fall, but Mr. T. received a kick while unhitching the horses from one of them which broke his nose, and it required surgical aid. There were no railings on the bridge.

14 October 1904
The Port Angeles Eastern road has passed to the ownership of the American-British Finance Company, and the promise is given that it will be completed by January, 1906. It will, of course, run through this city in connecting Port Angeles and Portland.

27 January 1905
The new schedule on the Northern Pacific went into effect this week. The Gray's Harbor train that now runs via Olympia will continue on the old schedule. The through train will run via the main line, but the Port Townsend Southern train will leave Olympia at 10:50, making close connection at Tenino for Portland. Returning it will bring Portland passengers and mail, leaving Tenino at 1:05 and arriving in Olympia at 2:00 PM. The new local train between Seattle and Olympia will not be operated on Sundays. It will arrive on weekdays from Seattle at 9:45 and leave Olympia at 4:45 PM. The Port Townsend Southern afternoon train will bring the Seattle and Tacoma mail at 2 o'clock. Therefore a change has been made in the opening hour of the Post-office on Sundays and holidays to between 3 and 4 PM.

7 February 1905
W. R. Trosper has again sued the county for $300 damages for alleged injuries received by his team falling through a bridge across the Union Pacific cut on the road between Tumwater and Black Lake. He lost a load of malt, broke his wagon, and sustained personal injury from a kick by one of his horses.

23 June 1905
Jack Hawthorne, an employee in the Olympia Lumber Company's camp, met with a remarkable escape from death Wednesday, in the camp near Tenino. His heavy glove caught on a knot of a rolling log and landed him over and underneath it, but he fell between the skids and escaped injury.

7 July 1905
The steamer Santa Barbara, to sail tomorrow, is taking in a cargo of lath at the Olympia Lumber Company's dock.

17 November 1905
Articles of Incorporation of the Port Angeles & Olympia Railway were filed yesterday. The capital stock is placed at $4,000,000 and Jacob Furth, Lester Turner and W. D. Hoffus, of Seattle, A. A. Arthur of New York, and M. J. Carrigan of Port Angeles are named as incorporators.

1 December 1905
The City Council of Tumwater has granted permission for a railroad track from the Port Townsend Southern to the [Olympia] brewery.

23 February 1906
The old Williamson [Olympia Logging Company] camp at Tenino, lately owned by the Mason County Logging Company, was sold this week to W. A. Weller and Robert McIntosh, who will begin operations soon by extending the logging railroad about two miles into a splendid tract of timberland. The road is a spur to the Port Townsend Southern. The new camp will give employment to 40 or 50 men.

23 March 1906
The sale of the old Union Pacific grade is to be held tomorrow at 10 o'clock, on foreclosure of tax liens. It is, however, said to be only an extra hitch its owner takes to make the title more secure.

13 April 1906
The sale of the remaining portion of the Union Pacific right of way will be made tomorrow at 10 AM at the court house door.

20 April 1906
The Northwestern Improvement Company [a subsidiary of the Northern Pacific

Railroad] Saturday bid in the old Union Pacific grade in this county through S. J. Pritchard, attorney for the Northern Pacific, for $300,000.

11 May 1906

Is It Another Sidetrack? – The plan now seems to be, from "straws" which are, however, not always reliable indications of real intent of corporations, for the Northern Pacific to select a new grade, farther east, for its mainline, and to divert the Port Townsend Southern, its "jerkwater" adjunct, to the route surveyed a couple of years ago long the eastern shoreline of Budd's Inlet and Puget Sound [the Union Pacific Railroad's surveyed, graded, but not completed Portland & Puget Sound Railroad] to Tacoma.

A notice filed with the Secretary of State this week designates intension [sic] to build a road "from some point near Tenino, in a northerly direction to the waters of Puget Sound; thence along Puget Sound to Tacoma, all of which will lie in Thurston and Pierce Counties, and be of an estimated length of fifty miles." This would be, of course, another practical side-track of our town as a community that the company has lost no opportunity to injure since it violated the contract with our people, over a third of a century ago, by removing its terminus after location in accordance with the report of its engineers that it was the best point to tap Puget Sound to secure the low gradients for the heavy trains of a transcontinental traffic. The building of another loop for trade through this city does not give the service our natural advantages justify nor our business importance demands. Our bay should be the point for transshipment, the place where land and ocean meet to transfer the trade of nations from rail to water. To haul the heavy freight some forty miles farther will be at a larger cost than it would in the holds of vessels, but it can be done, just as water may be made to run uphill, by expenditure of strength to overcome natural law, but it requires the operation of special machinery and power to do it.

It may be that the Northern Pacific has a call just now to shield its pet terminus from the aggressive policy of the Milwaukee, or other rival lines, and it may be deemed a wise movement to use the Port Townsend Southern as a check-rein to the prancing steeds of railroad opposition, but the effect upon the community [Olympia] for whom nature has done so much, will be the same; to retard the growth which is ours by right.

The Tacoma *Ledger* seems to think that this way-station loop will not even give Olympia the dignity of a "whistle-post"; that the new line "via Steilacoom and the Narrows" will strike the Sound "at or near the mouth of the Nisqually River at Sherlock." Well well; we'll see what we see.

Quite an excitement has been created the past week by railroad surveys now being made by a party of Northern Pacific engineers on the Nisqually River, whereby it is conjectured by some nervous people that the company, after all, may have under contemplation abandonment of its project for a new mainline through this city. It may not be so bad as that, however, and possibly it is only another move in the game of chess for commanding position and checkmate of some rival, or it may be to direct attention from a real object while the final preliminaries are arranged for building to Budd's Inlet, as has confidently believed to be its objective from surveys made a couple of years ago. Whatever the intent may be, it will in time develop, and we feel quite confident that we may all "be happy" yet.

31 August 1906

The Northern Pacific, under the name of the Port Townsend Railway, has filed several contracts for options on realty that may be used for right of way in locating its new line through Thurston County. Nothing definite is known, however, regarding the precise route.

7 September 1906

Parties of railroad surveyors keep our local quid nunc guessing what is going to happen. First it is some great Eastern road that is seeking the best terminal point on tidewater, then the interurban trying to secure new tributaries for Tacoma and Seattle, then the Northern Pacific trying to discover what it had bought in the "pig in a poke" purchase of the Union Pacific's leavings. Then again an electric line that is to connect Portland with Seattle. Then the whole thing is wiped from the slate and a new system of guesswork begun.

21 September 1906

Ex-sheriff George Gaston has been appointed to the place on the local police force, lately made vacant by the resignation of Robert McNair.

28 September 1906

The Port Townsend Southern Railway has bought a piece of land north of Tenino, just east of their right of way.

22 February 1907

The suit of the Tenino sandstone quarries and the Port Townsend Southern in condemnation proceedings, terminated this week in a compromise that seems satisfactory to all the parties, and the railroad will have an uninterrupted track through Tenino to its terminus on tidewater in Tacoma.

19 April 1907
The Tenino Sandstone Company has changed its name to the Hercules Sandstone Company, to avoid confusion with the Tenino Stone Quarries Company, doing business at the same place.

26 April 1907
The office of the Olympia Brewing Company has been moved from the Bottling Works at the Northern Pacific depot, to the new brew-house at Tumwater. The new spur of railroad [connecting to the Port Townsend Southern Railroad] enables the product to be handled from that point without transfer to the [Northern Pacific] station here.

31 May 1907
A new turntable is being constructed in the Northern Pacific yards of a much larger capacity than the one hitherto used, capable of handling the big mogul engines that sometimes haul trains through this city. The "Y" on the Westside, connecting the mainline with the Port Townsend Southern, is likewise to be renewed, a raft of 60 creosoted piles having been received to replace those destroyed by the toredo [worm].

28 June 1907
The Union Pacific, it is said, has actually begun construction in the southern part of this county and in Lewis County, on the Portland-Seattle Harriman line.

5 July 1907
George R. Cummings and Miss Clara Sheldon were married Sunday morning, at the residence of the bride's parents, Plum Station, Reverend Graham of Tumwater, performing the ceremony.

26 July 1907
Tumwater has made a formal demand upon the Port Townsend Southern Company for a side-track and station facilities in that enterprising little burg.

27 March 1908
The case against J. T. Thacker for attempting to blackmail the Olympia Water Company has been continued till Monday, to secure the attendance of the complaining witness, H. C. Heermans, who is now in the East.

2 April 1909
Mr. B. B. Turner was in the city Monday, and was heard to remark that considering the prices of life's necessities and the number of men out of employment in this country, the panic of 1907 is more severe than that of 1893; that he regarded President Taft incompetent to alleviate the situation.

20 August 1909
Northern Pacific agents are busily engaged in obtaining right of way for a double track between Tacoma and Kalama.

29 October 1909
Mr. J. F. McCorkle, who owns an extensive farm near Plum Station, visited the *Standard* this week. It is operated by himself and sons, and for a Republican he is an exceedingly companionable citizen.

27 May 1910
The people of Tenino have inaugurated an auto-stage service to this city to more conveniently serve their convenience in business matters. The stage makes two trips daily, Leaving Tenino at 7:30 in the morning and 2:15 in the afternoon and will leave this city at 9 AM and 5 PM, starting here from Fifth and Main Streets. The railroad time has compelled Tenino residents visiting Olympia to consume two days in making the trip of 15 miles and return, and arrive too late to meet any business matters requiring attention in the forenoon of the first day.

10 June 1910
Death of Isaac C. Ellis – One of the oldest and most respected citizens died at his home in this city, Wednesday evening about 6 o'clock, after an illness of only about a week. I. C. Ellis [was] known to almost everybody in the state, either personally or by reputation. He came to Olympia from Massachusetts in 1854. He has theretofore been a resident of this county 56 years, and for a long time was associated with George Foster in the logging business. He made and lost two fortunes, but at the time of his death his holdings were only moderate, consisting mainly of property in this city. About 15 years ago he established the race-track at Lacey, involving a cost of about $40,000, which he sold to Mr. George E. Huggins a couple of years ago. In the early 1880s Mr. Ellis was Mayor of this city and served a couple of times as Councilman. He was 78 years of age.

15 July 1910
It has been arranged by change of schedule on the Port Townsend Southern railway, so that our city will have two direct trains, to and from Portland, leaving at 5:30 PM, arriving at Tenino at 6:25 and connecting with the Puget Sound Limited. The Port Townsend Southern train will wait at Tenino till 7:35 to make connection with the local which leaves Portland at 3:30 PM, arriving here at 8:20.

Tenino News

24 February 1911
The Otis-Hartson Lumber Company has cleaned out the pond at their mill and on the arrival of the donkey engine, which is expected any time, work will be commenced, getting out ties being the first work in hand. The rails for the logging railroad are expected shortly, and on their arrival the road to the timber will be rushed to completion.

6 April 1911
The locomotive for the Hartson-Otis Lumber Company arrived this week, and commenced hauling logs to the mill yesterday, when the mill started. The smokestack on the locomotive was a little too high for the culvert under the Hercules quarry spur, and had to have the top taken off.

Washington Standard

19 May 1911
The Johns mill down on the west side have a force of seventeen men at work in the plant getting it ready to resume operations. Grading for the extension of the railroad spur to the mill is progressing rapidly. A large amount of new machinery is being installed.

15 March 1912
An effort is to be made to secure the old Union Pacific grade running between this city and Bush Prairie about nine miles south, and equip it with rolling stock to unite the Northern Pacific by water-grade connection.

22 March 1912
The Northern Pacific Railway is considering plans for a four mile cutoff on its Olympia-Tacoma line, which will eliminate the necessity of crossing the deep gully at the Nisqually River. George T. Held, attorney of the railroad, appeared before the County Commissioners Monday to discuss the situation. It is thought that the adoption of the suggested plan would solve the problem of right-of-way for the new State highway and amicably settle all controversy regarding the same. The action of the County Commissioners is deferred for a time to ascertain the sentiment of people about Sherlock, which will be side-tracked.

29 March 1912
Dr. P. H. Carlyon, representing the Olympia Terminal Railroad, has completed arrangements with the Northern Pacific for the transfer of the old Union Pacific right-of-way between this city and Bush Prairie to the terminal company. Work will begin soon and it is expected that the line will be completed within six months.

Morning Olympian

21 May 1912
BIG SLIDE ON TENINO BRANCH – *Embankment Caves In – Passengers To Be Relayed* – Passengers from Olympia and Tumwater to Tenino have to be relayed to their destination by stage from a point about one mile this side of Tenino, on account of an accident at that point. A big slide occurred along the track near Tenino, where the Point Defiance Line is building from Ruston to the southern Thurston County town, paralleling its tracks with those of the Port Townsend Southern. The slide came unexpectedly when the contractors on the new line were digging away earth and the embankment became too weak to withstand the weight. It will require several days to remove the dirt from the double tracks and during that time train service will not be suspended, but the trains will run to the slide from where the passengers will be taken to Tenino by stage. In the meantime workmen will remove the dirt from the tracks.

Washington Standard

5 July 1912
Pierce County has decided to have the Northern Pacific Railway people abate a mud hole they have created by changing their grade on the Nisqually Hill, on the Pierce County side of the river. The result has been that a short stretch of road has been almost impassable, especially for heavy automobiles, which sink to the hubs in the soft mud. No less than half a dozen cars had to be pulled out Sunday, and travelers are indignant that the aggressor has to be reminded of a duty that should have been rendered without a legal reminder.

9 August 1912
What Olympians believe indicates the intension of the Washington & Oregon Corporation to extend the Chehalis-Centralia interurban line to tidewater at Olympia came with the filing of a notice with the Secretary of State Tuesday authorizing an extension of the line to the southern terminus of the Olympia Light & Power Company's tracks at Tumwater. The company has recently purchased the Tenino Light & Power Company and the Castle Rock Electric Company, operating the latter under the name of the Independent Electric Company. The company also has obtained franchises in several of the small incorporated towns en route and also a right of way south of Olympia.

18 October 1912
Because of construction work on the Point Defiance cut-off, the southbound train [Tacoma to Grays Harbor] on the Northern Pacific, due here at 10:15, was routed down the mainline Tuesday morning, then across to Gate and the Harbor country, a local train made up here conveying passengers to meet it at Gate. As the result of the

change Tuesday morning's mails were two and a half hours late. The regular service was resumed in the afternoon, however.

25 October 1912
Holding that a grade crossing at that point would be dangerous, the public service commission has refused to grant the Northern Pacific permission to construct its Point Defiance line across the Tenino road [Old Highway 99] near the Milwaukee tracks. The fact that probably 50 trains a day will be operated over this line was an important factor in the commission's decision.

10 January 1913
SUSTAINS BROKEN NECK – *Phil Kratz, Native Son, Dies Instantly as Result of Accident* – When the horse he was riding apparently shied at the steam shovel working on the new Northern Pacific tracks near Plum Station, Phil Kratz, a native son of Thurston County, was thrown from his horse Wednesday, and sustained a broken neck, dying instantly.

23 May 1913
SEEK EXTENSION OF PORT TOWNSEND LINE – *Business Men of Upper Olympic Peninsula Want Rail Outlet* – *Enlist Portland Aid* – Portland, May 23 - Port Townsend's Commercial Club has issued an urgent appeal to the businessmen of Portland to cooperate with them in getting the Northern Pacific to build the 65 miles of line needed to give that community railway connection with the outside world. This appeal followed the visit of the Port Townsend businessmen to this community more than one year ago on the same mission. Rapid development of the Olympic Peninsula, the growing volume of commerce there, and the opportunity Portland would have to ship to Alaska without being held up in Seattle, are arguments used. In a communication to A. C. Callan, who was chairman of the reception committee when the Port Townsend businessmen came here a year ago, the northern club says: "Surely every shipper in your city is aware of the unfair discrimination at Seattle against Portland merchandise bound for Alaska, and that Portland shipments are loaded after all others, if there is still more room on northbound boats. Port Townsend bay is Portland's natural Alaska outlet, and Alaska's business is growing tremendously. Railway rates from Portland to Port Townsend would doubtless be the same as from Portland to Seattle, the distance in rail miles being practically the same. We feel that completion of the Port Townsend Southern is vital to your city and ours.

The extension of this line, as desired by the Port Townsend businessmen, would mean railroad construction out of Olympia through Shelton to the north, the only portion of the Port Townsend Southern now constructed being from Olympia south to Tenino to connect with the Portland branch of the Northern Pacific, and from Port Townsend to Quilcene. Should the Northern Pacific complete the extension, it doubtless would mean a heavy freight traffic through Olympia and the work on the proposed extension would very likely be followed by construction work by the Milwaukee through Olympia and up the Olympic Peninsula, according to the opinions of those said to be close to developments in railroad circles, to carry further the war instituted by the Milwaukee for the development of the peninsula by construction work on the northern end.

30 May 1913
EXTENSION TO SIMPSON – *Proposed Construction on Port Townsend Southern Overlooks Olympia* – Olympia is to be overlooked in the proposed extension of the Port Townsend Southern to connect Port Townsend with the Northern Pacific's Portland line so the Columbia River city will have another Alaskan outlet besides Seattle, according to the latest reports of the plans of the Port Townsend boosters. These plans propose the extension of the Port Townsend Southern from Quilcene through Shelton to Simpson [called Stimson in 2007] to connect with the Elma cut-off of the Northern Pacific. The Port Townsend businessmen are employing every effort to obtain the extension and have proposed this route as the shortest and cheapest.

4 July 1913
NEW RAILROAD IS SEEKING OLD UNION PACIFIC GRADE NEAR HERE *Olympia Southern Company, Just Incorporated, Starts Condemnation Suits - Willapa Harbor Prize?* – *Articles Make Puget Sound One Terminal* – *Concern Is Capitalized At $100,000.* Condemnation suits to obtain title to all of the old Union Pacific grade in the southern part of Thurston County from the point where it crosses the Milwaukee tracks nine miles outside of Olympia to the county line, were filed in the local superior court this week following the incorporation of the Olympia Southern Railway by F. R. Brown of this city and B. H. Rhodes of Centralia. The company is capitalized at $100,000, the papers being filed Tuesday. The company is authorized to construct either a steam or interurban line, but local reports have it that is to be a steam railroad tapping the Willapa Harbor country. The articles of incorporation provide for a line from the southern end of Puget Sound – Olympia – to the Columbia River in Cowlitz or Clarke County, passing through Centralia and Chehalis. Mr. Brown, the local incorporator, was at one time the owner of the Westside Mill, recently purchased by the McCleary Timber Company.

10 October 1913
The mill known as the Chain Hill Lumber Company has gone into bankruptcy. Every bit of the mill's property that was valued at anything has been attached by the creditors. This mill, under the management of its former owners [Mayes and

Helmink] was doing a good business. Many people lay the failure of the company to the fact that its present owners know very little about handling the business of a mill.

31 October 1913
TENINO - Two big steam shovels are now working on the big cut on the new Northern Pacific double track north of this city. The big slide continues to furnish plenty of dirt to keep them busy.

31 October 1913
James Swan, a former resident who went to Arizona four years ago in the hope of benefiting his health, died at Tucson last Friday morning, R. B. McIntosh of this city, a brother-in-law, who came West with him in 1884, and his wife and children, Mrs. Stella May Swan, Laura and Frederick, being at his bedside. Burial was made in Los Angeles. Mr. Swan was a member of the logging firm of McIntosh & Swan and a city councilman in 1906-7. Besides the widow and children he is survived by his mother, who is 90 years old, residing at his birthplace in Nova Scotia, a sister, Mrs. Mary Jane McIntosh of Tumwater, and a sister, Mrs. Beswanger, and two brothers, George and John, who live in Nova Scotia.

14 November 1913
O.-W. R. & N. WILL SPEND $1,000,000 ON NEW ROAD INTO OLYMPIA
Harriman Line to Build Terminals - ***Will Develop City as Exporting Point Assures Rapid Growth in Next Few Years*** - The announcement for which Olympians have been watching and waiting for several weeks came unexpectedly from Portland last Saturday when it was stated that the Oregon-Washington Railroad & Navigation Company had appropriated $1,000,000 for the construction of a branch line from the Tenino-Point Defiance cut-off eight miles into Olympia and would begin construction in January, adding that it would take over the holdings of the Olympia Terminal Railway Company [and] had already bought considerable terminal property here, and would buy more. Announcement was made at the same time of the company's intension [sic] to spend $4,000,000 in constructing a line from Centralia to Willapa Harbor.

27 March 1914
W. F. Lea of the Tumwater Lumber Company was out to his shingle mill at Black Lake Monday.

1 May 1914
Another new planer is being installed by the Chaen Hill Lumber Company and this company expects to go into the manufacture of silos on a large scale.

12 June 1914
TO START GRADING NEW RAILROAD SOON - ***Harriman System Will Be Operating Into Olympia By Early Fall*** - Twohy Brothers, contractors of Portland, who will do the grading for the Harriman system's new line into Olympia, expect to establish headquarters in this city within a few days to superintend the work and will begin the actual grading as soon as the necessary preliminaries can be arranged. Announcement of the awarding of the grading contract, made last Saturday, officially settled all question of whether the line would be built into Olympia this summer, and carried with it assurance that it would be in operation at the same time as the Northern Pacific's Point Defiance cut-off, over which the O.-W. R. & N. has trackage rights, which will be early in the fall. . . The new line will connect with the Tenino cut-off of the Northern Pacific. . . at Chambers Prairie Station, approximately 7.5 miles due east of Olympia. . . While this work is in progress the Northern Pacific is continuing activity on its Tenino cut-off, which it expects to have ready for operation by September 1. This line will complete the double track system between Portland and Puget Sound, and with greatly improved service. The O.-W. R. & N. company [Union Pacific Railroad] and the Great Northern both will use this road, under lease, in common with the Northern Pacific.

MILWAUKEE TO COME - ***Strong Likelihood for Another Railroad to Olympia Soon*** - That there is a very strong likelihood that the Milwaukee Railroad will be operating into Olympia within the next few months, bearing out rumors that have been persistent locally and making two new railroads for Olympia this year, is the opinion drawn from statements made here this week by J. F. Bahl of Seattle, special passenger agent of the Milwaukee Railroad, during a business visit to Olympia Wednesday. "The construction of the O.-W. R. & N. to Olympia may mean one of two things to our line," Mr. Bahl said, "either that we will come in here over their road by a trackage agreement, or that we will build an independent road." The fact that engineers for the Milwaukee have recently made surveys over the three mile stretch from Fir Tree [at the end of the Milwaukee Railroad's proposed spur to the Fir Tree Lumber Company] to the Chambers Prairie station where the O.-W. R. & N.'s new line connects with the Point Defiance cut-off is taken to indicate that the Milwaukee contemplates using the latter's road into this city, though it is also known that the Milwaukee looks favorably on the purchase of the old Union Pacific grade between Maytown and Olympia, which would be used if an independent line were constructed.

26 June 1914
START SOON ON RAILROAD - ***Contractors Assembling Equipment, to Begin Work Next Week*** - Rapid progress is being made in the establishment of the headquarters camps near the athletic park between Olympia and Tumwater, equipment is constantly arriving, and it is expected that some time next week

actual work will be started on Olympia's new railroad, with a crew of at least 125 men employed, which will be increased to 300 within a short time, as other camps are started and the construction work gains headway. Rajotte, Robert & Winters, contractors who specialize in heavy construction work, have sub-let the grading and tunnel contract from Twohey Brothers of Portland, who have the contract for the entire work, while J. A. McEachern & Company of Seattle will do the bridge and trestle work. The former will start first on the two tunnels, one under the bluff at the south end of Main Street [under modern Capitol Boulevard] and the other a short distance farther south [under modern Custer Way] and when these are well under way, will start on the actual clearing and grading of the roadbed. They expect to proceed with it as rapidly as possible and, given favorable weather, will finish on contract time, September 1.

10 July 1914
BUSH PRAIRIE – Fred Reichel and family attended the picnic at Crowell's bridge [on] the Fourth [of July].

17 July 1914
RUSH RAILROAD WORK – ***300 Men Will Soon Be Working on Olympia's New Line*** – With crews working day and night on the big tunnel under the bluff at the south end of the city, 120 men already employed in the three camps now established and additions being made daily that will bring the total up to 300 within a short time, work on the O.-W. R. & N. railway's new road into Olympia is being pushed rapidly. . . The big steam shovel is in place near the Hays school house and the work cars and engines are also ready for use, so that the two camps south of town and the third near Hays school house will soon be hard at work grading the roadbed.

4 September 1914
LOTS OF TALK IN RAILROAD CIRCLES – ***Considerable Speculation Over Assumption of Port Townsend Southern By Northern Pacific*** – What does the official taking over of the Port Townsend Southern by the Northern Pacific mean for Olympia? That is a question upon which there has been considerable speculation here for the last two weeks, since the official announcement that the Northern Pacific had assumed the line which it has been operating one way or another for several years. The talk that there is prospect of abandoning it is taken as simon-pure "bunk" by most people who see no reason why the Northern Pacific should swap its good stock for Port Townsend Southern holdings, as is usually done in such transfers, if it intended to throw away later what it had just bought in that way. One thing is certain: the assumption of the Port Townsend Southern by the Northern Pacific gives that railroad control of the Westside waterfront. And that means about $3 a car [savings] for the industries now located there, for under the old regime a switching charge of that amount was made when the Port Townsend Southern took a car down to the Northern Pacific and there is every assurance that this will be abolished.

What is Milwaukee Doing? – But the Northern Pacific has not cornered quite all the recent railroad gossip hereabouts. Quietly Milwaukee representatives have been circulating among local shippers and promising them the same service on the same basis as the Northern Pacific now offers and the O.-W. R. & N. Company will be in a position to offer as soon as the line now building is completed. This is taken as further evidence that the practice of the O.-W. R. & N. and the Milwaukee of working together throughout this Northwest territory is going to hold good in Olympia too, and that the coming of the O.-W. R. & N. means the entrance of both roads into this city. That's the talk, anyway.

30 October 1914
NORTHERN PACIFIC TO MAKE CHANGES – ***Opening of Water-Grade Line to Mean Better Freight Service for Olympia*** – Freight loaded in Seattle, Tacoma or Portland by 5 o'clock on the afternoon of one day will be delivered to Olympia merchants shortly after 8 o'clock the next morning after the Northern Pacific's new water-grade line is put into operation on or about November 8, according to reports current here this week as to the changes likely to be made when the new line is formally opened. From the business standpoint this is probably the most important immediate change in service that the opening of the Tenino-Point Defiance cut-off will make for Olympia. The junction between the new line and the old Grays Harbor route running through here will be made at a new station named St. Claire, about two miles beyond Union Mills, and it is expected that a switching crew will be employed between that point and Olympia to handle incoming and outgoing freight, bringing the former into Olympia by 8 o'clock in the morning, doing switching here and at Lacey and Union Mills during the day, taking the local outgoing freight to the mainline late every afternoon.

18 December 1914
NORTHERN PACIFIC USES NEW LINE – ***Point Defiance Cut-Off Officially Opened to Traffic Tuesday*** – The Northern Pacific's new Point Defiance line, built at an expense of some $8,000,000, from Tenino to Point Defiance and thence into Tacoma through a tunnel and affording virtually a water-grade from Tacoma to Portland, was officially opened to traffic last Tuesday, the principal event in the way of a celebration being an excursion of some 300 or 400 members of the Tacoma Chamber of Commerce from that city to Tenino, stopping at the various new stations along the line and being quite roundly entertained at Tenino. The only change in the local passenger service consists in routing two trains each way per day over a portion of the new line from Coylston into Tacoma, the other trains running over the old line, but considerably better freight service will be furnished local merchants,

as told in this newspaper some weeks ago. Trains on the local line first used a part of the new line last Saturday when they were routed over it from Coylston to Nisqually, the new station about a mile east of the old Sherlock depot, which has been abandoned.

16 July 1915

BELIEVE O.-W. WILL LAY TRACKS SOON – *Visit of Union Pacific Officials Tuesday Is Considered Significant* – That work will be started this summer to complete the new line of the Oregon-Washington Railroad & Navigation Company into Olympia before December 1, the date set in its franchise, is confidently believed to be the result of the visit to this city Tuesday of a number of prominent Union Pacific officials. How soon trains will be operating over the line, however, is a point upon which there is still doubt, but it is thought that this will be no later than next spring. . . To do this and to erect the new depot, the work will have to be started this summer. Another indication that "something is in the air" is seen in the report that the O.-W. and the Northern Pacific are negotiating an agreement for the joint use of the new line, the Northern Pacific to abandon that portion of the Port Townsend Southern between Olympia and Plum Station.

10 September 1915

COMPLETION OF NEW RAILROAD NOW UNDER WAY – *O.-W. R & N To Be Operating Into Olympia Within Six Weeks* – *Work Will Cost $100,000* – *New Line Believed Linked With Local Harbor Development* – Actual work on the construction of Olympia's new railroad, the O.-W. R & N, which will enable it to be in operation within the next six weeks, as announced the latter part of last week, was begun this week when the Northern Pacific began placing the "frog" in the Point Defiance line at Chamber's Prairie Station, where the new local line is to connect with the mainline of both the O.-W. and Northern Pacific between Portland and Tacoma. The laying of the rails will begin as soon as the "frog" is complete, according to Dr. P. H. Carlyon, local representative of the O.-W., and the track will be laid from the Point Defiance line toward Olympia as fast as the ties and rails, already ordered, are received. The work will be done by the railroad itself, the roadbed and the two tunnels under the Pacific Highway between Olympia and Tumwater having been completed some months ago by the contractors. Upwards of $100,000 will be spent on the completion of the new line and the erection of the depot at Fourth and Adams Streets, according to Dr. Carlyon. Plans for the depot were drawn and bids called for a year ago, but no definite announcement as to its construction has been made. It is estimated that it will cost from $25,000 to $30,000 and will be of brick. It is expected however, that the contract for it will be let within the next few weeks. When the line is completed, it is reported that hourly service by gasoline motor car will be furnished between Olympia and the mainline, over which there are 30 trains a day, affording travelers the best of train service. Similarly speedy freight service will also be offered local buyers and shippers and Olympia will henceforth be as freely served as if it were located on the mainline itself.

Is Milwaukee Coming? – Common report has it that the Milwaukee Railroad will also be operating into Olympia over the O.-W.'s new line, connecting with it from its line through this county only a short distance from the Point Defiance route. This is based on the fact that these two railroads have generally cooperated throughout the state, notably in the lines to Grays Harbor and Willapa Harbor, but it is also reported that, in the construction of the Point Defiance line by the Northern Pacific and O.-W., the latter road agreed, if it built a line into Olympia, not to permit any other transcontinental line except the Northern Pacific to use it. Reports are also current that the Northern Pacific will discontinue the Port Townsend Southern, which is now operated only as far as the junction with the mainline at Plum Station, and use the O.-W.'s line into Olympia instead, but no definite statements have been made concerning such an arrangement and surveyors have recently been over the Port Townsend Southern route, which must be improved, under orders from the Public Service Commission, if it is not abandoned.

31 December 1915

NEW RAIL SERVICE TO START SATURDAY – *Olympia To Celebrate* [on] *January 14* [the] *Coming of Union Pacific To City* – Marking an unusual coincidence in Olympia's railroad history, first trains over the Union Pacific system's new line into Olympia will be run next Saturday, January 1, 1916, exactly 25 years to the day from the date when the first Northern Pacific train from Tacoma reached the city, January 1, 1891. Olympia will not formally celebrate the opening of the new Union Pacific line, built here by the Oregon-Washington Railroad & Navigation Company, until Friday, January 14, according to a decision reached Tuesday noon by the special committee of the Chamber of Commerce consisting of George W. Draham, Frank M. Kenny, and George H. Funk. . . Olympia is peculiarly interested from other standpoints than the immediate one, in the opening of service on the O.-W. R. & N. next Saturday, in that 25 years ago the Union Pacific was building its Portland-Tacoma line through the city, and the residents of that day, having subscribed a large subsidy, had built great hopes upon the coming of this system only a short time later than the Northern Pacific, as they then thought. Considerable grading was done at that time in this city and in different stretches of the county, and the old "U. P. grade" has been mighty familiar during the intervening years. Much of it has been used in the construction of the new road, the entrance into the city from the south being identical with the old plans. . . the [Union Pacific] office is being moved today from its former location on Main [Capitol Way] between Fifth and Sixth to the new depot at Fourth and Adams, in preparation for the inauguration of service Saturday.

Schedule of New Service – The first train to go over the new line will be a freight train leaving here in the morning, picking up freight at Chamber's Prairie, official name of the station where the local branch joins the Point Defiance line, and returning here at 7:30. This train will be run daily except Sunday. The company's passenger schedule, as announced by F. L. Corkendall, Superintendent of this division, who is here arranging for the inauguration of the service, will be two trains per day, connecting with all Union Pacific trains between Seattle and Portland. The first train will leave Olympia at 11:25 in the morning, returning at 12:55, and the other will leave at 5:05 in the evening, returning at 6:10. The company does not contemplate a gasoline motorcar service.

14 January 1916

FIRST RAILROAD INTO OLYMPIA ABANDONED – *Northern Pacific Discontinues Train Service On Port Townsend Southern This Week* – After having been operated for almost 38 years, first as a narrow-gauge line constructed by local citizens to give Olympia a railroad outlet to the outside world, and then reconstructed to standard gauge 25 years ago this fall, train service on the Port Townsend Southern Railroad between Olympia and Tenino was discontinued last Monday by orders from Northern Pacific officials. It was Olympia's first railroad. What service the company proposes to establish in its place, if any, has not been announced. Residents along the line are protesting its discontinuance. The condition of the track was such that the company either had to rebuild the entire line between Olympia and the junction with the new Point Defiance line at Plum Station, or else abandon traffic over it, and chose the latter course. Ever since the Point Defiance line has been in operation only about half of the old Port Townsend Southern road has been used, the portion from Plum Station to Tenino having been abandoned. The construction of the Port Townsend Southern [as the Olympia & Tenino Railroad] in the early days of Olympia was a great event and was made possible by bonds purchased largely by local people. It ran from Long Bridge south on the west side of the channel through Tumwater and on to Tenino and regular service was first inaugurated over it August 10, 1878. It was made the occasion of a great celebration. During the railroad boom of the early [eighteen] nineties the line was taken over by the promoters of the Port Townsend Southern, who proposed to construct a line from Port Townsend down the Olympic Peninsula through this city to either a line from Tacoma to Portland or else direct to Portland to a connection with a transcontinental line. A considerable subsidy was raised here at that time, a portion of the line was built from Port Townsend south to Quilcene, and the line between this city [and Tenino] was standardized, but the panic of '93 "broke" the promoters and the line as projected was never built. Some years later [1902] the Northern Pacific bought the line, but it continued to be operated as a separate company until the Northern Pacific leased the Port Townsend end of it to the Milwaukee railroad about two years ago and formally took over the local branch.

Centralia Daily Chronicle

4 May 1922

TWO HURT WHEN ENGINES COLLIDE – *Emery Stockdale and Charles Osborne in Hospital With Injuries Sustained in Crash of Two Locomotives on Union Logging Road This Morning* – Emery Stockdale, brakeman, and Charles Osborne, fireman, both of this city, were injured this morning in a collision between two locomotives on the logging road of the Union Mills Company in the Hannaford Valley, northeast of Centralia. The two men were brought to a local hospital. Their injuries are said to be serious. The locomotives were badly damaged in the collision.

Thurston County Independent

7 Jun 1935

Opening of First Tenino Quarry Told by S. W. Fenton – The history of the sandstone quarries of Tenino is to a considerable extent the history of S. W. Fenton. . . After casting around [in 1888] for a time, they [Van Tine and Fenton] landed in Olympia, where they interested W. D. Derickson in financing a quarry. The I. O. O. F. Hall in Olympia was being trimmed with sandstone and the men determined to investigate the quarry [Manville Sandstone Company] from whence it came. The men were directed to a small quarry recently opened near Plum Station, and they rode out there on the narrow-gauge train. . . .

Morning Olympian

18 June 1935

OLYMPIA PIONEER CALLED BY DEATH – O. H. Hartson, 81, well known Olympia realtor and insurance agent, died at an early hour Monday at the home of his daughter, Mrs. C. L. Redman, on the Littlerock Road. Mr. and Mrs. Hartson had gone to the Redman home Sunday morning for the day, and the husband and Mr. Redman had gone to a nearby lake for a day's fishing. When Mr. Hartson complained of feeling ill they returned to the house and summoned a physician but death came within a few hours. Mr. Hartson was born in Jamestown, New York, March 11, 1854 and his early life was spent as a lumberman. He came to this city 29 years ago and on his arrival built the Hartson mill, on the Westside, operating it for several years. Later he was in the lumber business in Tenino for two years, retiring several years ago to engage in the insurance and real estate business.

Bibliography

Books and Periodicals

Armbruster, Kurt E. <u>Orphan Road, The Railroad Comes to Seattle, 1853-1911</u>. Pullman, Washington: Washington State University Press, 1999.

Asay, Jeff. <u>Union Pacific Northwest, The Oregon-Washington Railroad & Navigation Company</u>. Edmonds, Washington: Pacific Fast Mail, 1991.

Best, Gerald M. <u>Ships and Narrow Gauge Rails, the Story of the Pacific Coast Company</u>. Berkeley, California: Howell-North Books, 1964.

Cheever, Bruce Bissell. <u>The Development of Railroads in the State of Washington 1860 to 1948</u>. Bellingham, Washington: Western Washington College of Education, 1949.

Dwelley, Arthur G. "The Cannonball-Rails to the Capital via Tenino". *Columbia*, Tacoma, Washington: Washington State Historical Society, fall, 1987.

Dwelley, Arthur G. <u>Prairies & Quarries, Pioneer Days Around Tenino, 1830-1900</u>. Independent Publishing Company, 1989.

<u>First Annual Report of the Railroad Commission of Washington to the Governor</u>. Olympia, Washington: C. W. Gorham, 1907.

Gatke, Steven R. "Union Lumber Company, Part 3". *Timber Times*, Hillsboro, Oregon: Timber Times Inc., Number 6, Spring, 1994, pp. 24-26.

Hannum, James S. <u>Gone But Not Forgotten, Abandoned Railroads of Thurston County, Washington</u>, Olympia, Washington: Hannum House Publications, 2002.

Hannum, James S. <u>South Puget Sound Railroad Mania</u>, Olympia, Washington: Hannum House Publications, 2006.

Heitman, Francis B. <u>Historical Register and Dictionary of the United States Army, from Its Organization, September 29, 1789, to March 2, 1903</u>. Washington: Government Printing Office, 1903.

Leverty, Maureen Joyce. <u>Guide to Records of the Northern Pacific Branch Lines, Subsidiaries, and Related Companies in the Minnesota Historical Society</u>. St. Paul, Minnesota: Minnesota Historical Society, 1977.

McArthur, Scott. <u>Tenino, Washington: the Decades of Boom & Bust</u>. Monmouth, Oregon: Published by Scott McArthur, 2005.

Miller, Winlock Jr. "The Olympia Narrow Gauge Railroad". *The Washington Historical Quarterly*, Seattle, Washington: University of Washington Press, Volume 26, # 4, October, 1925, pp. 243-250.

Newell, Gordon R. <u>Rogues, Buffoons & Statesmen</u>. Seattle, Washington: Superior Publishing Company, 1975.

Palmer, Gayle L. <u>The River Remembers, A History of Tumwater</u>. Virginia Beach, Virginia: The Donning Company, 1995.

Palmer, Gayle and Shanna Stevenson. Thurston County Place Names: A Heritage Guide. Olympia, Washington: Thurston County Historic Commission, 1992.

Poor, Henry Varnum. Poor's Manual of Railroads. New York: Edition of 1890.

Prosser, William Farrand, Colonel. A History of the Puget Sound Country. New York and Chicago: The Lewis Publishing Company, 1903.

Ramsey, Guy Reed. Postmarked Washington: Thurston County. Thurston County, Washington: Thurston County Historic Commission, 1988.

Renz, Louis T. History of the Northern Pacific Railroad. Walla Walla, Washington: Louis Tucker Renz, 1980.

Robertson, Donald B. Encyclopedia of Western Railroad History. Volume 2, Mountain States, Volume 3, Oregon and Washington, Caldwell, Idaho: Caxton Printers Ltd., 1995.

Scott, Jessie Hartsuck. "Scrapbooks and Writings of Jessie Hartsuck Scott". Olympia, Washington: Washington State Library Microfilm NW 979.779 Scott, 1963.

South-western Washington, Its Topography, Climate, Resources, Productions, Manufacturing, Advantages, Wealth and Growth. Olympia, Washington: Pacific Publishing Company, 1890.

Stevenson, Shanna. Olympia, Tumwater, and Lacey, A Pictorial History. Norfolk, Virginia: Donning Company, 1985.

Tacoma Chamber of Commerce. Tacoma Illustrated. Chicago: Blakely Printing Company, 1989.

United States Interstate Commerce Commission. Interstate Commerce Commission Reports: Decisions of the Interstate Commerce Commission of the United States. Washington, D. C.: Government Printing Office, Volume 116, pp. 361-377.

Archives, Museums and Record Repositories

California State Railroad Museum. Sacramento, California.

General Administration, State of Washington, Division of Facilities, Maps and Blueprints. Olympia, Washington.

Henderson House Museum. Tumwater, Washington.

Jost, R. Dale, M.D. Archives of Western Railroads. Stockton, California.

Labbe, John. Photograph Collection, Oso Publishing, Hamilton, Montana.

Minnesota Historical Society Library. St. Paul, Minnesota.

Northern Pacific Railway Historical Association Archive. Minnesota Transportation Museum, Jackson Street Roundhouse, St. Paul, Minnesota.

Port Townsend Southern Railroad Company. "Corporate Records, 1890-1921," St. Paul, Minnesota: Minnesota Historical Society.

Southwest Washington Regional Archives. Olympia, Washington.

Tenino Depot Museum. Tenino, Washington.

Thurston County Roads and Transportation Services, Section of Engineering and Design. Olympia, Washington.

University of Washington Libraries, Special Collections, UW 23984z.

Washington State Archives. Olympia, Washington.

Washington State Historical Society. Research Center, Tacoma, Washington.

Indices

Index of People

Abrams, William	140
Ackerman, J. W.	81
Amos, J. D.	19
Anderson, Arthur	75
Anderson, E. M.	75
Anderson, Edward	75
Anderson, Kit	75
Anderson, Kurt	75
Arthur, A. A.	149
Bahl, J. F.	154
Baker, Charles	20
Barnard, David	140
Barnes, Nelson	138
Bartwell	140
Bee, Colonel	136
Bennett, Erasmus	40
Beswanger, Mrs.	154
Black, Superintendent	138
Blinn, Marshall	1
Bradley, Ira	1, 2
Blake, Frank G.	100
Bordeaux, Thomas	100
Brazel, Austin James	139
Brooks, Peyton H., Esq.	137
Brown, F. R.	139, 141, 153
Brown, Surveyor	90
Bush, Belle	82
Bush, George Washington	40, 42, 43, 81, 82
Bush, William Owen	9, 43, 81, 82, 84, 140, 147
Calan, A. C.	153
Canfield, Clarence	43
Cannon, James W.	77
Carlyon, P. H., Dr.	152, 156
Carpenter	140
Carrigan, M. J.	149
Clark, Delbert A.	118
Clark, J. Frank	118
Cogswell, L. S., Mrs.	146
Copeland, J. B.	146
Corkendall, F. L.	157
Coulter, Samuel	140, 141
Crosby, Clanrick	68
Cummins, George R.	43, 151
Cummins, Marcellus Ross	43
Cushing, C. A.	147
David, J. R.	141
Dennis, W. B.	145
Derickson, W. D.	157
Dick, James	131
Draham, George W.	156
Draham, Mark	100
Dwelley, Arthur	123
Eastman, Ellery	147
Easton, Roger	43, 68
Ellis, I. C.	140, 145, 148, 151
Fenton, S. W.	157
Ferris, Brian	27, 49, 56, 80, 90, 101, 129
Forbes, P. D.	141
Foster, George H.	4, 9, 81, 84, 139, 145, 147, 148, 151
Foster, Georgia	148
Fredrickson, Jim	27, 36, 49, 56, 96, 101, 109, 110, 131
Freitag, Charles R.	43
Funk, George H.	156
Furth, Jacob	149
Gaston, George	81, 82, 141, 144, 147, 150
Gatke, Steven R.	123
Giddings, George	140
Gilmore, Henry Harrison	56
Glover, A. D.	139
Graff, John W.	68
Graham, Reverend	151
Haase, Allan	96
Haines, Colonel	142
Hale, C. H.	138
Hanson, Charles	81, 87
Hartson, Orsal H.	61, 63, 80, 110, 157

Hawthorne, Jack	149
Hays, Smith	68
Heermans, H. C.	151
Held, George T.	152
Henry, Judge	148
Hoffus, W. D.	149
Hopp, George W.	146
Horr	145
Howard	140
Huggins, George E.	151
Huston, Billy	55
Irwin, Judge	144
Johnson, J. T.	118
Jones, David W.	40
Jones, Gabriel	40, 42
Judson, Charles P.	42
Kennedy	140
Kenny, Frank M.	156
Kevin, Ed	30
Kratz, Lawrence	136
Kratz, Phillip	153
Labbe, John	123
Laberee, A. E.	148
Larson, Ron	47
Larson, Ronda, Esq.	47
Lea, Charles W.	75
Lea, Mabel O.	75
Lea, William F.	75, 154
Lemon, Surveyor	148
Manville, Chester W.	96
Mason, Mr.	138
Mayes, George W.	101
McClelland, Samuel	145
McClintock, E. M.	146
McConnell, W. B.	148
McCorkle, Frank	49
McCorkle, James Fleming	90, 91, 146, 151
McIntosh, Mary Jane (Swan)	154
McIntosh, Robert B.	100, 148, 154
McLain	140
McLeod, Alexander	140, 144, 145
McNair, Robert	150
Miller, Edward	140
Miller, Winlock, Jr.	3
Mills, John	146
Mitchell, Frank	139
Mitchell, William	68
Morris, Frank M.	84
Morris, George W.	84
Morris, Philip Guy	84
Morris, Robert James ("James" or "R J")	84
Morris, T. B.	136, 137
Moyne, Thomas	140
Mullaney, Clara	49
Nedeau, I. A.	147
Nelson, Andrew, Mrs.	146
Nelson, Ron	47, 49
Oakes, Thomas F.	147
Ogle, William	91
Osborne, Charles	157
Otis, John T.	110
Ouimette, Esdras N.	3, 119
Perry, George	140
Phillips, A. A.	139
Pittman, W. E.	91
Plumb, Elihu Beman	43, 49
Plumb, William W.	49
Plummer, Mr.	136
Pritchard, S. J.	150
Redman, C. L., Mrs.	157
Reed, Charles L.	138
Reichel, Fred	155
Replinger, Peter J.	27, 123
Rhodes, B. H.	153
Richmond, Greg	90
Rice, Edmund	145, 146
Ricker, Cordelia	49
Salomon, Edward S., Governor	136
Scott, Jessie Hartsuck	90
Sheldon, Albert Elihu	43, 49
Sheldon, Alice Whitemarsh	43
Sheldon, Clare	43, 151
Sheldon, Earl	47
Sheldon Lela May	43, 46, 47

Sheldon, Roy	49
Simpson, Sol	147
Smith, Eugene	139
Spirlock (Spurlock) James D.	49, 146
Spirlock (Spurlock) Pearl	146
Sprague, John Wilson, General	1, 2, 4, 19, 139
Sprague, Otis	139
Stanley, Allen	123
Stewart, William	144
Stockdale, Emery	157
Sulley, Daniel	145
Sumption, Ellen	100
Sumption, George	100
Swan, Commissioner	138
Swan, Frederick	154
Swan, George	154
Swan, James	100, 154
Swan, John	154
Swan, Laura	154
Swan, Stella May	154
Taft, President	151
Thacker, John T. (Boss)	80, 151
Todd, Benjamin, Esq.	137
Townsend, Willis	68
Trosper, Will	149
Turner, Benjamin Buckman	4, 81, 87, 139, 140, 151
Turner, Lester	149
Walcott, George	146
Ward, Ira	68
Weller, W. A.	100
White, Allen	96, 100
White, Allen E. (A.E. White)	13, 96, 97
White, Henry W.	96
Whittaker, Lemuel Clarence	53, 100
Williamson, Eugene	100
Williamson, Frank	100, 148
Wingate, Robert	4, 139
Yantis, Alice	148
Young, A. L.	75
Young, S. C.	144

Index of Places

1st Street (Tumwater)	68
4th Avenue Bridge	4, 20, 22, 27, 35, 131, 137, 138, 143, 144, 146, 149, 157
4th Avenue Draw Bridge- see 4th Avenue Bridge	
4th Avenue	6
5th Avenue	135
25th Avenue NW	23, 24
73rd Avenue SE	42
79th Avenue SE	81
84th Avenue SE	43
88th Avenue SE	82
93rd Avenue SE	81, 82, 85, 86, 87
99th Lane	90
113th Avenue	92
143rd Avenue SE	101
Adams Street	156
Alaska	153
Anchor Lane	23
Angus Drive	15, 16, 53, 98, 101
Astoria, OR	42
Baldassin Road	101
Beaver Post Office, WA	42
Beaver Station – also see Bush Station	28, 29, 42
Bennett Street	40, 41
Big Skookum Inlet	140
Billings Bridge	146
Black Hills	23, 146, 147
Black Lake	81, 140, 149, 154
Bloom's Ditch	92, 93, 95
Bonniewood Drive	42, 80
Bordeaux, WA	23, 27, 43, 49
Boston Street Bridge	30, 36, 39, 68, 75, 77, 132
Brighton Park School	41
Brighton Park Station	29, 30, 40, 41
Brighton Park Subdivision	40, 41
Brooks Lane	85, 86
Brown's Wharf	1, 19
Bucoda, WA	144
Budd Inlet	1, 2, 4, 20, 21, 22, 23, 27, 30, 33, 40, 49, 61, 75, 81, 129, 137, 146, 150
Bush & Gaston Skid Road	16
Bush Prairie	81, 136, 137, 138, 139, 146, 152

Bush Prairie Station – see Bush Station	
Bush Station	9, 27, 28, 29, 30, 41, 42, 43, 44, 84, 129, 140
Butler Cove	1, 4, 5, 19, 20, 22, 23, 61, 142
Butler Cove Extension – see Port Townsend Southern RR, Butler Cove Extension	
C Street	36, 75, 77
Camp #1 (Foster)	82, 84
Camp #3 (Olympia Logging Company)	100, 104, 107
Camp #5 (McIntosh & Swan)	15, 52, 100
Camp #5 Station	29, 50
Capitol Boulevard Bridge	77
Capitol Boulevard (Tumwater)	20, 77, 80, 132, 155
Capitol Interpretive Center	66
Capitol Lake	20, 27, 33, 40, 81, 129, 131, 133
Capitol Way (Olympia)	156
Centralia, WA	126, 153, 154, 157
Chaen Hill – see Chain Hill	
Chain Hill	107, 108, 109
Chambers Prairie Station	154, 156, 157
Chehalis River	141
Chehalis, WA	144, 153
Cherry Hill, WA	141
Chicago, IL	148
Clark County, WA	153
Clark's Addition to Olympia	1
Columbia Hall (Olympia)	2
Columbia River	139, 153
Columbia Street	142
Cowlitz County	153
Cowlitz Landing	42, 43
Cowlitz Trail	104, 107, 109
Coylston, WA	155, 156
Crestline Drive	23
Crocker Lake, Jefferson County, WA	143
Crosby House	66
Crosby Plat of Tumwater	73
Crowell Lumber Company Mill	12
Crowell's Bridge	155
Crowell Spur – see Port Townsend Southern Railroad, Crowell Spur	
Crowell Station	29, 43
Custer Way	77, 155
Custer Way Bridge	36
Decatur, AL	1
Deep Lake	91, 92, 93, 96, 97
Dennis Street	80
Deschutes Basin	131, 133
Deschutes Parkway	63, 66, 67, 133, 135
Deschutes River	iv, 8, 43, 66, 67, 68, 72, 75, 77, 81, 82, 83, 84, 89, 131, 137, 139
Deschutes River, Lower Falls	67
Deschutes River, Middle Falls	30, 38
Deschutes River, Upper Falls	36, 68, 72, 75, 76, 77
Deschutes Waterway	148
Deschutes Way	36, 68, 72, 75, 78
East Olympia, WA	49, 131
Engine House (N P RR in Olympia)	6
Fenton Avenue	103, 104, 105
Fifth Street	142, 151, 156
Fir Tree, Thurston County, WA	154
First Mill Addition to Tumwater – see Mill Addition to Tumwater, 1st	
First Street – see C Street	
Fourth Street	156
Franco House	68, 72, 78
Gas Plant (Olympia Brewery)	7
Gate (City), WA	101, 144, 146, 152
George Foster Logging Spur – see Tacoma Mill Co., Foster Spur at Bush Prairie	
Gerth Street	80
Gilmore Station	16, 25, 27, 28, 29, 30, 53, 54, 56, 82, 101, 105, 106, 129
Grays Harbor, WA	1, 4, 100, 141, 152, 155, 156
Greer, SC	123
Hanaford Creek	59
Hanaford Valley, Lewis County, WA	123, 139, 157
Harbor View Drive	22, 23, 63
Hartson Mill	64
Hartson Spur – see Port Townsend Southern Railroad, Hartson Spur	
Hartstein Island	140
Helsing Junction, WA	101
Henderson Bay	140
Henderson Boulevard	63, 80
Heritage Lane SE	81
Hogden, Steven, Donation Claim	100, 106
Hood Canal	142
Hyatt Road	104, 105, 109
Interstate 5	36, 80, 135
Jamestown, NY	157
Jefferson County, WA	147

Jones Station – also see Brighton Park Station	28, 36, 40, 41
Jones Street	40, 41
Kalama, WA	136, 151
Kamilche, WA	141, 142
Klondike	145
Lakeridge Drive	63
Lacey, WA	155
Lakeview, Pierce County, WA	148
Lemon Hill	110
Littlerock Road	157
Littlerock, WA	146
Little Skookum Inlet	140
Long Bridge (Olympia) – see 4th Avenue Bridge	
M Street	80
Main Street	137, 151, 155, 156
Mason County Logging Company Log Dump	35
Massachusetts	151
Maytown, WA	154
McCorkle Road	v, 49, 90, 91, 92, 93, 95, 96, 119
McCorkle Road Spur – see Tacoma Mill Company, McCorkle Road Spur	
McDuff Road	16, 17, 53, 101, 102, 103, 104
McKenna, WA	100
Mill Addition to Tumwater, 1st	68, 72, 73
Millersylvania State Park	96
Montesano, WA	142, 144
Morris Brothers Camp	141
Moxlie Creek	142, 145
Mud Bay	140
Mud Lake	101
Mukilteo, WA	139
Nelson Road – see Hyatt Road	
New Hampshire	148
New York, NY	149
Nisqually Hill	152
Nisqually River	150, 152
Nisqually Station (N P RR)	156
North Bay	140
Northern Pacific Railroad Drawbridge (across Deschutes Waterway)	148
Nova Scotia, Canada	154
Odd Fellow's Hall (I. O. O. F., Olympia)	157
Offut Lake	97
Offut Lake Road	15
Ogle Lake	91, 92, 95
Old Highway 99	8, 9, 11, 12, 13, 14, 15, 16, 43, 47, 48, 49, 50, 63, 80, 81, 82, 83, 84, 85, 86, 87, 89, 92, 96, 108, 109, 112, 119, 153
Old Olympic Highway	80
Oldport Community	23, 25, 61
Olympia Airport	9
Olympia Brewery Spur – see Port Townsend Southern RR, Olympia Brewery Spur	
Olympia Harbor	19, 27, 31, 61
Olympia Station, 1st (O & T RR)	4, 6, 27, 31
Olympia Station, 2nd (O & C V RR)	6, 27, 32, 33, 143, 145
Olympia Station, 3rd (P T S RR)	6, 23, 27, 34, 35, 63, 123, 145, 146, 147
Olympia Station, 4th (N P RR at Water Street)	6, 27, 30, 36, 129, 148, 151
Olympia Station, Union Pacific Railroad	156
Olympia Street in Tenino	56, 57
Olympia – Tenino Road	43, 80, 81, 87, 90, 91, 104, 106, 107
Olympia, WA	1, 2, 3, 4, 5, 6, 19, 20, 21, 22, 25, 27, 30, 31, 32, 42, 49, 56, 59, 61, 63, 77, 80, 81, 87, 90, 100, 104, 119, 129, 131, 133, 134, 136, 137, 141, 142, 143, 144, 145, 146, 147, 148, 149, 150, 151, 152, 153, 154, 155, 156, 157
Olympic Peninsula	153, 157
Oregon	84
Oregon Trail	104
Oyster Bay	140
Pacific Export Mill Company Spur	5
Pacific Highway	104, 107, 156
Park Avenue	56
Patsy Drive	92, 95
Percival Cove	7, 27
Percival Creek	81, 133, 141, 143, 146
Percival Creek Railroad – see Tacoma Mill Company, Percival Creek Railroad	
Percival's Point (Percival Point)	4, 27, 31, 81, 146
Pierce County, WA	150, 152
Pittman Lake	91, 92, 95
Pittman, W. E., Farm	90
Plum – see Plumb, WA	
Plumb Station, 1st	i, 13, 25, 27, 28, 29, 30, 43, 48, 49, 90, 96, 100, 129, 146, 151, 157
Plumb Station, 2nd	13, 49, 51, 52, 84, 90, 96, 129, 131, 132, 156, 157
Plumb Station Post Office, WA	49
Plumb Station School	49, 50, 148
Plumb, WA	91, 97, 153
Point Defiance	129
Port Angeles, WA	149

Port Townsend, WA	20, 22, 121, 143, 145, 147, 153, 157
Portland, OR	20, 25, 129, 136, 142, 144, 145, 149, 150, 151, 153, 154, 155, 156, 157
Priest's Point	147
Puget Sound	1, 4, 81, 129, 136, 145, 147, 150, 153, 154
Quarry House in Tenino	56
Quilcene, WA	20, 22, 25, 123, 127, 143, 153, 157
Reserve Street – see Deschutes Way	
Rich Road	11, 12
River House	87
Rocky Prairie	49, 53, 136, 138
Rocky Prairie School	53
Roundhouse at Tenino – see O & C V RR, Roundhouse at Tenino	
Ruston, WA	152
Saint Claire, WA	155
Saint Paul, MN	129, 131
San Francisco, CA	3, 136, 145
Satsop, WA	42
Scatter Creek	99, 104, 109, 116, 136
Scott Lake	91, 92, 93
Seattle, WA	20, 25, 75, 119, 122, 144, 145, 149, 150, 153, 154, 155, 157
Seventh Street Tunnel (N P RR)	147, 148
Sheldon Road	12, 43, 81, 87, 88
Sheldon Station	12, 27, 43, 46, 47, 48, 49, 89, 90
Shelton, WA	20, 136, 153
Sherlock Station (N P RR)	156
Sherlock, WA	150, 152
Simmons Road	40, 68
Simpson, WA	153
Sixth Street	156
Skookum Bay	145
Skookumchuck River	59, 139
Smith Hays Donation Land Claim	68
Snohomish, WA	139
South Carolina	146
South Union Spur – see Tacoma Mill Company, South Union Spur	
South Union, WA	49, 82, 84, 90, 92
Springer Lake Road	87, 88
Spurlock - South Union Road	91
Spurlock Station	14, 28, 49, 52
Steilacoom, WA	150
Stimson, WA	153
Stone Quarry Station	29, 30, 43
Summit Slide	123, 124, 129, 130, 154
Summit, WA (near Tenino, WA)	17, 129, 136
Summit [Junction] WA (near McCleary, WA)	25
Tacoma, WA	1, 2, 25, 49, 72, 81, 129, 136, 139, 142, 144, 150, 151, 152, 155, 156
Tenino Station, 1st	ii, 4, 18, 55, 56, 57, 58, 59, 136
Tenino Station, 2nd [West Tenino]	18, 29, 30, 59, 60, 103
Tenino Station, 3rd (on Point Defiance Line and used only by N P RR)	129
Tenino, WA	vi, 2, 3, 4, 19, 20, 25, 26, 27, 28, 30, 49, 52, 56, 59, 61, 67, 77, 82, 87, 100, 103, 104, 105, 106, 107, 109, 110, 114, 116, 119, 123, 124, 129, 130, 136, 137, 138, 139, 141, 142, 143, 145, 147, 148, 149, 150, 151, 152, 153, 154, 157
Thompson Creek	59
Thurston County, WA	1, 3, 4, 25, 40, 50, 72, 81, 87, 96, 100, 104, 106, 150, 152, 153
Tilley Road	91, 92, 93
Tollner Ranch	90
Topeka, KS	40
Trosper Road	8
Tucson, AZ	154
Tumwater Bridge, Lower (between Tumwater and Olympia)	146
Tumwater, Crosby Plat of – see Crosby Plat of Tumwater	
Tumwater Falls Park	36, 75
Tumwater Station	7, 29, 30, 36, 37, 39, 41, 68, 129
Tumwater trolley station	30
Tumwater, WA	iii, iv, 3, 28, 36, 38, 43, 49, 53, 63, 66, 68, 69, 70, 72, 75, 77, 78, 129, 131, 132, 133, 135, 137, 138, 139, 144, 145, 146, 147, 148, 149, 151, 152, 154, 156, 157
Tumwater Hill	70
Tumwater Tunnel (U P RR)	143
Turntable (N P RR) at 4th Olympia Station – see Northern Pacific Railroad, Turntable at Water Street Station	
Turntable (O & T RR) – see Olympia & Tenino Railroad, Turntable at Tumwater	
Turntable (P T S RR) – see Port Townsend Southern Railroad, Turntable	
Union (City), WA	142, 143, 144
Union Mills, Thurston County, WA	123, 155
Vashon Island	140
Waldrick Road	13, 14, 48, 49, 96
Warbass Tract	139
Warren's Point	4, 7, 27, 31, 63, 137, 138, 141, 144
Washington State Capitol Building, Old (Washington Street)	144, 145
Washington State Capitol Campus	27, 33

Washington, State of 135
Washington Street 144
Washington Territory 1, 137, 141
West Bay (Budd Inlet) 4, 5
West Bay Drive 22, 23, 24, 63
West Olympia (Westside) 1, 6, 129, 131, 137, 146, 147, 155, 157
West Tenino 59, 60, 129
Westside Log Dump (Mason County Logging Company) 146
Westside Wharf 1
Whites, WA 100
Whittaker Station 16, 28, 29, 30, 53
Willapa Bay 123, 128
Willapa Harbor 42, 153, 154, 156

Index of Locomotives

Alaska Northern Railroad
#3 123

Columbia & Puget Sound Railroad
#5 120
#10 ....119, 120, 122

Northern Pacific Railroad
#119 119
#369 ....120, 123, 125, 126
#858 119

Olympia & Chehalis Valley Railroad
#2 (the Wallula) ....v, 119, 139
#3 (the Olympia) 119

Olympia & Tenino Railroad
#1 (the E. N. Oimette) ....ii, 3, 56, 119, 120, 122, 138

Port Townsend Southern Railroad
#1 ....i, 119, 123
#3 ....123, 124, 125, 126, 127, 129
#4 123
#6 ....iv, 27, 34, 36, 75, 123, 128
#858 ....iii, vi, 25, 26, 30, 37, 67, 112, 119, 121, 123, 147

Portland & Oregon City Railroad
#6 120

Union Lumber Company Railroad
#4 ....123, 126

Rogue River Valley Railroad
#6 120

Walla Walla & Columbia River Railroad
#2 120

Warren Spruce Company Railroad
#6 ....123, 128

Index of Railroads, Other Companies, and Organizations

Alaska Northern Railroad 123
Allison, J. P. & Company 72
American-British Finance Company 149
Anderson Brothers (of Seattle) 75
Baldwin Locomotive Works 119
Black Lake & Sherman Valley Railroad 81
Blackman Brothers 139
Burlington Northern – Santa Fe Railway 12, 13, 14, 15, 16, 17
                                                                      18, 53, 100, 102, 109
Bush & Gaston (Logging Company) 16, 82, 101, 141, 143
California State Railroad Museum 119
Capitol City Lumber Company 63, 80
Capitol City Shingle Mill 6, 63
Castle Coal Company 27, 34, 143
Castle Rock Electric Company 152
Central Pacific Railroad 3
Chain Hill Lumber Company 101, 153, 154
Chehalis-Centralia Interurban 152
Columbia & Puget Sound Railroad 119, 120
Corps of Engineers, US Army 133
Crowell Lumber Company 89
Crowell Spur – see P T S RR and N P RR
Currie & McDonald 140
Daily Chronicle 136
Deschutes River Boom Company 75

Dunlap Towing	23
Eagle Lumber Company	49, 51
Eastside Sawmill	146
Falls Terrace Restaurant	77
Gas Plant – see Olympia Brewery, Gas Plant	
Gelbach Flour Mill	30, 38
Grant Smith & Company	129
Great Northern Railway	25, 154
Gurney Cab & Transfer Company	148
Hartson Lumber Company	23, 157
Hartson-Otis Lumber Company (Tenino)	18, 104, 107, 109, 110, 118, 152
Hartson-Otis Lumber Company railroad	18, 105, 108, 109, 110, 112, 118
Hartson Spur – see P T S RR and N P RR	
Henderson House Museum	30, 36, 67, 68, 77
Henry McCleary Timber Company	61, 75, 153
Hercules Sandstone Company	18, 25, 109, 110, 111, 115, 117, 118, 151
Huston Hotel (Billy Huston's Railroad Hotel)	55, 56, 57, 58, 59
Independent Electric Company – see Castle Rock Electric Company	
Johns Lumber Company	63, 152
Johnson & Clark Lumber Company	116, 118
Jonis Spar and Lumber Company (Tenino)	18, 109, 112, 113, 114
Knap & Smith	140
Lake Superior and Puget Sound Company	2
Lakeside Industries	84
Lea Lumber Company	36, 72, 75, 76, 77, 148
Manville Sandstone Company	13, 96, 157
Mason County Journal	136
Mason County Logging Company	23, 27, 43, 49, 63, 84, 146, 149
Mayes & Helmink Lumber Company	16, 99, 101, 153
McEachern, J. A. & Company	155
McIntosh and Swan Logging Company	15, 50, 100, 154
McIntosh and Swan Logging Company railroad	15, 50, 98, 100
Milwaukee Railroad (The Milwaukee Road)	15, 25, 50, 98, 100, 150, 153, 154, 155, 156, 157
Minnesota Historical Society	20, 30, 56, 61, 63, 66, 91
Mitchell & Johns Mill	68
Morris Brothers	84, 147
New York Locomotive Works	119
North Pacific Railroad	1
Northern Pacific Railroad Company	1, 2, 4, 6, 7, 18, 20, 23, 25, 27, 30, 31, 36, 39, 42, 45, 55, 59, 63, 66, 67, 79, 89, 89, 90, 91, 96, 101, 112, 118, 119, 123, 125, 129, 131, 133, 135, 136, 137, 139, 142, 143, 144, 145, 146, 147, 148, 149, 150, 151, 152, 153, 154, 155, 156, 157
Northern Pacific Railroad, Lines, Divisions and Subdivisions:	
14th Subdivision of Pacific Division	129
Elma Cut-off	153
Grays Harbor Line	129, 134
Point Defiance Line	25, 49, 53, 56, 96, 100, 101, 110, 112, 116, 129, 130, 131, 152, 153, 154, 155, 156, 157
Prairie Line	25, 56, 59, 129
Tumwater Branch	43, 49, 80, 90, 129, 133
Tumwater Spur	74, 131, 132, 133, 134, 135
Northern Pacific Railroad, Freight House (Tenino)	56, 57
Northern Pacific Railroad, Spurs to Businesses:	
Chain Hill Lumber Company Spur	102, 103, 129
Crowell Lumber Company Spur	129, 132
Hartson Spur	129, 132
Hercules Sandstone Company Spur	118
Jonis Spar and Lumber Company Spur	109, 110
Olympia Brewery Spur	129, 131, 133, 134
Lea Lumber Company Spur	129
Tumwater Lumber Mills Company, West Bay Spur	63
Northern Pacific Railroad, Turntable at Water Street Station	30, 36, 151
Northern Pacific Railway Historical Association Archive	131
Northwest Fruit Products Company	131
Northwestern Coal Company	141
Northwestern Improvement Company	23, 119, 149
Ogle Lake Shingle Mill	91, 92
Olympia Airport	81
Olympia & Chehalis Valley Railroad Company	v, 1, 2, 4, 19, 20, 30, 59, 80, 82, 91, 96, 103, 139, 140, 141, 142, 143
Olympia & Chehalis Valley Railroad, Roundhouse (Tenino)	119, 141
Olympia & Tenino Railroad (generic term)	3, 6, 7, 8, 9, 10, 11, 12, 13, 14, 15, 16, 17, 18, 25, 27, 48, 58, 61, 81, 82, 87, 88, 90, 96, 101, 119, 129, 131, 137, 142, 146
Olympia & Tenino Railroad Company	ii, 4, 19, 22, 36, 42, 43, 49, 53, 56, 68, 75, 103, 119, 135, 138, 139
Olympia & Tenino Railroad, Turntable (Tumwater)	36, 138
Olympia Branch Railroad Company	1, 2, 3
Olympia Brewery	36, 66, 67, 68, 69, 70, 72, 131, 145, 146, 148, 149, 151
Olympia Brewery, Bottling Works	151
Olympia Brewery, Gas Plant	70, 71, 72
Olympia Brewery Spur – see P T S RR and N P RR	
Olympia Choral Society	2, 3
Olympia Iron Works	145
Olympia Light and Power Company	66, 67, 144, 145, 152

Entry	Pages
Olympia Light Guard Band	137
Olympia Logging Company	9, 17, 86, 100, 103, 104, 110, 148, 149
Olympia Logging Company railroad	105, 107, 108
Olympia Lumber Company	61, 62, 149
Olympia Mfg. & Building Company	6, 63
Olympia Railroad Construction Company	2
Olympia Railroad Union	3, 136, 137
Olympia Railway & Mining Company	2, 136
Olympia Sash & Door Company	146
Olympia Southern Railway Company	153
Olympia Terminal Railway Company	152, 154
Olympia Theater	145
Olympia Transcript	136
Olympia, Tumwater & Brighton Park Motor Railway Company	40
Olympia Tumwater Foundation	68
Olympian	129, 145
Olympia Standard	148
Olympia Tribune	144
Olympia Water Company	151
Oregon Improvement Company	20, 141, 142, 145
Oregon-Washington Railroad & Navigation Company – see U P RR	
Pacific Coast Steamship Company	145
Pacific Export Mill Company	5, 63
Pacific Pride gasoline station	43, 44
Percival Warehouse	142
Point Defiance Line – see Northern Pacific Railroad, Point Defiance Line	
Port Angeles & Olympia Railway	149
Port Angeles Eastern Railway	147, 149
Port Blakely Mill Company	81, 140, 141
Port Blakely Mill Company railroad – see Puget Sound & Grays Harbor Railroad	
Port Discovery Mill	147
Port Gamble Mill	140
Port of Olympia	77
Port Townsend & Southern Railroad (Port Townsend Southern Railroad)	40
Port Townsend Southern Railroad Company	i, iii, iv, vi, 5, 17, 18, 20, 21, 23, 25, 26, 27, 30, 31, 36, 43, 49, 50, 56, 59, 61, 66, 69, 72, 75, 77, 80, 86, 89, 90, 91, 98, 100, 101, 102, 103, 109, 110, 111, 112, 113, 114, 115, 116, 119, 123, 129, 142, 143, 144, 145, 146, 147, 148, 149, 150, 151, 153, 155, 156, 157
Port Townsend Southern Railroad, Divisions and Extensions:	
Butler Cove Extension	22, 23, 24, 25, 61, 63, 64
Northern Div. (Port Townsend to Quilcene)	22, 25, 119, 123, 127
Southern Div. (Olympia to Tenino)	22, 25, 49, 119, 123
Port Townsend Southern Railroad, Spurs to Businesses:	
Capitol City Shingle Mill Spur	6, 67
Crowell Lumber Company Spur	12, 43, 45, 47, 48, 49, 89, 90
Hartson Mill Spur (West Bay)	64, 65
Hartson Spur (Bush Prairie)	9, 63, 79, 81
Henry McCleary Timber Company Spur	61
Hercules Sandstone Company Spur	vi, 18, 114, 115, 152
Johns Lumber Company Spur	66
Jonis Spar and Lumber Company Spur	109, 111
Ogle Lake Shingle Mill Spur	91
Olympia Brewery Spur	iii, 7, 67, 68, 69, 70
Olympia Logging Company Spur (near Brooks Lane)	9, 85, 86
Olympia Lumber Company Spur	61, 62
Olympia Manufacturing & Building Company Spur	6, 67
Stone Quarry Spur	9, 85
Tumwater Shingle Company Spur	77, 78
Westside Mill Spur	5
Port Townsend Southern Railroad, Turntable	6, 27, 36, 40, 145
Porter Brothers Company	129
Portland & Oregon City Railroad	123
Portland & Puget Sound Railroad	8, 20, 40, 69, 80, 149, 150, 152, 153
Prairie Line – see Northern Pacific Railroad, Prairie Line	
Puget Sound & Grays Harbor Railroad (Blakely Railroad)	25, 142
Rajotte, Robert & Winters	155
Richardson Shingle Mill	146
Rogue River Valley Railroad	123
San Francisco Bridge Company	142
Seatco Coal Mine	141
Sheldon's Cabin	43, 44, 45
Sheldon's Café	43, 45, 47
Simpson Logging Company	147
Smith & Byrd	140
South Puget Sound Community College	80, 81
Southern Pacific Railroad Company	145

Southwest Washington Regional Archives	68, 77
State Farm Office	79, 80
Tacoma Iron Works	139
Tacoma Mill Company	4, 11, 81, 82, 84, 87, 90, 91, 139, 140, 141
Tacoma Mill Company, Spurs, Sidings and Railroads:	
Foster Spur at Bush Prairie	9, 79, 82, 83, 84, 91
McCorkle Road Spur	13, 79, 90, 91, 92, 93, 95, 96, 119
Percival Creek Railroad	80, 81
Siding at 93rd Avenue and Sheldon Road	11, 88
South Union Spur	9, 79, 82, 83, 84, 91
Tacoma *News*	140
Tacoma, Olympia & Grays Harbor Railroad (part of N P RR)	20, 21, 30, 152
Tenino Ace Hardware	59
Tenino & Hanaford Valley Railroad	59
Tenino Depot Museum	30, 47, 49, 56, 109, 110, 118, 119, 129
Tenino Light & Power Company	152
Tenino Manufacturing Company	101
Tenino Mill Company	118
Tenino Sandstone Company	110, 150, 151
Thacker Wood Company	80, 147
Thurston County Railroad Construction Company	3, 4, 119, 139
Thurston County Roads & Transportation Services	27, 40, 82
Tumwater Lumber Company	36, 68, 75, 154
Tumwater Lumber Mills Company	7, 61, 63, 74, 75, 77, 131, 132
Tumwater Paper Mills Company	131, 133, 134
Tumwater Shingle Company	7, 77
Twohy Brothers	154, 155
Southwest Washington Regional Archives	1
Union Lumber Company	123, 126, 157
Union Pacific Railroad	6, 7, 8, 20, 25, 101, 129, 131, 142, 143, 150, 151, 154, 155, 156, 157
United Stock Yards (Chicago)	144
University of Oregon Library, Photograph Collection	123
University of Washington Digital Archive	56
Walla Walla & Columbia River Railroad	119, 120
Ward & Mitchell Sawmill	137
Warren Spruce Company	123, 128
Washington & Oregon Corporation	152
Washington Coal and Transportation Company	136
Washington Public Service Commission	96
Washington Standard	136
Washington State Archives	25, 59
Washington State Capitol Museum	53
Washington State Department of General Administration	133
Washington State Historical Society	3, 4, 27, 36, 66
Washington State Library	136
Washington Utilities and Transportation Commission	96
West Bay Marina	61
Western Quarry Company	116, 118
Westside Mill	5, 61, 62, 63, 75, 77, 143, 145, 146
Weyerhaeuser Archive	100
Weyerhaeuser Company	100, 147
White, A. E., Inc.	96
White, A. E., Inc. (logging railroad)	13, 97
White Brothers Logging Company	96
White Logging Company	100
White's Mill	100
White Star Lumber Company	100
Whitemarsh Sawmill	148